SOTHEBY'S
CARING FOR
ANTIQUES

SOTHEBY'S
CARING FOR ANTIQUES

THE COMPLETE GUIDE TO
HANDLING, CLEANING,
DISPLAY AND RESTORATION

GENERAL EDITORS

METTE TANG SIMPSON · MICHAEL HUNTLEY

SIMON AND SCHUSTER
New York   London   Toronto   Sydney   Tokyo   Singapore

SIMON & SCHUSTER
Simon & Schuster Building
Rockefeller Center
1230 Avenue of the Americas
New York, NY 10020

First published in 1992 by Conran Octopus Limited
37 Shelton Street
London WC2H 9HN

Neither Sotheby's nor the publishers accept any responsibility for any damage caused
as a result of following any of the procedures in this book or otherwise.

Project Editor	Peggy Vance
Art Editor	Helen Lewis
Picture Researcher	Jessica Walton
Assistant Editor	Helen Ridge
Copy Editor	Patricia Bayer
Production	Sonya Sibbons
Illustrator	Andrew Farmer
Special photography	Lucy Mason

The publisher would like to thank Roy L. Davids, Ronald Varney, John Stair, David Battie, Ken Adlard, Julie
Armstrong, Roberta Hughes, Eric Emms, Polly Powell, Sandy Shepherd, Lisa Cussans, Lucilla Watson, Barbara
Mellor, Alistair Plumb, Mary Davies, and David Lee for their help with this book. Thanks also to all those in
Sotheby's London and New York who commented on the proofs, and to Antiquus, Sylvia Napier Ltd, Peter
Hurford Antiques, The Gallery of Antique Costume and Textiles, Mallett at Bourdon House, Guinevere Antiques
Ltd, and the Department of British Paintings & Drawings, Sotheby's London for lending items for photography.

Typeset by Servis Filmsetting Ltd
Printed in Great Britain by
Butler & Tanner Ltd Frome and London

10 9 8 7 6 5 4 3 2 1

Library of Congress Cataloging-in-Publication Data

Sotheby's caring for antiques : a guide to handling, cleaning,
  display, and restoration / general editors, Mette Tang Simpson,
Michael Huntley.
      p.   cm.
    First published in 1992 by Conran Octopus Ltd.
    Includes bibliographical references and index.
    ISBN 0-671-75105-0
    1. Antiques—Conservation and restoration.   I. Simpson, Mette
Tang.   II. Huntley, Michael.   III. Sotheby's (Firm)   IV. Title:
Caring for antiques.
NK1127.5.S67   1993   91-46689
745.1'028'9—dc20   CIP

CONTENTS

THE CONTRIBUTORS

DAVID ARMITAGE is Conservator to the Department of Eastern Art at the Ashmolean Museum, Oxford, England. He began his training in 1955 with Leeds City Museums, and has subsequently held a number of conservation posts at Liverpool Museum and Birkenhead Art Gallery. He is a specialist in the handling and repair of all kinds of oriental and occidental ceramics and is a Fellow of the IIC (International Institute for Conservation of Historic and Artistic Works).

LAURENCE BIRNIE is the Conservation Officer of Fine Metals at the National Maritime Museum, Greenwich, England, where he specializes in scientific instrument conservation and historic metal finishing. He is a Licenciate of the Institute of Metal Finishing, an Associate Member of the Institute of Corrosion Science and Technology, and has a Diploma of Archaeological Conservation from the University of London.

DAVID BOMFORD joined the Conservation Department of the National Gallery, London, in 1968, where he is now Senior Restorer of Paintings. He is involved with the treatment of pictures from all periods in the Gallery's collection, and has published widely on European painting techniques. He was, for ten years, editor of the international journal *Studies in Conservation*.

CHRISTOPHER CLARKSON was the conservator in charge of rare books and special collections at the Library of Congress, Washington, DC; conservator working on binding descriptions for a new manuscript catalogue at The Walters Art Gallery, Baltimore, MD; and conservation officer at the Bodleian Library, Oxford, England. He now runs one of the only workshops devoted to book conservation at the Edward James Foundation, West Dean, Sussex, England.

SANDRA DAVISON trained in archaeological conservation before working at the British Museum for fourteen years, specializing in ceramics and glass restoration. She has lectured and published widely, and practiced or taught glass restoration in museums and conservation schools in the U.K. and abroad. A Fellow of the IIC, she established The Conservation Studio in London in 1984, which specializes in ceramics and glass restoration. In 1989 she published *Conservation of Glass*, with Roy Newton.

RICHARD LANNOWE HALL began dealing in oriental carpets after completing his Bachelor of Arts degree in Fine Art at the Royal Academy of Arts, London, in 1976. He then worked in partnership with the firm of Marcusson, Hall & Meuse, dealers in tribal rugs and kilims and, after moving to Bath, founded Lannowe Oriental Textiles, which is now the largest independent workshop in England specializing in the washing, restoration, and conservation of oriental carpets and textiles.

JOHN KITCHIN is in charge of the Furniture Section of the Conservation Department at the Victoria & Albert Museum, London, which he joined in 1956. He has written a number of articles for professional journals and has lectured at the UNESCO International Course on Wood Conservation Technology, the London College of Furniture, and the Sotheby's Decorative Arts Course. He is currently President of the British Antiques Furniture Restorers Association.

MARION KITE is Senior Textile Conservator at the Victoria & Albert Museum, where she has worked since 1974. She is assistant coordinator of the ICOM (International Council of Museums) leather and related objects group, and has published articles and lectured on the conservation of textiles in the U.K. and abroad.

JOHN LARSON is Head of Sculpture and Organic Conservation at the National Museums & Galleries on Merseyside, England. For twenty-two years he was the Senior Sculpture Conservator at the Victoria & Albert Museum, responsible for the conservation of a large number of sculptures in a variety of media. He has also been an advisor to the National Trust, the Church of England, and English Heritage, and published and lectured widely on the subject of sculpture conservation.

JANE McAUSLAND set up a workshop for the conservation and restoration of prints and drawings in 1970 following a ten-year apprenticeship. A Fellow of the IIC and a founder member of the Institute of Paper Conservation, she contributes articles to journals and books. Her clients have included the Royal Library, Natural History Museum and the Henry Moore Foundation in England, as well as many others in the public and private sectors internationally. She is an advisor to Sotheby's.

ALLYSON McDERMOTT is a leading authority on the conservation and history of wallpapers. She left fulltime lecturing in 1988 to establish the Lintz Green Conservation Center, in County Durham, England, which provides facilities for scientific study and research, as well as undertaking a wide range of conservation projects for historic houses, museums, galleries and the National Trust, among others. She lectures on many aspects of wallpapers both in the U.K. and abroad.

ELIZABETH MARTIN has worked for the Conservation Department at the Victoria & Albert Museum since 1976, specializing in the conservation of photographs. She has lectured and written articles on photographic conservation, and is the author of *Collecting and Preserving Photographs* and a contributor to *A Guide to Early Photographic Processes*.

JIM MURRELL joined the Conservation Department at the Victoria & Albert Museum in 1961, where he is a conservator of pictorial and decorative art, with special responsibility for portrait miniature paintings and wax sculpture. He has written on the history of miniature painting materials and techniques, as well as on conservation practices.

DAVID NEWELL runs his own firm of clock, watch and music box restorers in London. He is a Fellow of the British Horological Institute and a member of the Antiquarian Horological Society. His work includes the conservation of clocks in the Wallace Collection, in London, and those of the National Trust in the London area, as well as those in private collections.

HAZEL NEWEY is Head of Metal Conservation in the Department of Conservation at the British Museum, where she has worked since 1972. She has published articles on various aspects of metals conservation and is a Fellow of the IIC, as well as being a founder member of the Metals Group of the United Kingdom Institute for Conservation.

ANDREW ODDY is the Keeper of Conservation in the British Museum, where he has worked since 1966. His conservation research has been mainly concerned with metals, stone, and waterlogged wood. He has also worked in the field of ancient technology, and he has lectured and published on gilding, tinning and wire-making in antiquity. In the numismatic field, he has studied the debasement of several gold coinages.

ALEXANDRA RHODES is the Director of Jewelry at Sotheby's London, which she joined in 1974. A Fellow of the Gemmological Association of Great Britain, she has given lectures on jewelry around the world. Her writing on the subject includes the book *Hatpins and Tiepins* and articles on 19th- and 20th-century jewelry.

METTE TANG SIMPSON has a Bachelor of Arts degree in Art History and a post-graduate Diploma in Conservation. She was the Director of the Textile Conservation Center at Hampton Court Palace, in England, before joining Sotheby's London in 1989, where she helped establish the Conservation and Restoration Department. A member of the ICOM and the IIC, she has traveled widely, undertaking conservation work for national museums, giving advice on the safekeeping of collections, and lecturing on many aspects of conservation. She has also assisted the Getty Conservation Institute in California on matters related to training in conservation. In addition, she is a specialist in the conservation of works of art on paper.

FREDERICK WILKINSON is President of the Arms and Armor Society, and Vice-President of the Historical Breech-loading Small-Arms Association as well as being consultant to Sotheby's Arms and Armor Department. He is currently being employed by the Royal Armories at the Tower of London on a program of valuation. This collection is known as one of the most extensive of its kind in the world. He is also the author of a large number of books and articles on arms and armor, and has lectured widely on the subject.

HAYDN WILLIAMS initially joined the British Watercolor Department at Sotheby's London in 1980, and subsequently specialized in the field of portrait miniatures. He is now the head of the Objects of Vertu and Russian Works of Art Department, and is responsible for sales in London and throughout the rest of Europe.

ILLUSTRATIONS

PAGE 2: *Various Greek and Roman coins on a vellum-bound volume of pen-and-ink drawings, attributed to Eneas Vico, c.1555.*

PAGE 8: *Conservation tools used in the treatment of a wide variety of materials.*

FOREWORD

" A thing of beauty is a joy for ever" only if you look after it. This means not breaking it, ensuring that it is kept in the right environment and getting repairs done in the most sympathetic way.

This book outlines the precautions you should take when handling, storing and displaying your antiques. These are not responsibilities merely to be handed over to someone else. The more you learn about your possessions, the better you can ensure their survival.

Firstly, you need to know as much as possible about the materials from which the objects are made and the way in which they are put together, since the type of deterioration depends both on composition and construction.

Secondly, it is vital to consider the environment in which you want to place the object. This may involve finding out how hot or dry your house becomes when the central heating is on, or making a note of which windows the sun shines through in different seasons and at different times of the day. Decisions have to be made about such basic issues as how often you would like to look at your collection, or whether you wish to use an object in the way that was originally intended. The information presented in this book should enable you to begin to take the correct action. The authors are all experts in their respective fields and are familiar with the many questions that owners of antiques need to ask.

An environment in which there are a lot of people will never be one that lengthens the lifespan of an historic object. People tend to prefer a warm atmosphere, which leads to conditions that are the principal cause of cumulative damage to antiques. Obviously it is important to enjoy and use your objects, so a compromise must be drawn, the owner making an effort to minimize the risks whenever possible. This may be as simple as turning the thermostat down a couple of degrees or making space in a cupboard to provide the best storage conditions. Caring always involves commitment. This commitment comes more easily if you understand the consequences of neglect and the benefits of positive action that are discussed in this excellent book.

DR JONATHAN ASHLEY-SMITH
HEAD OF CONSERVATION
VICTORIA AND ALBERT MUSEUM, LONDON

INTRODUCTION

*E*veryone who owns antiques and works of art should have an interest in their proper care and conservation. Passed down through time, whether purchased or inherited, they are effectively held in trust by a succession of owners whose pleasure it is to enjoy them but whose responsibility it must also be to ensure their survival. Collectively, these objects are an important part of our cultural heritage. Few would consciously seek to degrade it; yet, through unwitting neglect and a lack of knowledge or forethought, works of art in the home environment frequently suffer damage and deterioration that are easily avoidable and therefore quite unnecessary.

It is the primary purpose of this book to describe those obvious steps that owners should take to care for antiques in their possession, and to foster the kind of awareness and understanding that make for responsible ownership. Although primarily a guide to preventative care, written by professional conservators, the book also provides an insight into the effects of conservation and restoration on the survival of works of art that have suffered various forms of damage.

The following chapters deal with the care and conservation of the full range of objects likely to be found in private hands: furniture, ceramics and

A selection of fine works of art in a variety of media, none of which are in obvious need of restoration.

glass, jewelry, clocks and watches, scientific instruments, paintings and drawings, textiles, sculpture and much else. Where appropriate, each chapter recommends safe handling and transportation, while pointing out practices that invite disaster. Safe methods of cleaning are described, and suggestions given for appropriate display and storage. The insidious damage which can be caused by light and heat, by damp or dry conditions, and atmospheric pollution, is discussed in full, and advice is given on how to spot incipient problems. Each chapter also describes situations which can be dealt with by the layperson or by professional conservators.

Bad practices often stem from lack of knowledge or forethought. Paintings are frequently hung over fireplaces, the worst possible location since smoke, dust and heat all cause damage. Plates are often stacked one on top of another, which can lead to the enamel being worn away. The surface of silver that is polished regularly can be completely destroyed by this routine. A piece of garden statuary situated among foliage invites the damage that vegetation inflicts upon marble and other stones.

In most cases, good practice follows naturally from an understanding of the whole object, from the knowledge not only of how it is made, but also of the way the materials behave under various conditions. Knowledge of furniture construction and of the strength as well as the vulnerability of the wood promotes sympathetic handling and forestalls many problems, such as the loosening of joints and the lifting of veneer. Understanding atmospheric effects on a range of materials, from paper and textiles to metalwork, also encourages good housekeeping.

Included here is much common-sense advice, but also a great deal that is far less obvious — and may

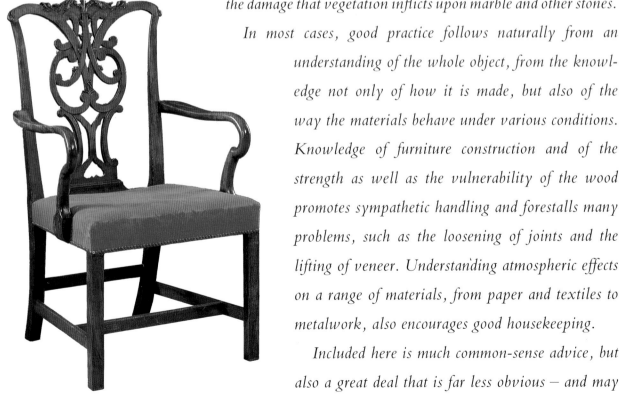

A carver from a set of English 18th-century mahogany dining chairs, c.1760.

require a little time and effort. However, such care will ultimately repay the trouble taken, both by enhancing the appearance of the object and by removing the need for costly conservation and restoration at a later date.

Despite reasonable precautions having been taken, cases will occasionally arise wherein professional conservation or restoration has to be considered. The purpose of conservation is to arrest damage and decay; that of restoration is to attempt to regain the original appearance of an antique or work of art. The roles of the conservator and restorer are in fact closely allied and frequently overlap. Both operate under a conservation ethic which places the integrity of the object above all else, dictating that all conservation or restoration work be reversible. Any work that is irreversible defaces an object and may possibly hamper future treatment. It is further recommended that all restoration that is carried out should be detectable.

It is essential to choose an experienced and sympathetic conservator or restorer. For each category of antiques with which this book deals, the text offers guidance as to advisable and inadvisable conservation procedures, discriminating between safe processes and those which are unacceptable and actually or potentially damaging. If it is deemed that professional work is required, the reader should feel better able to discuss with the conservator or restorer the nature and extent of the recommended treatment.

This book has been produced under the guidance of the Conservation and Restoration staff at Sotheby's London. The department came into

Chinese 17th-century underglazed blue-and-white porcelain ware with metal mounts.

A Roman 17th-century bronze group of the Laocoon.

being in 1989 in response to a growing number of queries from owners of works of art relating to care and preservation. Primarily it is a service that undertakes, on behalf of Sotheby's clients, the management of conservation problems of all types, any treatment being deemed necessary either carried out by the department itself or by a team of qualified, independent specialists whose expertise Sotheby's enlists. The department has wide experience of the special problems to which antiques of all kinds are prey and is aware of the desire of collectors to be well informed about the care of objects in their possession. It is hoped that this book will offer guidance as to when remedial action should be taken.

Sotheby's has been overwhelmed by, and is extremely grateful for, the enthusiasm with which the invitation to contribute to this book has been met. We are delighted that a team of such highly qualified professionals have lent their experience and knowledge to this volume. It is hoped that readers will be awakened both to the dangers of degradation to which antiques and works of art are exposed and to the many effective courses of action that lie open for saving them, thereby preserving important and beautiful objects for the benefit of future generations.

Graham Child
Head of Conservation and Restoration, Head of Furniture
Sotheby's London

A selection of fine French books with elaborate leather and gilt bindings.

FURNITURE

Furniture owes much of its great variety to the natural beauty and considerable versatility of wood. On this material are based the skills of joinery, cabinet-making and upholstering, the effects of veneer and inlay and those of carved and pierced decoration, the embellishments of ormolu, and surface finishes such as waxing, French polishing, lacquering and painting. Central to the good care of furniture is an appreciation of how it is both constructed and decorated, of the strengths and weaknesses of wood, and of the sensitivity of this natural material to favorable and inimical environmental conditions.

Virtually all forms of furniture, from the most basic joint stool to the finest satinwood table, are prone to damage from a few, relatively simple, causes. Rough handling and inappropriate usage can cause strain and structural damage; over-dry conditions and fluctuating levels of humidity will encourage splitting, warping and the lifting of veneer; spillages may leave surface marks and strong sunlight can cause bleaching; infestations of woodworm will weaken parts of, or even the whole of, a piece of furniture.

It is unlikely that any piece of furniture will have survived the passage of time completely untouched by one or more of these hazards. While the prevention of damage is of paramount importance, furniture nevertheless offers considerable scope for successful restoration, whether that is going to entail strengthening the joints of a table, repairing the inlay on a cabinet, polishing a dining table, or making a completely new leg for a chair.

Intarsia panel attributed to Fra. Damiano di Bergamo, dated 1536 INLAID WITH DIFFERENT WOODS, INCLUDING BURR-WALNUT, SYCAMORE, BOXWOOD AND OLIVE, THIS PANEL DEPICTS THE ANNUNCIATION, AFTER A PAINTING BY CARLO CRIVELLI. IT SHOWS FINE ARCHITECTURAL DETAIL AND PERSPECTIVE, AND IS DATED MDXXXVI (1536). TO MAINTAIN SUCH A PANEL IN FIRST CLASS CONDITION IT IS VITAL THAT IT IS KEPT IN A SUITABLE ENVIRONMENT AND TREATED WITH PARTICULAR CARE.

Most pieces of furniture are made predominantly of wood, so looking after them involves the care of, and by implication some understanding of, the wood. This material is susceptible to natural damage, such as splitting, distorting and being eaten by insects, and also to damage from human intervention, such as marking, bruising and breaking. It is also warm to touch, beautiful to look at, versatile, and amenable to repair.

Joints

Joints enable a structure to be built which is both light and strong. They can be fixed, as in a chair, or movable, as in a gateleg table. Joints can fail either through bad design, usage beyond the design concept, pest infestation, incorrect storage, the deterioration of glue and other fixings resulting from age, and, very occasionally from incorrect construction procedures.

If a joint has become loose because of bad practice in handling or craftsmanship, the options are either to avoid using the piece, or to allow a skilled craftsman to remake the joint.

INCORRECT USAGE
Dragging a drop-leaf table to the center of a room prior to setting it up as a dining table is a good example of incorrect usage. The assumption that the structure is sound in the same way that a solid object is sound is wrong. The frame is designed to accept vertical, not lateral, forces. Therefore, almost all furniture should be lifted when it is being moved, not dragged – even items on castors should be lifted where feasible. Snagging a carpet on an uneven floor can easily break the joint or split the leg.

Very little antique furniture is designed to be pushed or pulled, even if fitted with castors, which are often more decorative than functional (the small size of the screws used to attach them on the underside is evidence of this). The castors may also have been made inefficient by wear. The wheel has been used more successfully to cope with lateral forces, for example on the tea cart, where the larger wheel is better able to accommodate irregular surfaces than the castor.

PEST DAMAGE
Woodwork can be severely damaged by wood-boring insects. In temperate climates the common furniture beetle (*Anobium punctatum*) causes most of the damage. The joints of furniture, especially those pieces that are made of beech and walnut, often fail because of "woodworm" damage (see page 33).

Woodworm damage is not sufficient reason for discarding an object. In almost all cases the frailty of the timber can be attended to in a successful manner. Even if a damaged piece needs to be replaced, keep the removed part (having first treated it for woodworm), as it is important documentary evidence. There are resin preparations available that can be used by a restorer to strengthen weakened material, as well as more traditional remedies such as glue and sawdust. A conservator will advise a suitable course of action.

FAILURE OF GLUE AND FIXINGS
Joints are held together by pegs (sometimes called treenails or dowels), wedges, glue, and sometimes screws and glue. A joint will fail if the fixings fail or if either the pegs or the wedges fall out. Fortunately, their absence is easily detected and remedied by immediate replacement. If they are not treated at once, the joint may rock, bruise the socket edges, and consequently become permanently loose.

It is often thought that if an item is venerable, it must be vulnerable. This is not strictly true, for glues deteriorate with age, but timber may not. An example of this is the long-undisturbed funereal furniture of Tutankhamun and other Egyptian rulers, which has lasted in excellent condition for thousands of years.

POOR CONSTRUCTION METHODS
Sometimes incorrect joints have been used, and these will consequently fail. For example, the dovetail joint is designed to resist a pull in a certain direction, but drawers are occasionally made with the dovetails reversed, making them less effective. This is most likely to occur on some Italian and other Continental furniture, as well as on fake and altered pieces.

Furniture made with limbs that are too slender, in an effort to create the effect of grace and lightness, is less likely to last. These members are further weakened by the necessary constructional joints. Today much of this furniture shows its design faults in the legs, which are often found with repairs in the joint areas. An irregular dark patch in the proximity of the joint may be an attempt to disguise such a repair.

Seat Furniture

Seat furniture in the West is constructed with the seat raised on legs. This means that the legs have to be made stable, and in the past the answer was to use tight-fitting joints, with pegs or wedges inserted to stop them from pulling apart. This method was used until the eighteenth

Structural damage in chairs
THE BACKS OF REGENCY HALL CHAIRS, SUCH AS THE ONE ON THE
LEFT, ARE PRONE TO THE SORT OF STRUCTURAL DAMAGE SHOWN
ABOVE. THE BACK-TO-SEAT JOINT IS NOT STRONG ENOUGH TO
RESIST PRESSURE STRONGER THAN GENTLE LIFTING OR LEANING
BACK. THE GEORGIAN ARMCHAIR BELOW IS OF SOUNDER
CONSTRUCTION AND BETTER ABLE TO RESIST SUCH PRESSURE.

century, when gluing the faces of the joints became the
more common practice. (However, pegged joints did
become fashionable again in the William Morris-inspired
Cotswold School of furniture in the late nineteenth and
early twentieth centuries.) It is also the case that cabinet-
making practices developed differently in different countries: French cabinet-makers, for example, continued
using the pegged joint (although often with glue as well)
for a long time after the use of glue alone had become
normal practice in Britain.

Unlike many of the other objects treated in this book,
furniture is heavily used – and sometimes quite aggres-
sively – and any care program has to take this fact into
account. Chairs are subject to more abuse than almost any
other type of furniture, so a basic knowledge of the way
they are constructed is a prime requirement for owners
and curators.

LOOSE JOINTS
Whether they are glued, wedged or pegged, chairs are
particularly prone to looseness in the joints. Once this is
detected it should be corrected before the chair is used
again. The failure of one joint inevitably leads to failure of
other parts of the assembly. At worst, this is likely to

necessitate the complete rebuilding of the chair, and, at best, to require the replacement of broken components; both procedures that might have been avoided.

To check a chair, stand at the front and try to rock it from front to back or side to side. If any part of the frame does rock or exposes some part, however small, of the face of a joint (the timber will probably be lighter and unpolished on the faces of the joints), then that section of the frame needs to be disassembled, cleaned up and rejointed. If one joint has failed then the rest will probably need to be attended to in the near future, so it is a wise precaution to remake all the joints at the same time.

them refixed as soon as possible. Detachment may occur either because of glue failure – in which case check all the other blocks to see if any of them are about to drop off – or because of actual breaks in the timber. Do not, under any circumstances, attempt to marry up the two broken faces, even without glue, because further damage will probably occur to the torn wood fibers and make satisfactory restoration extremely difficult. Broken pieces should be put in a bag and tied to the item from which they came until the repair is effected. Do not handle the broken surfaces or let them get dirty; above all, do not try to bandage things up with adhesive tape. If tape must be

English early 18th-century walnut settee
FURNITURE WITH EMBROIDERED COVERS MAY APPEAR TO BE IN BETTER CONDITION THAN IT ACTUALLY IS. IF IT HAS RECEIVED HEAVY WEAR, HOWEVER, THE EMBROIDERY MAY ALSO BE SCUFFED AND THE GROUND FABRIC WEAKENED OR SPLIT. (LEFT)

English walnut bureau cabinet, c.1715
A PIECE OF THIS AGE AND COMPLEXITY MAY HAVE DAMAGED HINGES, LIFTING VENEERS OR A LOOSE INTERIOR, ALL OF WHICH CAN BE CORRECTED BY A SKILLED CONSERVATOR. (OPPOSITE)

DETACHED BLOCKS

The thickness of the timbers forming a chair can be built up for decorative or structural reasons by blocks, which are glued onto the frame of the chair. Attaching such blocks is a legitimate technique, the alternative to which, carving from the solid, would require the use of large-section timber and result in considerable waste. Internal corners are filled in with pieces called "ears," and external corners are built up with blocks to form "knees."

Glue blocks and corner blocks are fitted to the inside of the seat rails to add strength. If any of these become detached, it is most important to keep them safe and have

used, masking tape is less likely to damage the surface than more adhesive varieties of tape.

Amateur repairs are sometimes attempted using metal brackets, plates, straps, nails, screws, and even staples. It is not normally necessary to use such fixings to repair a chair, and they can considerably devalue and damage it. The exception is when a skilled metalworker has produced a purpose-made strap for an old piece. If such an improvement has been fitted with care and attention, and applied soon after the piece was made, then it is part of the historical documentary evidence of the piece and should be both valued and kept.

Upholstery

If a piece of seat furniture is covered with a textile of any merit, the seat should not be used, and the care instructions referred to on page 156 should be followed.

If the upholstery does not warrant avoidance of use, then good housekeeping and maintenance should be adequate care. Because seat covers are vulnerable to dust and attack by moths, carpet beetles and other pests, they should be regularly vacuumed. The nozzle of the vacuum cleaner should be covered with a net to prevent small, loose pieces, such as the buttons on button upholstery,

from being sucked up. Any loose pieces of cover or braid need to be secured as soon as they are discovered, and any loose or missing upholstery nails should be attended to. If the webbing sags or the stuffing is compressed, then the cover may become stretched. Old covers may be reused, and rewebbing and/or restuffing can add a further lease of life to tired-looking upholstery.

Care should always be taken that a drop-in seat is returned to its original chair after removal for cleaning or moving; if re-covered, the material should not be so thick as to require excessive force during replacement on the seat rail. A tightly fitting drop-in seat can break a rebate or force open a leg joint.

Loose covers can prolong the life of upholstery and should not be frowned upon. They protect the material from both dirt and light, and they may be removed when it is desired to display the original covers.

Carcass Furniture

Carcass furniture is furniture that encloses space, and includes coffers, cupboards, chests of drawers, pedestal desks, bureaus, bookcases, wardrobes and so on. Essentially, a carcass is a box that is accessible from the side or top. The top, base and sides of the box can be considered panels. The panels may be solid slabs joined together, or they may be set in a frame.

Conservators have to deal with the same problems of joint failure as occur on chairs, but their job is exacerbated by the panels, which are prone to splitting under certain conditions. In most instances where timber is used for panels in furniture (or, indeed, as a substrate for any work of art, such as a painting or a carving), internal stresses are set up as the timber absorbs and desorbs moisture as it adjusts to environmental changes.

SHRINKAGE

Carcass furniture should be examined for looseness in its joints, broken or missing pieces, and damage to the panels. The joint used in the top to sides and sides to base of most unframed carcass furniture is the dovetail joint. If, when examined, a chest of drawers shows slight regular protrusions along the top and bottom of the sides, then the dovetails used in the construction of the carcass are ''showing'' through due to shrinkage. Usually the surfaces are veneered, so only slight bumps in the veneer will be seen. The reason that the dovetails become apparent through the veneer is that the timber has shrunk more in its thickness than in its length. If there is any doubt that the wood has shrunk due to loss of moisture, then the

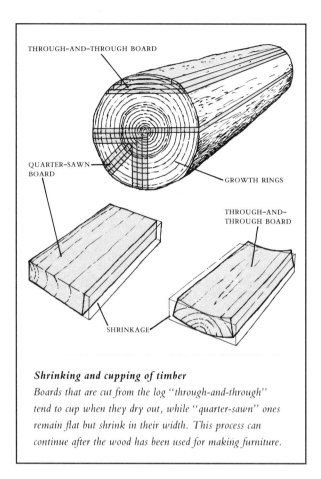

Shrinking and cupping of timber
Boards that are cut from the log "through-and-through"
tend to cup when they dry out, while "quarter-sawn" ones
remain flat but shrink in their width. This process can
continue after the wood has been used for making furniture.

HINGE PROBLEMS

Cupboard doors, being held on the hinge side only, are also subject to shrinkage, expansion and distortion. They may themselves distort, or the frame may be distorted, causing them to close unsatisfactorily. Likewise, if there is unevenness in the floor, this can be transmitted to the frame. Door hinges should always be properly secured. Loose hinge flaps can very easily pull away from the frame and, if the door is allowed to fall, it can be damaged or, in the case of a large bookcase, injure someone trying to find a book. The upper sections of bookcases should always be screwed to the lower ones, otherwise if all the doors were opened at once, it is possible that the top would become unstable and topple forwards.

dovetails showing in this way will settle the matter. It is not a major cause for alarm, as it shows that the carcass has been made using the best constructional techniques. Tearing and splitting of the veneer, which occur because of the underlying carcass construction, should be attended to, as should veneer that has cracked along the edges of adjacent boards forming the groundwork.

Other evidence of shrinkage is framed panels becoming loose and revealing unpolished surfaces, or splitting when they have been permanently fixed at the sides, thus not allowing them to expand and contract. Panel construction consists of specially grooved frame members, jointed together around the panel and designed to allow it to move freely within the grooves. Fixing the panel will not stop splitting; indeed, it will tend actively to promote it because the wood's capacity for expansion and contraction has been prevented. The force involved is enough to split a piece of timber with a loud crack, and an understanding of the causes of dimensional instability in timber is essential before any remedial or conservation work can be undertaken.

Another hinged panel that frequently shrinks and distorts is the fall of a bureau (the hinged writing surface). This can usually be straightened, but, if splits have occurred, the environment should be checked before any remedial work is carried out. Indeed, splits should be investigated as soon as they become evident, as should looseness of the hinge flaps, but take care not to tighten the screws and puncture the outside surface of the fall. The lopers, the pieces of wood that are pulled out to support a bureau fall, should be checked for looseness; they can become so worn away that open falls have to travel below horizontal in order to rest on them. This situation can put intolerable strain on the hinges, and the fall should not be used until the condition is corrected.

DRAWER AND FOOT DAMAGE

Drawers are prone to different problems, all of which can be improved or corrected, and should be attended to in order to prevent further damage. One is that over the years the runners – the pieces of wood on which the drawer slides – tend to wear away and need replacement.

Damage caused by unsuitable environmental conditions
THE TIMBER ONTO WHICH THIS VENEER HAS BEEN GLUED HAS SHRUNK, CAUSING THE VENEER TO SPLIT. BEFORE A REPAIR IS ATTEMPTED, BOTH THE OBJECT AND ITS ENVIRONMENT MUST BE STABILIZED. (OPPOSITE)

Anglo-Indian center table c.1840
THIS TABLE TOP HAS BEEN VENEERED WITH A VARIETY OF EXOTIC WOODS. WHEN VENEER LIFTS OR SPLITS, THE UNDERLYING CAUSE OF THE PROBLEM IS OFTEN WARPING OR SPLITTING OF THE SURFACE BENEATH IT (THE GROUNDWORK). THIS IS FREQUENTLY THE RESULT OF KEEPING THE OBJECT IN INAPPROPRIATE CONDITIONS. (RIGHT)

The edges of the drawer aperture can also become worn and may need patching. Also, the base of the drawer may become loose, and the front or sides may come apart.

From the early part of the eighteenth century an improvement in chest-of-drawer construction was the provision of a drawer stop. These are the little pieces of wood just inside the aperture that prevent the drawer from being pushed in too far. They may be missing, or they may have nails protruding from their top faces, which can damage the drawer base; both conditions require attention from a restorer.

Finally, the dust boards between the drawers may start to sag and impede the opening of the lower drawer, eventually preventing it from being opened.

Feet and cornices of carcass furniture are generally made up of shaped pieces glued together, and should be examined for soundness. Furniture should never be dragged along the floor, which is the surest way of breaking off a foot. Vacuum cleaners can knock against and damage the apron, the decorative pendent frieze between the feet of a piece of carcass furniture.

GLASS REPLACEMENT

The original glass used in old furniture tended to be particularly thin, and should therefore be treated with great care. Check a newly acquired piece to make sure that the putty or glazing beads (the little strips of wood that hold the glass in place) are present and sound. If they are not, call in a restorer, since the piece may be easily damaged by amateur repairs. If glass is missing, it should be replaced. If an original pane is cracked, but still firmly in place, it may be left as it is on the basis that all original features should be retained for as long as possible. Save all old glass, since a large broken fragment may be useful for replacing a smaller pane on the same or even another item. Glazed pictures, if worthless, can yield suitable glass.

Decorated Surfaces

Frequently the most visible surfaces of the timber used to make a piece of furniture are decorated in some way. Decoration should not be confused with surface finish, which is treated in the next section.

VENEERING

Veneering is not to be despised. In the case of fine furniture, it is not a method of producing pieces which look more soundly made than they are. Veneers are used for several reasons: because in some instances the method of cutting the veneer is the only way to reveal the required decorative grain features; because it would be wasteful to employ a rare, exotic species to form the basic carcass of an item; or because the constructional details require solid timber to be used in such a way that the grain and lines of the joints will, in the designer's view, detract from the overall appearance of the piece.

Veneer is similar to wallpaper, in that its final appearance is dependent on the surface underneath it. It is essential, then, that the groundwork onto which it is glued is solid and undistorted. Many repairs to veneered work are repairs to this groundwork. The groundwork warps and splits because it has dried out and, as a result, the veneer suffers. The glue can also dry out and fail, and in damp environments an excess of moisture can enter into the surface of the veneer, either through a damaged polish layer or through cracks, causing the veneer to swell and the glue to weaken and fail.

As prevention is better than cure, it is important to ensure that furniture is kept in the correct environmental conditions (see page 180). If splitting or lifting of the veneer has occurred, it should be attended to. If it is dealt with soon after it has happened, it is usually possible to make a repair that is almost invisible. Any loose pieces should be put in a clear plastic bag (so that the contents can be seen easily) and taped to the inside of a drawer or tied to the leg of a table or chair. Only use an "invisible" matte self-adhesive tape or painter's masking tape for this purpose; no tape with stronger adhesion should ever be used on furniture. Try to avoid sticking tape to a polished surface, but if, for example, some veneer has lifted but not become detached, it is better to cover the edges with a strip of tape than to risk the veneer being broken by dusting or some other contact. The four-part rule is: do not force it back; do not try to reglue it; protect the edges; and contact a restorer as soon as possible.

Marquetry (a design forming a picture) and parquetry (a design forming a geometric pattern) are both forms of applied decoration that can be treated in the same way as veneer. They are prone to pieces lifting, especially when formed of many different woods, so beware of losing pieces. Make sure that any detached pieces are put in a bag that is then attached to the item.

String lines (or stringing) are the long, thin strips of single or multiple contrasting colored woods that are inlaid into a surface, usually near an edge. It is a form of applied decoration which can lift up, and is then vulnerable. Tape the lifting section with masking tape, and get the item attended to by a restorer.

BUHL OR BOULLEWORK

Boullework (a composite veneer of brass, other metals, tortoiseshell and horn, all glued to the groundwork) is very prone to lifting. This is due mainly to the different rates of movement of brass, shell and wood; the difficulty of gluing metal to wood; and exposure to unsuitable environments. Once lifted, the brass inlay is particularly vulnerable. If it becomes bent in any way it is extremely difficult to re-lay satisfactorily. If there is a loose end of the metal inlay it may be taped down, but do not try to force bulges down; instead, protect them with a loose web of tape, and contact a restorer. Boulle restoration is very time-consuming, and therefore costly, work, but it is a false economy not to have damage attended to as soon as it is discovered. Whatever happens, do not try to nail or pin the brass down. Because of the different materials involved, controlling the temperature and humidity is very important. Pieces incorporating boullework should be kept in as stable an environment as possible.

CARVING, MOLDING AND FRETWORK

These are all forms of decoration which usually rise above the surface of the wood. As such they are likely to be knocked, and it is common to find bruises, losses and evidence of early restoration. The rule of putting broken-off pieces, including all splinters, in a plastic bag and fixing it to the object applies. Do not try to fix or tape the piece back, as this can further damage the edges; it is most important that these edges are kept unharmed and, if appropriate, a bandage of ordinary tissue or absorbent paper toweling could be applied around them.

Carcass furniture often has strips of molding applied at the top and bottom of the front and sides. At the corners these moldings are each cut at 45° so that the pair of moldings forms a 90° corner, which is called a miter joint. If the top has shrunk, then the mitered corners of the molding will be exposed, freeing the side moldings to project beyond the front molding. Even the very smallest projection provides a hazard that may well result in permanent damage. The tip of the molding, where it comes to a fine point, is easily broken off. If the miters are exposed on a piece of furniture, contact a restorer. Whether the whole molding has come off or is just loose, a house visit may suffice during which the restorer can refix the molding.

Italian mid-18th-century painted bombé commode with ormolu mounts
PAINTED AND LACQUERED SURFACES SHOULD BE TREATED WITH EXTREME CARE. NO CLEANING FLUIDS SHOULD BE USED, AND LIMIT CLEANING TO A LIGHT DUSTING, TAKING CARE THAT THE BRUSH DOES NOT DISLODGE ANY PIECES OF THE SURFACE. SUCH OBJECTS SHOULD BE KEPT IN LOW LIGHT, AND AT APPROPRIATE TEMPERATURES AND LEVELS OF HUMIDITY. CARE SHOULD ALSO BE TAKEN NOT TO ABRADE THE SURFACE BY PLACING UNSUITABLE OBJECTS ON IT, OR BY KNOCKING AGAINST IT.

Fretwork is a sheet of wood pierced with a design. It can be applied to a surface as a flat overlay, when it is known as "blind fret," or it may be free-standing, as in the case of a gallery around a table-top. Free-standing fretwork is vulnerable to pressure from the side. Therefore, it should be cleaned not with a cloth but with a soft brush – usually a 2in decorator's brush with soft natural bristles. Then apply polish with a different brush and, finally, rub with a burnishing brush, just as you would when cleaning a pair of shoes. Cover the metal ferrules of all brushes with masking tape so that they do not accidentally scratch the wood. Blind fret is much less vulnerable than free-standing fretwork, but should still be cleaned in the same way. This technique of dusting and polishing with a brush also applies to carvings and any deeply incised decoration.

LACQUERING AND JAPANNING

Lacquering is a technique used on furniture produced in the East, whereas japanning is the attempt to copy that technique in the West. In caring for both surfaces, keep the objects away from sunlight and free of dust. Use a brush as described for carvings, molding and fretwork. Do not allow water or any liquid onto the lacquered or japanned surfaces. Lacquer can be damaged by fingerprints, so wear cotton gloves when handling it. Provided there are no loose or flaking pieces, it will not be harmful to use a light microcrystalline wax on such surfaces once or twice a year (though it is not essential). If there is any evidence of flaking, take the item to a conservator. Some Oriental lacquer has raised and applied decoration – such as gold foil, mother-of-pearl, soapstone or coral – so take care when dusting or polishing not to dislodge these.

GILDING

Gilding is the application of gold leaf to an object. Gilded furniture, frames, works of art and ornaments are vulnerable to loss of adhesion between the preparatory layers for gilding and the woodwork (for ormolu and other gilded metals see page 58).

There are two types of gilding on wood: oil gilding and water gilding. Water gilding is vulnerable to water, so unless you can recognize the different types of gilding, keep water away from gilded objects. Recognizing the type of gilding is essential for correct conservation. Old items have often had past repairs in oil gilding to a surface that was originally water gilded. Make sure that your gilder is a competent specialist, especially as unburnished water gilding can look like oil gilding.

The care of gilded objects is simple. Dust them regularly, and do not let them get knocked. Whereas a wooden object will bruise when knocked, a gilded (or japanned) one will probably crack or flake. Such a surface break will allow dirt and moisture in, which in turn will bring about a loss of adhesion of surrounding areas.

Composition decoration, which very often is gilded, has a habit of fissuring at 90° to its length. This is a normal condition, and distinguishes a composition frame from a carved wooden one. It will be aggravated by changes in

English giltwood and gesso wall mirror, c.1765
CARVED WOOD COVERED IN GESSO IS OFTEN GILDED TO PRODUCE THE RICH EFFECT SEEN IN THE FRAME OF THIS MIRROR. BOTH THE GOLD LEAF AND THE FRAME ARE VERY FRAGILE, AND WILL HAVE A TENDENCY TO CRACK OR FLAKE IF KNOCKED. CLEANING SHOULD BE LIMITED TO GENTLE DUSTING WITH A BRUSH; WATER SHOULD NEVER BE USED.

relative humidity: the composition decoration will not expand or contract in the same way that the wood base will, and therefore the bond with the base will be weakened, but otherwise it will remain stable. If pieces do become loose – regular gentle dusting will offer you an opportunity to check them – they can be kept wrapped in a box, then given to the conservator to be reglued. In any event, do not attempt to clean with water. Treatment for carved and gilded wooden frames and composition frames is basically the same, but the latter are extremely vulnerable to vibration and, if transported, should be cushioned from shocks with several layers of bubble wrap over acid-free tissue.

OTHER SURFACE DECORATION

Mother-of-pearl, ivory and tortoiseshell can be used for surface decoration. These materials are very prone to lifting, and should be checked for good adhesion before being cleaned. Loose dust should be removed with a soft brush, followed by an application of microcrystalline wax. Papier-mâché is another material which should be treated in the same way. Water should not be used to clean these substances as it may harm them or weaken the glue.

Surface Finishes

Bare wood is absorbent and will mark easily, so most furniture has a surface finish of some kind. This finish generally comprises four or more distinct layers, which bind together to give the overall effect. They are, from the wood outwards: grain filling, coloring, sealing and, if applicable, wax (it is possible, as described later, for one substance to do two jobs). The ageing of these layers, sometimes called patina, should not be removed. Problems occur when these layers are damaged.

GRAIN FILLING

When wood is cut, however carefully, the ends of the cells which carried the vital fluids up and down the trunk and branches are bent over. These open cells with bent ends are part of the grain, hence filling them is known as grain filling. Treating them is important because if the ends of the cells are not smoothed with specially fine abrasive paper and the holes are not filled, then it will be impossible to obtain a totally flat outer layer to the finish.

Polish sinks into the grain over a period of weeks, so it is vital that when fresh polish is applied to, for example, a table-top, the grain has first been filled. If a very flat, mirror-like finish is desired, confirm with a restorer that the grain will be filled.

COLOR

Not only does the color of timber vary considerably from species to species, but indeed there is color variation within individual logs and boards from the same tree. The original cabinet-makers also applied and painted coloring agents onto the surface of the wood to achieve the appearance they desired.

When restoration work is being carried out on the surface of a piece of furniture, it is necessary to be aware of, and to be able to respond to, these different aspects of color

Italian side cabinet inlaid with ivory, c.1880
A VARIETY OF DECORATIVE MATERIALS, BOTH ORGANIC AND INORGANIC, CAN BE USED TO DECORATE FURNITURE, AS IN THIS CABINET INLAID WITH IVORY AND WOOD. THESE MATERIALS ARE PRONE TO LIFTING, AND BEFORE CLEANING IS CARRIED OUT A CHECK SHOULD BE MADE FOR GOOD ADHESION. DUST GENTLY IN ORDER NOT TO DISLODGE FRAGMENTS OF INLAY.

in timber. Good restorers will discuss with their clients what color and finish are appropriate before starting work on the pieces.

WAX, SHELLAC AND VARNISH

The sealing agent used over the grain filler and color applied onto the wood acts almost like a kind of "skin" that protects the main visible surfaces of the object. The protective "skins" likely to be encountered are wax, shellac and varnish. In England, oak and country-made furniture is often wax-finished. Shellac and varnish tended to be used on the finer-surfaced woods, such as mahogany, satinwood and rosewood.

Furniture that has a wax finish is not very easily marked, and the surface is relatively easy to look after. The wax is vulnerable to heat, so insulating mats should be used on tables. Spillages of cold water and alcohol should be mopped up as quickly as possible using absorbent paper, which should always be kept handy if food and drink are to be consumed anywhere near valuable furniture. Wax finish is a much more "tolerant" finish than shellac: if you were to leave a spillage on it inadvertently for ten minutes before mopping it up, it is unlikely that any serious harm would be done. Wax finishes will also accommodate bruising better than shellac or varnishes.

Shellac is a natural resin which becomes soft when mixed with denatured alcohol, and which dries hard as the alcohol evaporates. The dried surface can be waxed to give a mellow look, or it can be finished and burnished to give a smooth and shiny surface known as French polish.

As alcohol is the solvent for shellac, it must be kept away from the finished surface. Like wax, it is vulnerable to heat, and must also be kept free from water lying on the surface. The layers of shellac are also easily scratched. Fresh shellac takes three to six months to harden, so be careful how you use a recently polished table or chest of drawers. Fabric mats with an obvious weave will leave an impression if used under a vase on a newly polished surface. Although the list of detractions for shellac is long, it is also relatively easy for the skilled polisher to repair. It may take numerous applications of very thin layers of polish, but a good surface can usually be built up again.

The same cannot be said for varnish. Damaged varnishes almost always have to be removed and the surface refinished. If such is the case, considerable thought should be given as to whether it is better to keep the original surface and alter the way the piece is used. For example, it may be possible to use a plate-glass top on the item and thereby save the original finish (see page 30). Always

Polishing

THE USE OF SHELLAC TO
FORM A "SKIN" OF POLISH IS
A SKILLED JOB INVOLVING
MANY GENTLE APPLICATIONS
OF POLISH WITH A "RUBBER"
(WADDING AND CLOTH) AND
THEN BURNISHING, TO
PRODUCE THE FINE PATINA
SHOWN ON THIS BUREAU
CABINET. (LEFT)

consult an expert to establish the best course of action. Varnishes are rarely used these days, and it is almost always acceptable to replace them with shellac.

Modern lacquers and varnishes are to be avoided unless there is a particularly compelling reason to use them. Heavy family use of a mid-Victorian dining table might be such a reason, but professional advice should always be sought, and only reversible finishes should be used. Reversible means that one can undo the work that has been done, leaving the option of returning to a nineteenth-century finish. It must be stressed that a piece can be totally ruined by injudicious finishing, so always consult an acknowledged expert.

Other types of finishes are sometimes used on timber, such as graining and ebonizing. A native wood, such as beech, may be painted to resemble the grain of a rare exotic species, such as rosewood, and the texture and appearance of ebony may be recreated by applying an opaque black polish to a pale wood. These finishes are very sensitive to overcleaning and abrasion and, if damaged, require professional help. Their restoration calls for considerable skill in order to capture the appearance of the grain of the simulated timber.

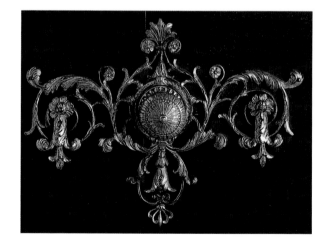

Gilded Adam-style Door Handle

MANY INTRICATE AND GRACEFUL BRASS AND GILT-BRASS FITTINGS WERE MADE IN THE EIGHTEENTH CENTURY. DETAIL AND GILDING MAY BE REMOVED BY LIQUID OR ABRASIVE CLEANING; DUSTING WITH A SOFT BRUSH IS THE ONLY TYPE OF CLEANING RECOMMENDED FOR THIS TYPE OF MOUNT.

Cabinet Fittings

The essential metal fittings found on furniture are usually made of brass, but they are sometimes made from iron or steel. Handles, hinges and locks are perhaps the most obvious fittings.

The handle may be attached to a drawer by a post with a pommel on the outside end and a nut on the inside. Both pommel and nut should be tight; sometimes a split pin is also used. Missing parts of a handle, or, indeed, any brassware, can be cast using a companion part as a pattern for a mold. Hinges should also be securely fixed, with all screws in place, the leaves undistorted, and the pin sound.

There are a huge variety of locks and keys, many very decorative and complex. As a general rule, locks should not be oiled. Lubrication should be carried out using powdered graphite; because it is dry, it does not form a sticky paste of dust and dirt as oil does. Keys should be labeled. This is not just a practical precaution: a label bearing a former owner's annotation forms a tangible link with the item's past. Restorers are often asked to preserve such labels or mementoes which have always accompanied a particular piece of furniture.

Castors should be checked for excessive wear and for the soundness of all screw fixings. Old castors can be refurbished, and should never be thrown away. Secretaires with patent or cantilever hinges supporting the fall need to be examined carefully, to establish whether they are still working properly. These mechanisms are very prone to distortion, wear and consequent failure.

Simple brassware may be safely cleaned with polish-impregnated wadding, but avoid overcleaning and removing the mellow appearance of old brass: shiny brass on antique furniture is not ethically acceptable. As all metal cleaners remove some portion of the surface of the object, and therefore will in time remove the detail, cleaning should be kept to a minimum. A coat of microcrystalline wax will slow down tarnishing. Well-fitted dressing cases, writing boxes and the like often have gilded fittings – do not attempt to clean them, as it is likely that the gilding will be removed.

Mounts

Most mounts on furniture are golden in color, but they are rarely made from solid gold. The mounts are usually solid brass or gold-plated metal, usually called ormolu. Sometimes bronze, pewter, copper or silver are also used, and even iron or steel. Most of the solid metals referred to here are dealt with on page 58.

ORMOLU

In ormolu, the thin, extremely delicate coating of gold is fixed by mercury gilding or electrical bonding to the base metal, which is usually brass or bronze. Several factors can affect the color of the gold, the most obvious being a gradual accretion of dirt over time. Early gilding often left minute pinholes in the layer of gold, through which atmospheric pollution can corrode the underlying metal and produce black or green spots.

A slight darkening resulting in a mellow appearance is acceptable and, indeed, is sought after by many collectors. However, if left uncleaned and unchecked, this darkening can continue until it is hard to tell that the mount was ever gilded. Sometimes the gold is physically worn away by overzealous or injudicious cleaning or use.

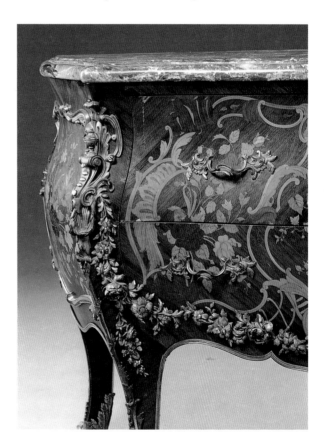

French commode with gilt-bronze mounts, c.1880
INTRICATE AND EXTENSIVE MOUNTS OF THIS TYPE ARE DIFFICULT TO KEEP CLEAN. BECAUSE OF THE FRAGILITY OF THE GOLD LAYER, ONLY AN EXPERT SHOULD ATTEMPT TO CLEAN THEM WITH ANYTHING OTHER THAN A SOFT DUSTING BRUSH. ONCE THEY HAVE BEEN THOROUGHLY CLEANED, IT IS POSSIBLE TO LIMIT DETERIORATION BY THE APPLICATION OF A COAT OF LACQUER OR MICROCRYSTALLINE WAX.

Because of the delicacy of the layer of gold, any attempt to clean mounts other than with a soft dusting brush must be done by an expert. A soft brush is used because dust is abrasive, and to use a cloth for regular cleaning would scratch the gold. Cleaning solutions and detergent are extremely damaging to the gold layer. It is very easy to remove entirely the original gilding from a mount by uninformed but well-meant cleaning. Never use any proprietary wet or dry abrasive cleaners on the mounts on

Frequently the appeal and attractiveness of gilding come from the contrast of matte and burnished surfaces. Reburnishing to bring back life to a piece is a very skilled job, and should not be attempted by the owner.

Everyday Care

Furniture is made to be used. Provided that the material from which it is made is still sound, there is no reason why

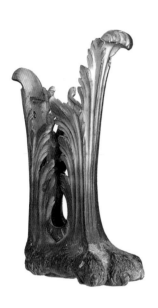

Restoration of gilded mounts
THE GILDED FOOT (FAR LEFT) HAS SUFFERED FROM CHEMICAL REACTION TO THE BASE METAL AND LOSS OF THE GOLD LAYER FROM THE OUTER SURFACE. AFTER EXPERT CLEANING AND RESTORATION IT IS REBURNISHED (LEFT), A SKILLED TECHNIQUE WHICH RECREATES THE CONTRAST OF MATTE AND REFLECTIVE SURFACES THAT IS SO CHARACTERISTIC OF SUCH PIECES.

a piece of furniture, and never ask anyone but an experienced conservator to do it for you. This applies to all mounts, whether solid or plated, ormolu or iron.

Unless the piece is kept in a carefully controlled environment, it is usually beneficial to have the mounts lacquered. A lacquer made from shellac, similar to that used in the eighteenth century, would be appropriate. Eventually the lacquer will fail and need to be replaced, but at least some protection will have been gained. Unlacquered, ungilded mounts must be kept clean, dusted and waxed (with microcrystalline wax), or they will lose their luster and become dark and pitted.

It is preferable to save the original gilding wherever possible. Usually the biggest problem will be relatively small bare areas that have lost their gilding from repeated handling. However, much can be done by skilled restorers to color-match bare areas to the original without undertaking a process of regilding.

antique furniture should not be used and enjoyed. If the material and the joints have been examined for failure or weakness, and any problems attended to, then considerate use should ensure that the object enters the twenty-first century with minimum wear (and increased value).

Objects should be used for the purpose for which they were intended. Chairs should not be tilted back or stood on. Drawers should not be overloaded, and only opened with both handles simultaneously – otherwise the drawer becomes twisted in the carcass. When using a ball-point pen, always protect the table or writing surface by placing some padding under the paper. Ornaments should also not be placed directly on surfaces without a layer of protective padding. Plate glass may be used to protect surfaces. If felt pads are used to raise it from the surface, do not apply undue pressure to unsupported areas. Ensure, also, that damaging liquids and abrasive grit are not trapped under any glass or felt covers.

DUSTING AND POLISHING

Dust and extremes of humidity are the enemies of fine furniture. Furniture should be dusted weekly, but there is no need to wax with the same frequency. Wood does not need "feeding." The surface can lack luster and detail of figure (grain), may be excessively dry, moist, bleached or stained, but it is never "hungry." Sometimes the layer of polish has been worn through in places, or has degraded and taken on a blotchy appearance. In these instances a skilled polisher can smooth out the unevenness and apply extra polish to the surface, which may have the appearance of "feeding" the raw areas. Preparations for "reviving" or cleaning furniture that has ring marks, ink stains or deep scratches should only be used by experienced polishers.

High-gloss French-polished furniture should be dusted regularly, and every three months given a firm rub with a clean, soft rag to remove airborne greasy deposits. Check first that the polishing cloth is free of grit or any abrasive substance. No other polishing is necessary.

Waxed furniture should be dusted weekly. Any food residues may be removed with absorbent paper towels dampened with lukewarm water. Several applications may be required for stubborn residues, but ensure that water does not lie on the surface any longer than absolutely necessary. Other residues may be softened with paper towels containing a small amount of mineral spirits (but test the finish first in an inconspicuous place). The clean surface should be waxed, if necessary, and then buffed up with a soft cloth. Spray polishes should be directed into the applying cloth and not directly onto the item, which should then be buffed up with a soft cloth. Alternatively, a light coat of beeswax polish may be applied (three or four times a year) and then buffed up. The manufacturer's instructions on the tin should be followed, as they can vary from brand to brand.

If you are in the habit of "damp dusting" your furniture – and have used this technique successfully in the past – there is no reason not to continue. Always ensure, however, that moisture does not lie on the surface of the timber, but is wiped away.

Desk leathers can be revived and protected by an application of microcrystalline wax. Baize linings on desks and tables, and on the underside of boxes and ornaments, should be vacuumed. As with upholstery, take care to ensure that poor adhesion does not allow the baize to be pulled away from the object which it is part of. If baize is not fitted to objects that are to be stood on polished surfaces, consideration should be given to making small, individual baize pads for the objects to be placed on, or to using small plate-glass or clear plastic mats.

REMOVING CANDLE WAX

Spilled candle wax should be eased off very gently with a Teflon spatula as soon as possible after it has cooled. Do not push down *into* the wood, as this may leave a bruise; instead, push *along* its surface in the direction of the grain. If there is still a residue of wax, lay blotting paper over the area and place a warm hot-water bottle on the blotting paper. The wax will be drawn up into the blotting paper. Make sure that no water is spilled.

English papier-mâché tilt-top table, c.1845
PROFESSIONAL CLEANING OF INTRICATE PAPIER-MÂCHÉ WORK SUCH AS THIS SHOULD BE FOLLOWED BY REGULAR DUSTING.

Candle wax also has a use in lubricating wooden parts that move against each other. Drawers, for example, can be made to run more easily if their runners and sides are lightly rubbed with a candle.

PROPER LIFTING AND MOVING

Much damage occurs when furniture is moved (often to the furniture mover as well as to the object). Objects should be raised by lifting from a point or points on the lowest, strongest structural member.

Any moving process should aim for maximum stability, and large objects may require three or more people: two to lift and one to help balance the object. To lift something by the top inevitably puts the component hanging from it at considerable risk. Drop-leaf tables should have a tie put around the leaves before moving. Check that the leaves hang vertically first; otherwise, tying them will damage either the leaves or the hinges.

Objects should be lifted by a part of the main carcass or frame, never by something attached to it, such as any ornament or moldings. Chairs should be lifted by the seat rails, not the crest rails nor the arms, and chests of drawers should be lifted from the base of the carcass, not from under the rim of the top. Chests and other large objects can be made much lighter by removing the sliding trays, drawers or shelves first. Mark them in chalk or pencil with a number on the back or base (and the same number on the carcass area), so that they can be inserted in the right place. Keep the fittings and keys safe in a labelled plastic bag tied to the object to ensure that they are not separated from it.

Extremely heavy objects can be made much easier to lift by sliding webbing underneath them and gripping the loose ends at a comfortable height. This also keeps the object nearer to the ground, which may reduce the amount of damage to all concerned in the event of an accident.

Marble tops should always be removed from furniture before the item is moved. The marble should be turned through 90° onto its edge and carried in the vertical position, never horizontally. Large marbles should be raised on webbing slings, but still kept on their edge.

Check an object carefully to establish whether it separates into its component parts, starting from the top. Cornices almost always lift off; if not, get up on a stepladder to see if they are screwed to the top board, and check for any doors held by pins (see below) at the same time. Next, look at the middle section and see if it is screwed to the base. If so, remove the screws, taking care to mark the holes and the screws with masking tape and an identity number. This is important as when the object is reassembled a screw that is too long could puncture a surface, while one that is too short will be too weak to hold the sections together.

Doors, especially glazed doors, should be tied shut, not just locked, with a soft woven tape at least 1in wide. The width of the tape will spread the load so that bruising of the edges of the piece is avoided (this would happen if string were used). Check for other moving parts (such as lopers, which may slide forwards), and remove all drawers from the fitted interiors of bureaus and secretaires. Some

Ensuring suitable environmental conditions
Rapid fluctuations or extremes of temperature, bright sunlight, and cold drafts can all contribute to the deterioration of furnishings. Whatever its period or style, antique furniture can be protected from excessive light and changes in temperature by a few simple precautions. Here light is screened by a combination of net curtains, a blind and heavy curtains. Such curtains are especially useful in winter, when they can help reduce the temperature differential between the center of the room and its edges.

from the fitted interiors of bureaus and secretaires. Some doors are fitted with pins instead of hinges. The top pin is located in a socket in the cornice, and the lower pin in a matching socket in the frame. When the cornice is lifted, the door will fall forwards unless supported. Such doors should always be removed before any attempt is made to move the item.

When packing objects for transport, make sure that they are well wrapped. Old blankets are ideal for this purpose. Cushions make good spacers, and can be used to separate objects or to protect edges from being marked by rubbing against the sides of vehicles. Remember that things will slide if you stop suddenly, and any grit on the vehicle floor or the wrapping may leave a furrow which could be impossible to remove.

Handling and Care

In order to be able to provide appropriate conditions for the use and storage of furniture, the reaction of wood to heat and moisture and the process of seasoning need to be taken into account.

HUMIDITY AND WOOD

Seasoning is the process of drying timber before it is used for constructional purposes. If the timber is allowed to season gradually, then most splitting and twisting forces due to internal stresses can be removed from the timber before it is cut to the approximate finished size. However, when the completed object is moved from one environment to another where there is a difference in local moisture content, then the timber will either give out, or take in, moisture. This causes the cells of the timber to expand or contract, which in turn alters the balance of internal forces – as well as the cross section of the timber. Moving from a well-ventilated old house to a centrally heated environment, perhaps with sealed double glazing, would constitute such a change. In such circumstances most panels suffer splits and distortion of their plane surfaces, damage that is far more common – and preventable – than people think. Stability of local conditions is very important; if an object has been stable in its previous environment, then attempts to recreate that same environment as closely as possible at its new location should be made.

Local weather conditions should be taken into account. For example, in temperate climates the general trend of timber is to dry out and shrink, but in humid climates other responses will be prevalent. When examining objects for indications of environmental damage, it should be remembered that thin sections of timber respond much more quickly than larger ones.

PEST INFESTATION

Pest infestation usually refers to wood-boring insects and, in particular, to woodworm. In temperate climates the furniture beetle and the pinhole beetle are the most likely insects to cause damage to furniture.

The pinhole beetle favors new wood with coarse grain, such as oak, beech, chestnut or ash, for laying its eggs. The furniture beetle is attracted by many timbers native to Europe, and will lay its eggs in any suitable crevice, such as a loose joint or split.

The most obvious evidence for the existence of woodworm is generally the presence of small holes in the wood, about 1mm in diameter. In truth these holes are evidence of the absence of the "worm" that produced them: they are the emergence holes of the beetle, called flight holes, made after the larva has pupated. (Though entomologically inaccurate, the word "worm" is used here, as it is within the furniture trade in general.)

If the entrances to the flight holes do not appear to reveal freshly exposed timber, but instead contain house dust and wax, then it may be assumed, but not guaranteed, that the infestation is non-active. Light-colored dust may be "frass," the residue left by the larvae. It may also be the dust from wearing drawer runners, bases, or some other moving joint. Remove all drawers and check for wear before concluding that the piece is infested with woodworm.

Some timbers are affected more badly than others. Mahogany, teak and cedar are rarely attacked, whereas walnut, lime and the sapwood of European timber are particularly prone to woodworm. However, this should not be taken to mean that walnut furniture always contains worm, or that the opposite applies.

In an ideal world, collections of furniture would be kept in an environment that is known to be beetle-free, and all new additions would be treated with a poison to eradicate the beetles. Obviously, such precautions are not easy in a domestic environment. Recently emerged beetles fly towards the light, so if the tiny beetles are observed on a windowsill, it is worth examining all the furniture, starting with the most recently acquired objects, to see if flight holes are present. If flight holes are found in an object, ask a restorer to assess whether they are recent or not and what action should be taken. The beetle may have emerged many years ago and there may be no sign of its having returned.

If there has been recent beetle activity in a piece of furniture, in some countries it is permissible for a good-quality, low-odor woodworm fluid to be applied by the restorer. This should kill emerging larvae and deter reinfestation. The fluid should be applied with care, as it is toxic and may damage the surface. If the piece is upholstered and its inner members are not reachable, fumigation carried out by a specialized company may be considered.

CERAMICS

Pottery and porcelain, two of the most ancient of man-made materials, are remarkably durable. Unglazed pieces, because they are porous, are slightly more vulnerable than those coated with a glaze. Both, however, are generally impervious to the kind of environmental factors that degrade most other materials. The survival of the beautifully painted Tang and Song wares of ancient China is testimony to the inherent stability of the ceramic body, and to the ability of most decoration to retain its color and brightness for many centuries.

Being easily broken, ceramics all too readily suffer the consequences of clumsy handling. From the moment they are picked up to the time they are put down again, pottery and porcelain are always at some risk from minor mishaps, which cause disfiguring cracks, chips and fractures, and from major accidents, which can reduce an object to fragments. While decoration under the glaze is well protected, painting over the glaze – in colored enamels, in silver and copper luster, and in gold – is exposed and can be highly sensitive to rubbing, scratching and moisture.

Fortuitously, pottery and porcelain's vulnerability to breakage finds partial compensation in the highly developed restoration techniques which now exist to dissimulate cracks and fractures. Sometimes even complete reconstructions are possible. Frequently, however, restoration tends to involve overpainting, and thus obliterating, some of the original surface of the piece. For the serious collector of ceramics, there is therefore nothing so precious as an undamaged piece, and nothing so important as maintaining its condition.

Figures from an early set of the Meissen Monkey Band
THESE 18TH-CENTURY FIGURES HAVE BEEN MOLDED IN HARD-PASTE PORCELAIN AND DECORATED WITH GILDING AND OVERGLAZED ENAMELS. THIS TYPE OF FIGURE SHOULD BE CLEANED BY IMMERSION IN WATER USING A SOFT-BRISTLED BRUSH, BUT BEFORE DOING SO ENSURE THAT THE PIECE HAS NOT BEEN RESTORED. WATER CAN EASILY SOFTEN SOME ADHESIVES AND REMOVE OVERPAINTING.

Ceramics were the first truly man-made objects. At their most simple they consist of clay and water, subjected to sufficient heat to harden the clay. By changing the ingredients and the temperature of the fire, however, different bodies can be created that have distinct qualities, presenting collectors and restorers with a variety of problems. It is a testimony to the durability of the resulting material that a good number of examples have survived in near-perfect condition to the present day.

Types of Ceramic Body

The crudest pottery, simply mixed clay and water, has been created by most cultures and is still made by some peoples. A fired pot is suitable for cooking and storage but, to be watertight, it must be covered with a glaze – usually transparent – which can be made from a wide variety of substances. Glazing demands a kiln, and therefore assumes a certain complexity of social organization.

By refining the clay of the body, its strength and appearance can be improved; examples of the resulting earthenwares include Islamic pottery, Italian maiolica, French and German faience, Dutch and English delftware, and English Staffordshire pottery, including ironstone, Victorian majolica, creamware and pearlware. The glaze on all these should render them nonporous, but in practice this is rarely so. Unglazed foot rims and crazing, chips and cracks in the glaze can provide a channel for moisture to enter the piece. Earthenwares are fired at about $1,472°F$, but if the temperature is raised to $2,192°–2,552°F$ they become stoneware.

Stoneware was first used in the Yueh wares of China. Although it is made from a single clay, it has the capacity to vary greatly in color and texture, sometimes even on a single piece. When fired to a high temperature, the body and glaze fuse together with no porosity, to produce a vessel that is immensely strong and extremely practical. Among the stonewares produced in Europe are Wedgwood's jasper and basalt wares.

The Chinese in the Tang Dynasty (AD 618–906) discovered that a mixture of china clay (kaolin) and china stone (petuntse), fired at about $2,552°F$, produced a strong, nonporous body that gave a musical note when struck. This was true, or hard-paste, porcelain, which formed the basic material of Chinese and Japanese wares and was later produced by Meissen, at Sèvres, in France, and in British factories. Parian can be considered a form of hard paste. Like stoneware, hard pastes tend to be strong, making them among the easiest and most satisfying ceramics to conserve and restore.

Soft-paste, or artificial, porcelain resulted from European attempts to produce a hard-paste body without being aware of the vital ingredient, petuntse, otherwise known as feldspar. Crushed quartz or glass was mixed with a white clay and fired at a temperature below that of hard paste, producing a translucent body. Various ingredients and manufacturing techniques, often closely guarded factory secrets, led to great variation in the hardness and porosity of the body.

At the end of the eighteenth century in Staffordshire, England, a hybrid paste was developed, only supplanted after about twenty years, by bone china. Developed by Josiah Spode (1754–1827), this is a modified hard paste (replacing the china stone with bone ash) and still forms the basic body of British porcelain. Soft-paste, hybrid hard-paste, and bone china bodies are reasonably strong and tend to be relatively water-resistant.

Forms of Decoration

GLAZING

Unglazed ceramics leave the kiln "in the biscuit" with a dry, matte surface. Glazing is carried out primarily for two reasons – to put a waterproof coating onto a porous body, and to improve the appearance of the surface. The glaze may be opaque, white, colored, or transparent and provides a receptive surface texture for further decoration. The disadvantage is that the glaze may obscure fine modeling and incised or impressed decoration. The Tang potters made both glazed and unglazed pieces, the former relying on their bold modeling and bright colors, the latter on detailed work. They also combined the techniques, glazing the bodies of the figures and leaving the head and hands unglazed.

In the Ming Dynasty, the problem of glaze obscuring detail was turned to advantage in anhua, or "secret" decoration. Here a design was engraved into the thinly potted, unfired porcelain body and the piece glazed. When fired, the design is all but invisible, only appearing in strongly raking light. The subtlety of this form of decoration makes restoration virtually impossible.

Early in the fourteenth century, Chinese potters were responsible for painting oxide of cobalt onto the porcelain body, covering it in a glaze and firing it at a high temperature. This was the beginning of underglaze blue, undoubtedly one of the most enduring and popular forms of decoration. Protected underneath the glaze, the cobalt blue has the strength to withstand many of the rigors of everyday use.

English delftware plate (probably Bristol), c.1760
THE PLATE IS SUSPENDED BY AN ACRYLIC PLATE HANGER. THE
PRESSURE FROM THE THREE SUPPORTS CAN BE ADJUSTED SO NO
DAMAGE IS CAUSED TO THE RIM OR SURFACE OF THE PLATE.

OVERGLAZE DECORATION

After the main firing, porcelain, stonewares, and some of
the finer earthenwares may be decorated with a wide
range of pigments, which are fixed to the surface by firing
the vessel a second time at a lower temperature. The colors
of these overglaze enamels may be transparent, others
opaque. Textures vary from smooth and imperceptible to
the touch, to others that are raised from the surface and
are, therefore, more prone to wear.

"Lustering" is the term used to describe the process of
depositing metal oxides (usually gold or platinum) over
the glaze. When fired, this technique produces a thin
iridescent film of metal on pottery or porcelain. It is safe to
wash, but very easily abraded.

GILDING

The ultimate embellishment of a ceramic object is the
addition of gold. Various methods have been used over
the last three hundred years; most require an additional
firing, whereas others are applied cold, as leaf, secured by
oil or size. As gilding is soft and very susceptible to wear,
handling should be kept to a minimum and cold gilding
kept away from water.

APPLIED DECORATION

Relief decoration, known as "sprigging," is produced by
the application of contrasting clay to the body of a ceramic
object. Perhaps the best-known examples of this technique are the jasper ware products of Wedgwood,
featuring bas-relief cameos. In the pâte-sur-pâte ceramics
produced by Sèvres and Minton in the second half of the
nineteenth century, the handcarving of the clay makes
each piece unique. Care should be taken not to knock the
reliefs on these objects, as they easily fracture.

At various times in China, Meissen, and Staffordshire,
particularly in the nineteenth century, porcelain was
decorated with ceramic flowers or fragments of clay. If
there are no structural weaknesses, the conservation
problems with these objects are no worse than with
comparable unencrusted objects, apart from fragility.

A rare form of decoration known as "jeweling" was
used at Sèvres on both hard- and soft-paste porcelain from
1780 to 1786. Minute blobs of transparent and opaque
colored enamel were fired onto prepared gold foil. These
were stuck to the porcelain with enamel and fired at a low
temperature. The technique was reintroduced in the 1860s
for imitations of Sèvres. Jeweling represents the most
delicate of all fired decorating techniques.

A style of decoration that fits uncomfortably into any
category is *cloisonné*. Normally this is practiced on metal,
but in late nineteenth-century Japan, the technique was
applied to porcelain. Copper or brass wires are attached to
the body, which then had the resulting cells filled with
colored clays or enamel and then fired.

Handling, Use and Display

Unlike most other works of art, ceramics do not react to
normal environmental changes of humidity and temperature. Dirt and dust may be visually unattractive, but rarely
put the object at risk. The greatest cause of deterioration is
accidental damage, and all precautions should be taken
when handling, using and displaying ceramic objects.

HANDLING

The careful handling of ceramics comes down to common
sense and the adherence to a few simple rules. Gloves
should rarely be worn as they can be slippery, or may snag
intricate porcelain or damage a friable surface. It is
important, however, that hands be clean and dry,
especially when handling unglazed pottery, which has an
absorbent surface and is easily marked. Hands perspire,
and the perspiration contains oils which may discolor the
body, also acting as a trap for dust.

Chinese 17th-century plate displayed on an acrylic stand
THE RIM OF THE PLATE SHOULD SIT COMFORTABLY IN THE TWO INDENTATIONS AT THE BOTTOM OF THE STAND, WHILE BEING SUPPORTED IN A NEAR-VERTICAL POSITION. FOR SECURITY THE BACK SUPPORT SHOULD BE THE SAME HEIGHT AS THE PLATE.

Before picking up an object, look carefully to establish how many elements make up the piece. A lidded vase on a ceramic stand may be of three separate pieces intended to look as one. Never try to pick up more than one piece at a time, or to lift lids by the knob or teapots by the handle. All too often these parts have been repaired, and the adhesive may fail. Mounts should be wriggled gently to ensure that they are not loose, and vases raised slowly, as they may have separate bases which are temporarily stuck.

With a hollow object, carefully remove the lid, if there is one, and set it to one side. Lift the piece with the fingers as far inside as possible and with the thumb out. On raising it, the free hand should immediately cradle the base. When replacing lids, observe whether they have locating lugs or slots, as they may fit in only one way. Some lids, particularly on Chinese teapots, are often ill-fitting and may slide off very easily.

Equal care should be taken when putting a ceramic object down. Before lifting anything, ensure that there is a clear and safe space in which to set it down, and lower it slowly to avoid jarring.

At antique fairs and markets there may well be hundreds of objects on a table, and it is most important to avoid the dangers inherent in stretching and lifting a piece over others, if at all possible, as a falling part may do double damage. The best method is to ask the owner to display the object to you. Be careful, too, of accidents caused by necklaces, scarves, bags, and falling eyeglasses.

USE

Many people buy decorative ceramics intending to use them. While some objects have been made only for display, the vast majority were intended for functional purposes, and were consequently made in relevant forms. If general guidelines relating to cleaning and conservation are followed, the ceramics are unlikely to come to harm. There are, however, a few important points that should be considered before an object is used. Any crazing of the glaze may allow the body of the object to be penetrated by liquids or fats, such as cream or butter, that may cause discoloration; the acids in fruit may attack and discolor enamels; and cheese should be removed from plates and dishes soon after use. Ceramic objects should also never be put in the refrigerator, where thermal shock can cause them to split, nor in conditions where there are rapid and extreme changes of temperature, such as near a hot stove.

DISPLAY

There are many ways of displaying ceramics. The European tradition of collection differs markedly from the practices of Oriental collectors. The latter generally store their collections in silk-lined boxes, keeping them for private display on specific occasions. In the West, it is far more common to place valued objects on open shelving. The ideal method of display would be dust-proof, vibration-proof, burglar-proof, regulated for humidity and temperature, and well lit. Few collectors can afford to create such desirable conditions, but they must nevertheless ensure that their prizes are at as little risk as possible.

Because modern cabinets are small and light in construction, it is important that they stand firmly on the floor and do not vibrate when people walk past, causing items to creep to the edge of the shelf or towards each other. If the shelves are adjustable, check that each corner is firmly supported. Make sure that lids do not rattle or items rock. A small ball of temporary adhesive may be sufficient to steady them. A great deal of cleaning time can be saved by ensuring that the display cabinet is as dust-proof as possible.

Some ceramics are liable to damage highly polished furniture. A felt pad, cut to the size of the foot-ring of bowls or vases, or the base of figures, will protect furniture from scratches, although it may increase the risk of creeping. This method should also be used when standing a ceramic on a hard floor. Vases used as umbrella stands should also have the inside of their base protected, for which a piece of foam rubber cut to shape suffices.

Plates can be displayed on dressers or stands, or hung on the wall. If a piece has been fitted with a fixed wire suspension, this should be removed, but do not attempt to bend the hooks back over the edges as this risks damaging the rim; snip wires at the rear and remove. Unless the piece has either been cracked or restored, it is unlikely to come to harm if hung from modern sprung hangers of the correct size which have plastic-coated wires. Also, be sure that the nail is well hammered in, and is of suitable size and strength.

A better hanging system, and the only one recommended for softer ceramics such as slipware and delft, uses an acrylic fitting. These hangers have no sharp edges and, since they are transparent, allow the whole of the plate to be seen. The most important factor is that the tension on the rim is adjustable, making it suitable for use on cracked, or otherwise vulnerable restored plates.

Bowls decorated on the inside pose a different problem. To be seen to best advantage they need to be supported in a near-vertical position, raking slightly backwards onto the support, which should be higher than the top of the foot-ring. Before the invention of plastics, the Orientals produced beautifully carved wooden stands complementary to the porcelain. These are still obtainable, and make an attractive and traditional alternative to the modern acrylic variety.

Cups and saucers are best displayed in the acrylic stands designed specifically for them. These come in two varieties, one of which tilts the cup, or tea bowl, backwards or forwards for better viewing.

Storage and Transportation

Ideally, ceramics should be stored in cupboards that are easily accessible; neither too high nor too deep. Plates should be stored on wooden racks, similar to drying racks, padded with felt to prevent abrasion to the rims. Bowls and dishes should all have their own place on the shelf to avoid stacking and overcrowding. If cups and saucers are kept together, place a pad of acid-free tissue paper in the well of the saucer and invert the cup on top. This affords a greater degree of stability and protects the surface of each object from contact abrasion.

If a ceramic object needs to be transported any distance it is advisable to use a container. A shallow basket or a strong cardboard box is best. Line the bottom with a layer of foam, and pack crumpled acid-free tissue paper around the object. Carefully study the shape of the object, and decide upon its most stable position. Although many ceramics will sit on their foot-ring, greater stability may be obtained by placing them upside down. For example, a stem bowl with a flared rim and only a small base is less likely to rock if transported inverted. Always transport lids separately and carry containers with both hands to ensure that the object does not slide within.

This method, while being suitable for moving ceramics from room to room, will not suffice over greater distances. Once a ceramic needs to be taken to another building or on a journey, the whole procedure changes. If a number of pieces have to be transported, consideration should be given to employing a firm that specializes in fine-art packing, but if this is not feasible, tough, rigid boxes or tea chests should be used. The base of the box should be lined with bubble wrap or expanded polystyrene, if available, or (for temporary storage only) masses of newspaper loosely crumpled, sheet by sheet. Each piece must be individually wrapped in acid-free tissue and then wedged tightly with further packing or other objects. Obviously, weighty items should be packed at the bottom, plates and dishes resting on their rims, bowls on their foot rim. Lids should never be stuck down with tape, as the slightest jar could cause a crack or chip, and tape can lift gilding and enamels. Nor should two objects ever be wrapped in the same piece of paper as, on unwrapping, there is a chance that one of them might be dropped. Miniature items can be wrapped in colored tissue (for easy identification) and packed into rigid boxes, which are then sealed and their contents listed on the outside. The box should be firmly taped down, numbered, and marked with a list kept of what has gone into it. After unpacking, check that all items have been retrieved.

Cleaning

Today's atmospheric pollution, together with normal household dust, deposits a layer of surface grime onto ceramic objects. On open display, dusting will remove some of this deposit, but over the years a residue can build up. This should be removed, but as each ceramic represents a different cleaning problem, according to its type and condition, only broad guidelines can be given. With all pieces, check for restoration, since moisture can easily soften some adhesives, and overpainted or replacement areas may discolor.

WASHING CERAMICS

For those types of ceramic object that may be immersed (see below), washing should be done in large plastic bowls where a good supply of hot and cold water is available. A two-wash procedure should be followed, the first containing a hand-hot solution of non-ionic detergent (1 tsp to 1 quart of water) that will help to remove greasy dirt, the second a warm water rinse. The bottoms of the bowls and the draining boards should be coverd with old towels to provide cushioning. Each object should be washed and dried individually. If there is a danger of snagging, use a soft-bristled brush rather than a cloth. After draining, cups, saucers and plates should be thoroughly dried; leave more complicated shapes to dry naturally.

Dishwashers should never be used; they scour surfaces and reach unacceptable temperatures.

Where immersion is not recommended, but ceramics may be cleaned with a little water (see below), place a folded towel on a firm table to cushion the item to be washed and soak up any excess moisture. Dampen a cotton-tipped swab with non-ionic detergent solution (1 tsp to 1 quart), and work over a small area. With a new cotton swab, rinse the same area, trying to prevent water from running over unglazed or damaged areas.

UNGLAZED CERAMICS

Unglazed ceramics with a porous body should only be dusted. Water, applied to such a body, would soak in, taking with it the surface dirt, causing discoloration. Unglazed ceramics, such as Tang tomb figures, are sometimes decorated after the firing of the body, using water-based cold pigments that could easily be removed, even with a damp cloth. Occasionally the molded harness impressions on equestrian figures still bear traces of gold leaf. Such decoration could also be instantly removed with a damp cloth, so moisture should never be allowed to come in contact with this type of ceramic.

Derby porcelain figure of Minerva, c.1765
WITH ITS MANY NOOKS AND CRANNIES TO COLLECT THE DIRT, ITS FRAGILE APPENDAGES, AND ITS DELICATE, GILDED DECORATION, THIS FIGURE DEMONSTRATES THE DIFFICULTIES INVOLVED IN CLEANING INTRICATE PIECES. IT IS FURTHER COMPLICATED IN THIS CASE BY THE STRESS CRACK TO THE NECK, WHICH COULD ALLOW WATER TO PENETRATE THE BODY.

Group of Chinese 17th-century underglazed blue-and-white porcelain with metal mounts
LIQUIDS USED DURING CLEANING SHOULD NOT BE ALLOWED TO COME INTO CONTACT WITH ANY METAL COMPONENTS. (LEFT)

Detail of Chinese silver mount
THIS VASE WAS SO BADLY DAMAGED (PROBABLY IN CHINA) THAT THE OWNER DECIDED TO CUT OFF THE BROKEN UPPER PART AND ADD A SILVER RIM. (BELOW)

LOW-FIRED CERAMICS

Low-fired earthenware is sometimes porous due to cracks in or crazing of the glaze. Cleaning should be carried out with cotton-tipped swabs (see above), since the immersion of objects of this type is not recommended.

HIGH-FIRED STONEWARE

If these ceramics are in good condition, immersing them in water will do no harm (see above), but stoneware pieces that have been decorated over the glaze should only be cleaned with a cotton-tipped swab. Various enameling techniques found on these pieces, from a second firing to cold painting, may also be vulnerable if immersed.

HARD-PASTE PORCELAIN

Hard-paste porcelains are generally the easiest ceramics to clean. If a piece is in good condition, it is not likely to be harmed by immersion (see above).

SOFT- AND HYBRID-PASTE PORCELAINS

Although generally robust, soft- and hybrid-paste can be porous through damaged and unglazed areas. Immersion should therefore be avoided (see above). A small artist's sable brush is useful for the cleaning of delicately modeled decoration. Pierced or molded decoration should be cleaned in the same manner.

BONE CHINA

The bone ash in this type of ceramic can cause natural discoloration, Bloor Derby being particularly prone to this problem. This is generally irreversible, but staining of a similar appearance may be caused by penetration from fats or liquids. If it is a modern, inexpensive, and/or replaceable piece, try soaking it in a highly diluted solution of biological washing powder and warm water (with added water softener if in a hard-water area). Pieces that feature any type of decoration and/or are valuable or irreplaceable, should be taken to a conservator for treatment.

METAL ELEMENTS

Repairs to ceramics often have metal rivets holding the broken pieces together. Porcelain in this condition should always be kept dry. Iron rivets will rust if exposed to moisture and this causes them to expand, resulting in further damage and staining. A restorer will remove the

Conservation of a damaged 19th-century Continental porcelain basket

CERAMICS ARE ESPECIALLY VULNERABLE TO BREAKAGE, AND A DELICATE OBJECT SUCH AS THIS PORCELAIN BASKET MAY ALL TOO EASILY SHATTER INTO PIECES. HERE, AN EPOXY RESIN ADHESIVE IS PAINSTAKINGLY APPLIED TO ONE OF THE BROKEN EDGES BEFORE

THE TWO PIECES ARE PLACED IN POSITION. THIS KIND OF ADHESIVE IS EXTREMELY STRONG BUT TAKES ABOUT TWENTY-FOUR HOURS FOR THE RESIN TO CURE, DURING WHICH TIME THE PIECE SHOULD BE TAPED TOGETHER AND NOT MOVED. GREAT CARE MUST BE TAKEN TO ENSURE THAT NO GILDING IS LIFTED WHEN THE TAPE AND ANY EXCESS ADHESIVE ARE REMOVED.

metal, and repair the piece using a modern adhesive. Copper rivets do not react to moisture in the same way as iron ones, but may corrode and may cause staining to the white body of the porcelain.

For hundreds of years, many ceramics have been mounted with metal components. The more common examples include German tiger ware, Dutch and English delft, and nineteenth-century English Doulton. Ensure that fittings are firmly attached to the body, and keep them as dry as possible so as to prevent corrosion. To clean the body of the ceramic (if it is of a type that is washable), use equal quantities of water and colorless, industrial methylated spirit (to aid evaporation), applied with cotton-tipped swabs, avoiding contact with the mounts.

Silver-mounted ceramics may have a residue of dried metal polish around the edges of the mount. The most effective instrument for removing this and other deposits is a wooden toothpick. Hold the object firmly on a padded working surface, and gently work the point of the toothpick at the deposit, having moistened it first with a

little of the mixture of water and methylated spirits solution. Only soft pressure should be applied, and the deposit should be removed a little at a time.

Ceramics decorated with *cloisonné* enamel should generally only be dusted, but if particularly dirty may be cleaned by the cotton swab method (see above), using a minimum of water. They should then immediately be dried as thoroughly as possible.

Damage

Ceramic objects with simple breaks – such as handles and spouts that have fractured cleanly – should be wrapped in acid-free tissue and packed into a rigid box to await the attention of a ceramics restorer.

A ceramic object that has dropped on the floor and broken into many pieces should be retrieved methodically to ensure that all the pieces are found. Place the broken pieces on a tray. Sweep the whole floor with a dustpan and brush to ensure that no fragments are overlooked. All crumbs and slivers should be put into a small container and placed with the wrapped fragments. Lay the pieces out and wrap individually in acid-free tissue before placing in a box. Resist any temptation to fit the pieces together as any friction between the broken edges can cause further chipping. If a photograph of the undamaged object is available, it should accompany the shards (see page 183). If more than one item is involved in the accident, do not try to sort out the pieces – this is better left to a professional.

Damage is sometimes difficult to detect. To discover whether unseen cracks have occurred in hard-paste porcelain plates, saucers or bowls, listen to the sound of the ring. Porcelain vessels have a resonance similar to a bell. Holding smaller vessels in the open palm of the hand and standing larger ones on the surface of a table, tap the rim with your fingernail. The resulting sound will indicate if any cracks are present. A dull sound means further examination is necessary. A bell-like ring would indicate no cracks, although a piece that has been broken in half and stuck together very tightly will have much of its ring restored.

There is a further useful test that can be used to discover previous repairs that have been made to porcelain. An ultraviolet lamp is needed. The porcelain should be illuminated by the lamp in total darkness. The difference of the absorbency of the ultraviolet rays between the original material and later synthetic substances may be seen. There is a chance, however, that the whole surface may have been sprayed with a thin coat of clear glaze medium, which would negate any effect from the lamp.

Restoration

Damaged objects are more than ever likely to be a financially viable proposition to restore than was once the case, and it is inadvisable for an untrained person to repair even simple breaks. Modern adhesive technology has resulted in the disappearance of many unsightly and damaging rivets, and missing areas can be filled with materials matched as closely as possible to the hardness and color of the orginal body.

Figures may have lost arms or legs: modeling skills are required to produce satisfactory replacements. In the case of very large ceramics that have sustained such damage that their structure is irreparably weakened, the additional support of a bronze or stainless steel armature may be necessary. In such cases, the minimum possible foreign material will be incorporated into the repair.

It is most important for a full discussion between owner and restorer to take place before any work is embarked upon. The owner should be in no doubt that to disguise a crack or a break so that it is barely detectable may well involve covering all or some of the original surface. Complete overspraying is disliked by many museums and some collectors. The best restoration procedures keep overpainting to an absolute minimum.

Owners of broken Oriental ceramics may prefer an Oriental-style repair, whereby contrasting materials, such as gold, silver and lacquer, are used to replace missing pieces. Repaired fractures are covered with a thin line of Oriental lacquer mixed with fine gold powder, an addition which may stand raised from the surface. The repair is, therefore, made a feature of the object, which, in the opinion of the Oriental connoisseur, enhances the original appearance.

Japanese 17th-century Kakiemon-style vase
A GOLD LACQUER LINE EMPHASISES THE SEAM BETWEEN THE ORIGINAL PORCELAIN AND THE RECONSTRUCTED HANDLE.

GLASS

Glass is a material that, over the centuries, has inspired an enormous range of applications and a vast repertoire of decorative effects. It is made from the fusion of flint or sand with soda (producing soda glass), potash (potash glass) or lead (lead glass). Calcium, which acts as a stabilizer, is sometimes also included. Generally, glass is relatively inert but, in those rare types that have a pronounced tendency to deteriorate, cloudiness and crizzling develop. While these sort of conditions can be stabilized, they cannot be reversed.

Being light and fragile, glass demands careful handling. Of all materials, it is the least amenable to repair; as it is thin and translucent, cracks cannot be disguised or fractures mended in ways that are effective with other materials such as ceramics. Glass that is in good condition, however, needs relatively little attention, provided that it is safe from accidental damage. Simple cleaning and polishing are all that is necessary to restore the sparkling translucency to pieces such as decanters, bottles and drinking glasses, or chandeliers hung with lusters.

Mirror glass, though equally straightforward to maintain, may suffer from deterioration of the silvering. Likewise, reverse painting on glass can be prone to detached or flaking paint. Stained glass and leaded windows, which are exposed to the elements, may become discolored and increasingly brittle; repairs to their supports and surrounds are often needed. Enamel, a form of opaque glass used in the decoration of metal surfaces, is mostly at risk from chipping, cracking and crazing, leading in turn to damage of the underlying metal.

Glassware by Maurice Marinot, 1926–31 ART DECO STUDIO GLASS SOMETIMES FEATURES DECORATION INTRODUCED DURING MANUFACTURE. MARINOT, THE MAKER OF THESE VESSELS, FREQUENTLY USED CHEMICALLY INDUCED METALLIC AND COLORED STREAKS, VEINS AND TRAILS, RICH CRACKLED EFFECTS AND TRAPPED AIR BUBBLES. UNLIKE DECORATION APPLIED AFTER MANUFACTURE, THESE EFFECTS DO NOT PRESENT ANY SPECIAL CLEANING PROBLEMS, AND SUCH OBJECTS DEMAND LESS CONSERVATION.

The majority of antique glass objects that survive today will probably be stable in terms of their chemical composition, since glass is not generally readily subject to variations in the environment. However, being light and fragile, glass items are easily cracked or broken, often as a direct result of incorrect handling or packing. Glass should be carefully examined for cracks, chips, flaking enamel, unfired paint and gilding, as well as any previous repairs which may well be very difficult to see with the naked eye.

It is worth noting that there are four man-made vitreous (glassy) materials: glass, glaze, enamels and faience. Glass may be formed into vessels and other decorative objects, or used in association with other materials to form items such as chandeliers, mirrors and windows. Glaze is applied as a coating over a supporting material, such as fired clay; faience is used to form objects in its own right; and enamels comprise colored, fritted glass fused to a metal backing.

Deterioration

All aspects of glass deterioration should be referred to an experienced conservator, who will be able to recommend the most suitable course of remedial action.

IRIDESCENCE

Excavated glass may exhibit many different signs of deterioration, the most common of which are colorful iridescent layers, which may be thick and flake off. Layers of iridescence, flaking or not, should never be removed, even though in doing so the original color of the glass may be revealed. Iridescence and other deterioration layers are actually decayed glass and thus part of the object itself. A conservator may need to consolidate the glass surface. This strengthening process is usually carried out through impregnation with a synthetic resin.

LIME AND MOLD

Glass vessels used to store liquids, such as vases and decanters, may exhibit a cloudiness on their interior surface. This is usually a lime deposit often associated with a deterioration of the glass itself; unfortunately, it is virtually impossible to remove without risk of damage to the glass. There are many documented treatments for lime-scale removal, such as swilling the interior of affected glass with water and sharp sand or even lead shot. Although such treatments may have limited success, they can also cause further damage; they are certainly not recommended for collector's items.

If mold growth is noticed – for instance, on animal-glue restoration – it must be removed with a dilute solution of disinfectant. It may sometimes be necessary for the vessel to be dismantled and restored, using a more suitable adhesive. This work should always be carried out by a trained conservator.

CRIZZLING

There is a deterioration phenomenon, often referred to as "diseased" or "sick" glass, which occurs on some antique glass, most notably on Venetian *cristallo* (a colorless soda glass) and early English (lead glass) pieces made by George Ravenscroft (1618–81), and more recently on late nineteenth- and early twentieth-century beads. Diseased glass, which weeps (sweats) and may eventually crizzle (crack), is the result of a chemical imbalance during manufacture, and repeatedly generates a slippery surface or droplets of moisture if the glass is exposed to humid conditions. Crizzled glass surfaces have diminished transparency owing to the formation of very fine surface cracks. Maintaining a suitable environment of 42% relative humidity for glass affected in this way seems to be the most suitable conservation procedure to prevent further deterioration (see page 181).

Handling

Because of its light weight, and sometimes its lack of color, glass is easy to knock over. When items have to be moved they should be placed on another adjacent surface and not merely pushed to one side, especially if the shelf is crowded. Never reach over glass vessels to move others at the back of a shelf. Before moving a glass, check that it does not consist of more than one piece, or that any previous restoration is not failing, in case removal may cause a breakage. Glass with a flaking surface or flaking decoration should be handled as little as possible.

Glasses should never be picked up by the rim. Rather, the bowl should be cupped in one hand and the base supported in the other in order to cradle the glass against knocks. Vessels should be carried one at a time unless a box is being used, in which case the box should be padded with cotton wool or foam covered with tissue paper, and the objects separated from one another by twists of tissue paper. When glass objects are being unpacked, they should be placed on their most stable plane on a surface thinly padded with material or foam, ensuring that they cannot roll. Never turn away while setting a piece of glass down, since the distance between the base of the object and the table-top will almost certainly be misjudged and

Islamic 11th- or 12th-century glass bowl
THE IRIDESCENCE ON THE SURFACE OF THIS BOWL IS THE RESULT OF DETERIORATION THROUGH BURIAL. THE SEPARATE PIECE HAS BEEN REMOVED AS IT HAS COME FROM ANOTHER SIMILAR BOWL AND HAD BEEN INSERTED DURING A PREVIOUS RESTORATION. IT WILL BE REPLACED WITH SYNTHETIC RESIN POURED BETWEEN WAX SHEETS.

the glass may be broken. Glass objects should never be placed near the edge of a surface where they could easily be brushed against and knocked over, particularly as they are sometimes difficult to see.

It is advisable to wear clean cotton gloves during handling to prevent leaving fingerprints on the glass. Caution must be taken not to let the glass slip, however, which it is more prone to do in gloved hands.

Cleaning

ANCIENT GLASS

A conservator should be consulted concerning the cleaning of ancient archaeological glass. Antique bottles such as those excavated from Victorian rubbish dumps are often impossible to clean adequately because of either the presence of metal corrosion products from metal objects buried with them or damage due to burning. However, general dirt can be removed by soaking the bottles for two or three hours in warm water containing a small amount of water softener and a biological washing powder. The solution should loosen dirt, though a bottle brush may be needed to clean the interior surface. After cleaning in this way, the bottles will need to be rinsed several times in clear water and allowed to dry naturally. It is important to remember that any wet treatments will remove remains of original labels and perhaps damage their print.

PERFUME BOTTLES

Stale perfume residues can be removed from glass perfume bottles with alcohol (methylated spirit). The alcohol should be left in the perfume bottle for an hour or so and then replaced, possibly several times. If necessary, to remove the smell of alcohol the bottle may be washed out with warm water and non-ionic detergent. The bottle should then be rinsed with clean water and allowed to dry out thoroughly before replacing the stopper (or it may become stuck in the neck), or filling with perfume. Metal fittings should be cleaned in the appropriate manner (see page 54): if cleaning involves wet treatments, the metal must be completely dry before attaching it to the glass, to prevent it from tarnishing.

CHINESE SNUFF BOTTLES

Chinese glass snuff bottles were frequently carved extremely thinly and painted on their interior surface with unfired pigments. The decoration is seen through the glass. On no account should these items be washed; they must be taken to a conservator, although it may well be the case that no cleaning will be possible without the risk of disturbing the painted decoration.

GENERAL WASHING

Historical and utilitarian glass objects can usually be washed in water, but there are many exceptions. Some of these are crizzled glass, glass with worn or flaking painted or gilded decoration, repaired or restored glass with metal or ormolu mounts, and deteriorated archaeological glass. Other than utilitarian household pieces, glass should not be placed in a dishwasher, as it may become chipped;

moreover, lead glass may develop an irreversible surface bloom. If in doubt, professional advice should be sought.

Glass that is in good enough condition to be able to be washed safely, should, ideally, first be dusted using an artist's sable or hogshair paintbrush, holding the object steady with one hand. It is advisable to wash glass objects one at a time, and to wrap the faucet with cloth or foam plastic so that the glass does not chip or crack if accidentally knocked against it. The bottom of the sink should also be covered with a soft material if a plastic bowl is not available. The water should be tepid, never hot, with a few drops of liquid soap added to it. Ideally, a non-ionic detergent should be used. A soft brush may be used to dislodge dust and dirt trapped behind handles and other appendages. No pressure should be placed on the glass, especially the rim, during washing and drying.

After washing, the glass should be rinsed and then left to drain on a cloth- or absorbent paper-covered surface so that it does not slide. Once the free water has drained off, the glass can be further dried and, if necessary, polished, using a soft, lint-free cloth. Stemmed glasses should be supported by holding the bowl and wiping up and down the glass rather than using a twisting movement.

Decanters in regular use should, after washing and rinsing, be left in a plastic bucket to drain overnight. Stoppers should never be left in decanters or they may stick in the neck. It may be possible to free a stopper by spraying a small amount of thin penetrating oil between the stopper and vessel neck. The oil should penetrate the crack and allow the stopper to be gently twisted out. The remaining oil can be removed by washing as described above. Force should not be applied, since it is easy to break the neck of the container. Fortified wine left in decanters may form a deposit; if this is removed with a bottle brush, take care not to scratch the glass with the exposed wire at the tip of the brush.

Commercial glass cleaners should not be used on any glass except utilitarian household items, since these contain unspecified chemicals which may cause damage to the glass or fitments and frames. Polishing the interior of utilitarian items mechanically or with hydrofluoric acid, which is highly dangerous, must be carried out by an expert. Since there is a danger of the glass breaking, this method is not recommended for collector's items.

Display and Storage

For obvious reasons, glass on open display should not be placed directly beneath objects hanging on the wall. It should also be kept away from flapping curtains or heavy

Bohemian late 19th-century cased and cut glass with gilded and enameled decoration; detail of chipped rim
ONLY EXPERTS SHOULD REPAIR SUCH COMPLEX PIECES. (ABOVE)

Late 19th-century acid-etched lamp bowl
THE GLASS BOWL HAS BEEN REPAIRED BY A CONSERVATOR. (OPPOSITE ABOVE)

Turko-Persian 18th-century ewer
THIS DAMAGE WAS PROBABLY CAUSED BY DRILLING THROUGH THE GLASS TO ATTACH THE HANDLE. (OPPOSITE BELOW)

doors, which may slam and cause a draught sufficiently strong to dislodge light glass.

Reverse paintings on glass and mirrors (see page 50), as well as glass bearing unfired pigments, should be hung or displayed away from sources of heat, light and moisture. The condition of chains, wires, cords and metal fittings that are used to hang them should be checked routinely, and the frames and backboards checked for signs of insect attack. Normal household conditions are suitable for displaying glass, that is, a relative humidity of 45–60% and the temperature at about 65°F.

Display cases and the shelves within them should be stable and level so that glass cannot move due to external vibrations, however caused. If necessary, glass objects may be supported by acrylic mounts, and mirrors may be used to reflect light upwards onto decorative details so that the subjects need not be placed immediately over light bulbs. Lighting should be of the cool variety or external and properly situated so as not to cause a heat build-up. The effects of heat build-up can be very serious on certain types of glass, for example, pieces with incipient crizzling or painted surfaces, or weathering products. A conservator can advise on the special conditions necessary for storing and displaying unstable glass.

Ideally, glass should be stored in glass-fronted cabinets so that the contents are readily visible. The shelves should not be overcrowded, and the glass vessels should not be allowed to touch one another. Vessels that have more than one component need special care; lids and stoppers should either be stored separately (and identified), or bound in place with cotton so that they cannot fall when the vessel is lifted. Dust can be prevented from entering such items by covering them loosely with acid-free tissue paper or muslin. Objects stored on their sides should be bedded in tissue to prevent them rolling. Treated excavated glass, although robust, should be stored in stable atmospheric conditions. Shards should be stored horizontally in perforated plastic bags. Tissue may be necessary to prevent the shards rubbing together. Vessels must be stored in dust-free cases or boxes with adequate packing of inert foam or acid-free tissue paper (never newspaper or cotton wool). If glass is patinated or iridescent, its handling must be kept to a minimum to prevent further damage to the surface.

Packing and Repair

Temporary packing of glass vessels for transit within a building has been dealt with above (page 46). For external transport, glass should be extremely well packed in sturdy wooden boxes. The services of a professional packing company may be sought.

Any important broken object requires professional restoration; it is advisable not to attempt a repair as this will only increase the eventual cost due to the extra restoration work involved. All fragments should be collected and individually wrapped in acid-free tissue so as not to damage each other. The packages should then be placed in a box until taken to a conservator.

Small chips in the rims of utilitarian glass objects can be ground out by a specialist, provided that this does not destroy any decoration and that there are no cracks running from the chip. This course of action is not recommended for collector's items as it will further devalue them. Ground and polished edges are not always possible to detect with the naked eye. New decanter stoppers and blue-glass liners can be custom-made.

Chandeliers and Other Lighting

Glass chandeliers and other types of lighting, such as lamps, candelabra and candlesticks, quickly lose their sparkle when covered with dust, wax and nicotine. Before any cleaning is undertaken on electrical lights they must be unplugged or, in the case of chandeliers, isolated from the main electrical supply.

Lamps, candlesticks and simply designed chandeliers (those with few glass lusters), can be dusted, cleaned with some non-ionic detergent on a damp cloth, and then rinsed. Make sure that no solution enters the interior of the hollow arms (especially if these are electrically wired). Large chandeliers, which are often intricate in design, will require specialist attention. They may be cleaned annually by removing chains of lusters and other glass decoration, and then washing as above. Every ten years or so they will need to be fully dismantled to enable a thorough inspection of the construction and the electrical wiring, as well as a more in-depth cleaning program.

Broken glass components can be repaired by a conservator; it is sometimes possible to buy replacements, particularly the lusters, from suppliers or antique shops specializing in chandeliers. Individual small lusters and prisms may also be found in junk shops.

Mirrors

The need to protect valuable mirror plates has resulted over the years in a vast array of styles and shapes of frame. Until modern techniques became available, silvered glass was a rare and expensive commodity. Mirrors range from small hand-held examples to enormous wall mirrors, such as overmantels and pier glasses. The general condition of wall-hung mirrors, in particular, should be routinely checked. If the mirrored surface is showing signs of peeling or flaking, the mirror should be referred to a specialist. However, it may not be possible to improve the appearance, except by the insertion of a reflective sheet behind missing areas of mirroring. Although it is possible to resilver glass, the appearance of even "antique finish" will differ from the original. Resilvering may reduce the value of a mirror, as may alterations to the frame. If a plate is replaced, the original plate must be retained.

Glass mirrors in good condition can be cleaned with a soft, lint-free cloth and water with non-ionic detergent or alcohol, then polished with a soft dry cloth. Small mirrors should be taken off the wall before cleaning, to prevent their becoming dislodged. Carved frames should be checked for structural stability before being cleaned or moved, and subsequently handled with great care. Large mirrors, attached to the wall with mirror plates, may be cleaned *in situ* provided there is safe and easy access by stepladder.

Paintings on Glass

Paintings on glass, usually framed, are painted on the back of a sheet of glass in reverse order (details first, then the ground), and viewed through the glass. Paintings of this kind were combined with mirroring in nineteenth-century Chinese work, and may also be gilded. Depending upon the pigments and media used, the painting may lift from the glass so that air introduced between the design and glass obscures the details; or paint may flake off. It is difficult to correct either of these processes, particularly if the glass itself is broken.

Glass paintings often are broken as a result of either pressure applied to the glass when cleaning or during framing, or accidents during hanging. Since these were produced in many countries, using an enormous range of techniques and materials, they are not easy to restore; thus, professional help is most important.

Window Glass

Window glass suffers from the same problems as other glass objects – but to a greater extent, since it is often exposed to the elements. Glass windows *in situ* become discolored and brittle, building up layers of weathering products, combined with dust and other airborne dirt. Colored window glass was either colored right through in

Reverse painting on glass
PAINTING ON GLASS IS A DELICATE TECHNIQUE INVOLVING
BUILDING UP THE IMAGE ON THE BACK OF THE GLASS IN REVERSE
ORDER. PROBLEMS INVOLVING LIFTING OR FLAKING PAINT SHOULD
BE REFERRED TO A PROFESSIONAL.

its molten state and/or decorated, once hardened, with fired-on enamels and/or silver stain. Stained glass has come to be the term used to describe all types of colored and leaded glass, although "painted" glass is more accurately applied to glass decorated after manufacture.

Leaded glass is composed of glass fragments joined together with lead rods (cames) secured with putty. The putty usually deteriorates more quickly than either the glass or the lead, becoming brittle due to its oil drying out. The lead usually remains in shape as it is supported around the edge by the window frame itself. However, as the lead begins to deteriorate, the window may bow out of shape and will need to be releaded professionally.

Ancient glass, badly deteriorated window glass, and glass that is surface-decorated should always be inspected by a conservator before being cleaned, and will usually require professional attention. Each color on the glass must be tested for stability by either gently brushing or rolling a damp cotton-tipped swab over its surface. If pigment is removed, cleaning will not be possible. Heraldic designs and other ornate decoration may be particularly vulnerable. Household cleaners should not be used since the chemicals contained in them may attack the lead and putty as well as the glass itself.

If the paint is soundly attached to the glass, the surface should first be gently brushed to remove loose dust. Then, depending upon the size and condition of the glass panel, water – with the addition of a little non-ionic detergent – can be used to clean it. The water can be applied with a cotton-tipped swab, soft lint-free cloth, soft sponge or chamois leather. Large panels or windows should be cleaned starting at the base and working upwards, repeatedly cleaning and rinsing. This way, dirty water does not run over uncleaned glass and cause staining. Care should be taken not to let excess water run beneath the leading, or to put pressure on the leaded glass.

DISPLAY AND STORAGE

Unframed examples of stained glass should be leaded around the edge or supported in a metal frame for display. Organic materials, such as oak wood, which give off acid vapors, should not be used for framing or for storage cabinets since the acid will attack the lead. If the glass is to be hung in a window, it should be protected by an ultraviolet, light-absorbing acrylic sheet that is placed between the panel and the window.

Panels in good condition can be stored vertically if well supported, but horizontal storage is preferable. Bowed or distorted panels must be stored horizontally and padded with acid-free tissue-paper or foam.

Enamels

Enamel is composed of metallic oxides (colors) mixed with a glassy frit of finely powdered glass, and fused to a metal base (copper, silver or gold). Since it is essentially glass, enamel can exhibit many of the same signs of deterioration, including, in rare cases, weeping.

Enamel shatters easily if it is knocked or dropped. Once the enamel breaks, it can flake away from the base. Loss of enamel could allow moisture to enter, causing copper-alloy backings to corrode and push yet more enamel off. Antique enamels should be kept in a stable atmosphere to prevent damage by differential expansion and contraction between the "glass" and its metal backing. They should be examined for cracked, crazed, broken or chipped surfaces, for previous (and discolored) restoration, and for damaged metal fittings. Damaged enamels should be referred to a professional restorer.

Displaying enamel objects in glass-topped cabinets will help to keep them clean. Otherwise, display and storage conditions are the same as for other glass objects.

METALWORK

Although metals are to an extent justifiably associated with durability and resistance, they are in fact susceptible to various forms of damage and degradation, and therefore need as much care as most other materials. Exposed to humidity, to various pollutants present in the atmosphere, and to the acidity of fingerprints, most metals are likely to corrode or tarnish. Handled carelessly, they may become bent, dented or scratched. Polished too vigorously, their surface may be worn away and delicate decoration completely erased.

The greatest enemies of arms and armor are rust and unsightly patches of corrosion caused by fingerprints on their highly polished surfaces. Corrosion also affects coins and medals, especially those made of silver and copper and their alloys, when they are stored in damp conditions, exposed to harmful substances present in a polluted atmosphere, or, ironically, kept in contact with many of the materials in which they are traditionally stored or displayed.

In jewelry, the combination of metals with other materials demands that special consideration be given. Relatively hard gemstones, such as diamonds, rubies and sapphires, as well as softer pearls, coral, shell, amber and jet, are variously prone to scratching and to damage from moisture, dirt, soap, creams, perfume and hair spray: everyday hazards that it is difficult to remember to avoid. Gold, silver and enameled snuffboxes and objects of vertu must be handled with care and treated as the precious personal possessions they were originally intended to be.

Detail of a German wheel-lock sporting rifle, c.1600

THE METAL OF THIS LOCK IS CHISELLED AND PIERCED, AND SOME OF THE PARTS ARE EMBELLISHED WITH GILDING. SUCH A PIECE EXEMPLIFIES THE DELICATE SKILLS OF THE GUNMAKERS OF THE 16TH AND 17TH CENTURIES. THERE ARE MANY WEAPONS WITH WORK OF COMPARABLE QUALITY, WHICH MAKES ARMS AND ARMOR AN ATTRACTIVE FIELD FOR THE COLLECTOR, BUT ONE WHICH DEMANDS CAREFUL CONSERVATION.

METALS

Metals are not as tough and resistant as they may appear or as their various uses suggest. In varying degrees, they are all vulnerable to scratching and denting, some to fracturing, and many to wear from handling and polishing. They may also experience chemical damage which causes them to tarnish and corrode. This necessitates cleaning or polishing, which in turn cause further wear.

Removing the causes of tarnish and corrosion, thereby obviating the need for frequent cleaning and polishing, is

Cleaning

There are no short cuts to cleaning metalwork safely and satisfactorily. It is never simply a question of quickly applying a metal cleaner and buffing to a shine.

First, examine the object in a good light to identify the metal from which it is made as this is not always obvious if the hallmark or maker's mark is obscured. A combination of metals and decorative finishes, and the presence of other

Detail of a 19th-century horse trapping from Turkestan
MADE OF STEEL OVERLAID WITH THIN SILVER STRIPS, THIS HORSE TRAPPING DISPLAYS TWO IMPRESSIONS OF FINGERPRINTS ON THE SURFACE OF THE SILVER — A RESULT OF THE OBJECT BEING HANDLED WITHOUT GLOVES.

the first step towards preserving metalwork, the natural beauty of its surface sheen, or its patina, and its incised, embossed or applied decoration.

Handling

The softer the metal, the greater its vulnerability to wear simply through handling. When handling significant metal objects, it is important to wear white cotton gloves (that should be washed periodically to remove a build-up of perspiration and other deposits) or surgical gloves. Rubber gloves, which may contain sulfides, are not recommended for use with metals.

To reduce the risk of scratching, and of denting if accidentally dropped, objects should be handled over a padded surface, preferably at table height. Lift the object using both hands, supporting it from below. Avoid lifting an object by the neck, handle or other protruding part (often its weakest point), and refrain from unnecessary manipulation of moving parts, such as lids; this may further weaken worn hinges. Also, ensure that detatchable parts are secure before turning an object over.

materials, such as ivory, wood or gemstones, dictates the choice of cleaning methods and materials used.

DUST REMOVAL
Removing dust is the first step in the correct procedure for cleaning metal. Use a clean, soft-bristled brush or photographer's air brush. Probe gently into crevices with a soft wooden cocktail stick (or toothpick), if necessary. It is preferable not to use a feather duster.

WASHING
Washing with water and a little non-ionic detergent is the gentlest way of cleaning most metals. It is, however, inappropriate for antique bronze, iron and steel, and for objects made of metals combined with other materials.

Wash the object in warm water in a plastic bowl or on a draining board padded with foam, toweling or some other thick, soft material. Use only a soft sponge or cloth, and a soft brush or cocktail stick to remove dirt from engraved areas and crevices. Food stains can often be gently sponged off with warm water and non-ionic detergent. Deep stains usually need to be removed chemically or polished out, and this should only be done by an experienced conservator.

After washing, rinse the object well inside and out to remove all traces of soap and detergent. Dry it at once with a soft absorbent cloth. It is most important to pay equal attention to both the inside and the outside of hollow objects. Water or other cleaning solutions trapped inside an object may set up a chemical reaction that in turn will lead to corrosion, while moisture on the outside will mark the surface of the metal. A warm hair dryer may be used to dry intricate parts. Do not dry a metal object by placing it in full sunlight, or in front of any source of direct heat.

Pair of Sheffield silver-plate candlesticks, 1796
THE SILVER LAYER HAS COMPLETELY WORN AWAY IN CERTAIN AREAS AS A RESULT OF EXCESSIVE POLISHING. TRACES OF CLEANING MATERIAL CAN BE SEEN AS A WHITE DEPOSIT IN THE GAPS BETWEEN THE SCONCES AND THE STEMS. IF LEFT, IT COULD ATTRACT MOISTURE AND CAUSE FURTHER CORROSION.

REMOVING WAX AND TARNISH

Remove deposits of candle wax by warming the object very slightly in an oven, or with warm water, until the wax softens and lifts off cleanly. If the object cannot be warmed, or if warming fails to produce results, use a cotton-tipped swab dipped in turpentine or mineral spirits, taking care to follow health and safety precautions.

Heavier tarnish and some light corrosion may be removed with polish-impregnated wadding, liquid metal cleaner, or other commercial products specifically intended for the metal. These products remove a small amount of the metal surface in the form of silver or copper compounds. They should therefore be used as infrequently as possible, and never on metals such as Sheffield plate and electroplate as the silver plating will be gradually worn away, revealing the underlying metal.

POLISHING

When preparing to polish a metal object, cover the working surface with a soft padded material, such as a towel. Read and follow the instructions given by the manufacturers of metal polishes, to avoid damage to the object and risk to health. Many cleaners and polishes contain chemicals that can be harmful unless the correct health and safety precautions are taken.

Apply the polish with a soft cloth or soft-bristled brush. Keep a separate cloth or brush for each metal. Test the reaction of the metal on a small, inconspicuous area. If in doubt, seek professional advice. If not, proceed to clean the object by applying polish using a gentle circular motion, and do not exert pressure on thin or heavily pierced areas, which are likely to bend or fracture. If necessary, support delicate areas with padding. Dirt caked into engraved areas, applied decoration and other intricate parts may be removed with a soft-bristled brush, a cotton-tipped swab dipped in liquid metal polish, or a piece of polish-impregnated wadding wound around a wooden cocktail stick. Try to avoid spreading polish onto other materials such as ivory or wood, since it may stain them.

Using a soft cloth, gently polish the object to a lustrous finish, though taking care not to exert unnecessary pressure. Vigorous polishing has a wearing effect on most metals. It gradually dulls the outline of engraved and embossed decoration, and wears away the silvering on Sheffield plate and electroplate and the gilding on silver-gilt. After polishing, wash the object, rinse it thoroughly, and dry it immediately with an absorbent cloth. Any residues of polish left on the metal will continue their chemical action, acting as a point from which further corrosion will spread.

Once an object has been polished, regular washing should keep its surface lustrous and free from tarnish, thus removing the need for frequent chemical cleaning processes detrimental to the surface of metal. After polishing, some metals, such as silver that is not in frequent use, may be lacquered to protect them against tarnishing. A coat of microcrystalline wax may be applied to copper and brass to retard tarnishing, and to steel and cast iron to protect these metals against rust.

In cases where stubborn staining or tarnishing do not respond to cleaning with proprietary metal polishes, the object should be taken to a conservator, who will be able to treat it under laboratory conditions.

Composites

Objects made of a mixture of materials are known as composites. Metals, for example, may be set with gems and semiprecious stones; they may also be enameled or combined with organic materials such as wood, ivory, horn, bone or amber. They need special consideration as many cleaning treatments for metals can damage non-metallic materials or affect the settings of gems.

Before cleaning, it is advisable to discover whether an object can be dismantled to separate the different materials. An object should only be taken apart if it is clearly intended to be so, that is if there are easily unscrewable nuts holding the additional material to the metal. Having

dismantled an object, keep all pieces carefully and make sure that it is subsequently reassembled correctly. Each piece should be completely dry and all traces of cleaner removed before reassembly.

If an object cannot be dismantled, do not immerse it in water or any other cleaning solution. Clean it with a cloth moistened with water and non-ionic detergent, or dipped in methylated spirit. Take care not to run any moisture or cleaning materials over organic materials; a cotton-tipped swab may be necessary to clean areas around wood or ivory, for instance.

Display

Ideally, metal objects should be displayed in a dust-free environment, where temperature and humidity are stable, and acidic vapors and tarnish-inducing sulfides in the atmosphere are at a minimum.

It is inadvisable to place metal objects on a mantelpiece or above a radiator, where heat lifts and deposits dust. Heat and direct sunlight also encourage tarnish to form, as do sulfides given off by gas and wood fires; these are particularly harmful to silver, brass and copper. Direct heat and sunlight are also harmful to painted metals, causing the paint to crack.

Copper and its alloys, such as bronze, are not ideally suited to display in bathrooms or conservatories, where they may become damp and are at risk from being splashed with water. A damp floor may also damage brass, copper and lead objects unless they are separated from it and placed on a cork mat, plastic sheet or wooden slats.

Small metal objects are best protected by being displayed in a glass or Plexiglas case. Avoid wooden cases, which emit organic acid vapors, and do not display metal objects – silver in particular – on felt, wool or velvet, which contain sulfides. All cause some degree of tarnishing on metals.

Special consideration should be given to metal objects containing organic materials such as wood, bone, ivory or amber. All these are more vulnerable than metals to sunlight, and to warm, dry and damp conditions, particularly when those conditions fluctuate. Ideally, these objects should be kept at a constant temperature of about 68°F and a constant level of 50–60% relative humidity.

Storage

Metal objects should not be packed for storage immediately after cleaning. Leave them in a dry, dust-free place for up to two days in order to reduce the likelihood of moisture being trapped inside the packaging. Choose a storage space where relative humidity can be maintained at 45–55% and temperature at about 68°F.

Where possible, wrap items individually to prevent them from abrading one another. Use acid-free tissue paper to inhibit the formation of tarnish (silver and brass benefit particularly from this protection). Silver may, in addition, be placed in specially designed bags made from sulfur-free baize and impregnated with tarnish-retardant. Do not use ordinary felt, wool or velvet to wrap metal objects in; these materials all contain sulfides, which attack metal.

Bubble wrap over the acid-free tissue gives extra protection from physical damage. Wrap each piece loosely and place in perforated plastic bags. Do not store pieces in sealed bags or plastic wrap since this may trap moisture, which will in turn promote tarnish and corrosion to set in.

Large objects, such as bronze or lead statues that cannot easily be wrapped and put away, should be placed on a layer of cork or plastic sheeting, or wooden slats, to protect them from damp floors, then covered in plastic sheeting (pierced to prevent moisture from accumulating) to protect them from dust.

Do not store objects that have started to corrode; if possible, remove the corrosion first or take the object to a conservator. Tarnish, being stable, is not harmful to metals either on display or in storage.

Conservation

The main concern of metal conservation is to arrest chemical damage caused by corrosion, to remove corrosion products, and to treat objects in various ways so as to prevent corrosion recurring. Corrosion that is too advanced or too difficult to remove by cleaning at home

English silver teapot, 1829
IF THE METAL IS SOUND, THE DENTS CAN BE REMOVED BY A SKILLED SILVERSMITH, BUT NOT BY SOMEONE UNUSED TO SUCH WORK. (RIGHT)

Late 19th-century Fabergé photograph frame
WHERE SILVER AND WOOD ARE INSEPARABLE, TAKE CARE TO KEEP METAL CLEANER OFF THE WOOD. (OPPOSITE)

When storing several objects in one bag, do not pack them too tightly or they could bend or dent one another. Also, ensure that those objects at the bottom of the bag are not crushed by those on top.

It is possible for metal corrosion to stain other materials such as ivory or wood if they remain in contact with one another for long periods of time. It is therefore important to check objects in storage regularly to ensure that no deterioration is taking place.

Similarly, avoid storing metal objects in wooden cases or cardboard boxes without regularly inspecting them. Even when they are wrapped in acid-free tissue and placed in perforated plastic bags, metals are still vulnerable to sulfides and acids given off by wood and cardboard.

can usually be removed by a conservator by manual or mechanical abrasive techniques or with the aid of chemicals too powerful for use by the layperson. If conservation is not carried out on unstable corrosion, such as that occurring on iron or lead, there is a risk of losing or seriously disfiguring the whole object.

Restoration

It is virtually impossible for amateurs to carry out successful repairs to badly damaged metals. It is also inadvisable since the danger of damaging pieces is great. Old and valuable objects should always be repaired by a professional restorer.

Simple, reversible repairs, however, may be carried out at home using adhesives that can easily be removed. This is suitable, for instance, for repairing figurines from which heads, arms or other details have broken off. Resist the temptation to use stronger glues like epoxy resin and superglues. These are not so easily removed if it is later decided that the object should be restored professionally. Do not use any woodworking adhesives on lead or pewter as they can cause corrosion.

In the hands of a qualified restorer (but never in those of a layperson), welding and soldering are the most satisfactory way of repairing fractures. The wrong treatment can irrevocably damage an object and detract from its historic integrity. Likewise, dents should only be taken out by a trained and experienced conservator.

For virtually all antique plated metalware, neither regilding nor resilvering is advisable. The original condition of a piece is prized above its restored condition; replacing lost gilding or silvering with modern gold or silver is really an act of vandalism that no good restorer would recommend. Apart from ethical considerations, the color of modern plating differs noticeably from antique gold and silver. Resilvering is, however, allowable on canteens of cutlery that are in regular use, although a conservator should be consulted first. Home treatment with solutions purporting to cover metals with a layer of silver is inappropriate for fine pieces.

Other metals can be chemically stripped and highly polished. However, the result is complete loss of patina and a new appearance to the metal. It is nearly always an inadvisable practice on antique pieces.

With regard to wooden or ivory handles that have deteriorated, it is always best to have them conserved and, if possible, repaired to preserve the integrity of the object. In cases where deterioration makes them irreparable, they may be replaced by modern replicas as near in shape to the original fitting as possible. A record of any modern replacements in an object should always be kept, as this is helpful in any future restoration work.

Lacquering and Waxing

Lacquering and waxing are two separate methods of protecting certain metals from dirt, tarnish and corrosion by sealing their surface from the surrounding atmosphere.

Lacquering is suitable for silver-gilt, solid and plated silver, brass and copper. Correctly applied, it should give protection for up to five years. Reducing the need for periodic cleaning, lacquering is recommended for fine pieces of metalwork not in regular use.

Because the process involves the use of organic solvents and lacquers that emit toxic fumes, and because it requires considerable skill, lacquering should be carried out by a conservator. Firstly, the surface of the object is scrupulously cleansed of dirt, grease and deposits left by fingerprints. Secondly, lacquer is brushed or sprayed onto the metal, thinly and evenly coating the object. Unsightly iridescence develops in areas where lacquer gathers or is applied too thickly. In any areas inadvertently left unlacquered, tarnishing will appear.

Once a piece has been lacquered, handle it with care. Though lacquer is an effective sealant, it is vulnerable to scratching and degradation from fingerprints, which in turn allow the atmosphere to penetrate through to the metal and tarnish to develop. It is also recommended that a record be kept of pieces which have been lacquered, so that they are not inadvertently polished and the lacquer abraded. A note of the date of lacquering is useful for timing the date on which relacquering should take place. Both the removal of old lacquer and relacquering should be carried out by a conservator.

Waxing, usually by the application of a thin layer of microcrystalline wax, is suitable for copper, brass, steel and cast iron. Applied to copper and brass, it gives protection against handling and tarnishing. On steel and cast iron, it protects against rusting.

Waxing can safely be carried out at home. Apply the wax with a pad of soft cloth or a soft brush, using a circular motion. Work on one small area at a time, buffing the wax before it dries. If the wax is allowed to dry out and harden too quickly, remove it with a cloth dampened with mineral spirits and rewax the area.

Gold, Gilding and Ormolu

In its pure state, gold is very soft and lustrous, and it neither tarnishes nor corrodes. Being so soft, as well as very costly, pure gold is rarely used to make metal objects. It is more usually alloyed with silver (which produces a white gold); or with copper (which gives a reddish gold). An alloy of gold, silver and copper produces a yellow gold.

The proportion of gold to other metals in the alloy is indicated in terms of carats: 24-carat gold is pure, a 20-carat alloy consists of twenty parts of gold to four parts of a baser metal and so on down the standard scale of 18, 14 and 9 carats. Gold of a lesser quality may display the corrosion products of the baser metal with which it is alloyed.

Very gentle dusting is usually all that is recommended for cleaning gold. If dirt and grease are present, these can normally be washed off solid gold with water and non-ionic detergent. Care must be taken to dry the metal thoroughly since gold is particularly vulnerable to impurities in tap water, and may discolor. Polishing is both unnecessary and harmful.

Gilding, in which a thin layer of gold is applied to a baser metal, should not be polished regularly as it will eventually be worn away. Again, very gentle dusting should be all that is needed. Should cleaning be necessary, gently wipe the object with a cloth dipped in water and non-ionic detergent. Before doing so, however, inspect the gilding to check that it is well attached. If, as is the case in much poor-quality gilding, the gold does not adhere well, water may penetrate between the layers and cause a chemical reaction. Given its delicacy and vulnerability, gilding is one type of metalwork that benefits the most from a protective layer of lacquer.

Ormolu, which consists usually of gilt-brass or gilt-bronze, was used to make objects such as candlesticks and

Handle of an 18th-century Italian silver-gilt ewer
THE DARKER AREAS OF TARNISH IN THE DEPTHS OF THE DETAIL CAN BE CLEANED USING A SOFT-BRISTLED BRUSH OR COTTON SWABS MOISTENED WITH WATER AND DETERGENT, OR SILVER CLEANING SOLUTION, THEN RINSED AND DRIED. THIS IS ESPECIALLY IMPORTANT IF THE OBJECT IS HOLLOW, AS TRAPPED CLEANING SOLUTIONS CAN LEAD TO INTERNAL CORROSION. (ABOVE)

Russian silver and niello box
THE LAYER OF GILDING HAS WORN THROUGH ON THE HIGH POINTS, AS A RESULT OF EITHER HANDLING OR EXCESSIVE CLEANING AND POLISHING. (RIGHT)

mounts on furniture, clocks and other pieces. To clean it, no more than very gentle dusting is once again recommended. Providing, however, that the gilding is firmly attached to the base metal, ormolu can be washed carefully with water and non-ionic detergent and then thoroughly blow-dried with a hair dryer. If it has a heavy black deposit that does not respond to washing, consult a conservator. Do not try to scrub off the deposit with an abrasive material (see also page 29).

Silver and Silver Plate

Like gold, silver is too soft a metal to be used in its pure state, so it is usually alloyed with copper. British sterling silver contains 92.5 percent silver, whereas Britannia silver has 95.8 percent silver.

Silver was also used extensively to plate baser metals. Sheffield plate consists of copper plated with silver on one or both sides by means of heat and pressure; electroplate consists of base metal coated with silver by electrolysis.

The majority of silver items will be clearly marked, plated pieces having identifiable stamps. These provide the most straightforward means of distinguishing between solid and plated silver.

TARNISH
Silver, whether solid or plated, is especially susceptible to tarnishing. Tarnish, or silver sulfide, results from a chemical reaction occurring between the silver and sulfur in the atmosphere. Sulfur is also given off by organic materials such as felt, wool and velvet, and these should be kept away from silver.

Tarnish first appears as a thin, iridescent or yellowish-brown deposit, which turns blue and eventually black. While it is not damaging to silver, it is usually thought of as spoiling the appearance of an object and thus as undesirable. Light tarnish can be removed by washing in water with soap or non-ionic detergent, and heavier tarnish with a proprietary cleaning solution.

CORROSION AND WEAR
If the surface of the metal becomes covered with a green crystalline deposit, this usually means that the copper in the alloy is corroding, and the object should be treated chemically by a conservator. Green corrosion can also develop on Sheffield plate, and should be treated in the same way. If, however, the green layer is dark and waxy, it may be verdigris, a copper acetate, which can be removed by wiping with methylated spirit.

Whether solid or plated, the surface of silverware is

inexorably worn away every time it is cleaned. Particularly fine or intricate pieces may therefore benefit from lacquering, which obviates the necessity of cleaning, and therefore a major cause of wear, for many years.

ADDED EFFECTS
Silver is sometimes decorated with niello, which is a black waxy compound that is pushed into the recesses of incised decoration. Comprising silver, lead and copper sulfides, and borax, niello is commonly used in Russian silver. Silver-cleaning solutions that remove sulfides will also remove niello. Proprietary silver polish should therefore be used, but great care should be taken not to overpolish and destroy thin areas of niello.

Deliberate tarnishing or oxidation on silver was a technique used to bring out designs on the metal, particularly on Art Deco silver. Lack of observation can easily lead to this effect being mistaken for ordinary tarnishing and removed by polishing. If there is any doubt at all as to whether a piece has been treated in this way, consult an expert in the subject before any cleaning is done. The cleaning will have to be done by a professional to preserve the effect.

Copper, Brass and Bronze

Copper is a soft, pinkish metal that is usually hammered or rolled into sheets to make a variety of vessels. In the case of cooking pots it is usually coated in tin to prevent its corroding and contaminating food. Copper was also used as the base metal in Sheffield plate and electroplate. Tarnish on copper is brown, but in the presence of pollutants a layer of green corrosion will form which is relatively stable. Tarnish can be removed with a proprietary cleaner and its formation can be retarded by an application of microcrystalline wax.

Brass is an alloy of copper and zinc, sometimes containing a proportion of lead. It is usually cast and is also one of the base metals used in gold plate. Tarnish on brass first gives the metal a matte surface, then turns a greenish-brown. Advanced tarnish is very dark and difficult to remove with ordinary metal polish.

To clean copper and brass, first wash in water and non-ionic detergent. If a bright surface is to be obtained, proprietary cleaners of the wadding or liquid type are suitable. They are, however, abrasive and therefore suitable only for sound and robust objects such as copper and brass vessels. Beware of alkaline solutions, such as caustic soda and ammonia-based chemicals. Alkalis attack the zinc content of brass, removing it from the surface of the alloy and leaving a bright pink copper color, which can be misleading.

Heavily tarnished brass and copper can be cleaned professionally by chemical stripping. This is usually quite unacceptable for antique brassware, as it destroys the patina and gives the object a pristine appearance that is actually very undesirable.

Brass door furniture and brass and copper inlaid into wood should not be heavily polished. Often they do not require a high sheen and should only be lightly rubbed with a soft cloth. In any case, metal polish can damage the fine woods into which brass and copper are usually inlaid, and it is therefore recommended that, if possible, the cleaner be applied locally on a soft cotton-tipped swab (see page 56). Brass and copper inlaid into silver can be polished by the usual silver-polishing methods.

Bronze is an alloy of copper, tin and small amounts of other metals (most usually lead, since this was often added to facilitate casting). Variations in the nature and proportions of the alloys in bronze produce a corresponding variation in color.

Russian silver and niello box, 1827
MANY SILVER CLEANING SOLUTIONS WILL ALSO REMOVE NIELLO, AND MUST NOT BE USED WITH THIS TYPE OF INLAY. HERE EXCESSIVE POLISHING SHOULD ALSO BE AVOIDED, AS IT WOULD DAMAGE THE TEXTURE OF THE GILDED PARTS. (OPPOSITE)

17th-century bronze group of the Laocoon
THE DARK BROWN PATINA, DELIBERATELY PRODUCED BY A CHEMICAL TECHNIQUE, HAS GRADUALLY WORN, BECOMING A PALER COLOR. THE MAJORITY OF SUCH PATINAS WILL BE UNAFFECTED BY SIMPLE CLEANING METHODS, BUT IT IS IMPORTANT TO CHECK THE EFFECT ON A SMALL CONCEALED AREA BEFORE PROCEEDING. (RIGHT)

Bronze usually has a brown or dark brownish-green patina. This patina may have been intentionally produced by means of a chemical process, and removing it seriously disfigures the object. Therefore, do not use any metal polish on bronze, and do not wash it in water. The only cleaning that bronze is likely to need is careful dusting and gentle rubbing; avoid rubbing raised parts, where patina can gradually be worn away. Accumulations of dust in crevices can be removed with a cotton-tipped swab moistened with saliva.

Although bronze is relatively resistant to corrosion, it occasionally develops green powdery spots of cupreous chloride. This is a condition known as bronze disease. It occurs particularly on archaeological bronzes and should be treated by a conservator as soon as possible to prevent complete deterioration of the metal.

Lead

Lead, the softest of all metals, is susceptible to the effects of organic acid vapors; these can be emitted by fresh paint, unseasoned wood, paper and cardboard. They cause a white powdery corrosion to form, which is highly poisonous and must be dealt with immediately.

If the object is merely dusty, wipe it with a cotton-tipped swab moistened with water and non-ionic detergent. If it is corroding, seal it inside a plastic bag and take it to a conservator; do not attempt to treat it yourself. Lead corrosion can also look like the corrosion on tin and aluminum, so if in doubt, seek professional advice (see also page 71).

Tin, Tinplate and Toleware

Tin is a soft metal which, beaten into thin sheets, is easily bent. It was used to coat the inside of copper cooking vessels to prevent the copper from contaminating the food. As tinplate – a coating of tin on iron to stop iron rusting – it was often used to make toys and models.

Tin is reasonably stable. Corrosion, when it does occur, produces a white surface on the tin. This can be washed off, after which thorough drying is of vital importance. Corrosion that cannot be washed off is more serious and should be treated by a conservator.

Toleware, which is tinplate covered with a black or green varnish, is usually painted with simple motifs. Although the varnish is resistant to heat, the paint on toleware may crack if left in direct sunlight or near fires or radiators. It is also easily chipped and scratched.

Toleware can be washed in water and non-ionic detergent, although it must not be soaked. Thorough drying is vital. If dirt remains after washing, remove it with a cotton-tipped swab dipped in methylated spirit, but only after first testing a small painted area to check that the paint is not affected by the spirit.

Rust can be removed by very careful scraping with a scalpel held flat or slightly oblique to the surface. Take great care not to scratch any of the paint or cut into the surface. Waxing is excellent protection against rust.

Pewter and Britannia Metal

Antique pewter is an alloy of tin and lead; modern pewter an alloy of tin and antimony. Like tin, pewter is stable. It can, however, develop a "warty" corrosion which it is best not to remove. Removing these "warts" is likely to leave pits that are more unsightly than the "warts" themselves. If a powdery deposit develops, this may be the result of the lead content in the pewter reacting with acids in the atmosphere, so a conservator should be consulted.

Opinions differ as to the most desirable finish on pewter. Most conservators today recommend light cleaning with water and non-ionic detergent, which preserves the naturally matte surface of the metal. Some collectors,

by contrast, have tended to polish their pewter, giving it a shine that lasts for decades.

Britannia metal, used for silver-plated items, is an alloy of tin and antimony, with a small percentage of copper added. It has a similar appearance to pewter and slowly tarnishes to a gray-brown color. It may be carefully cleaned with water and non-ionic detergent.

Iron and Steel

Iron is alloyed with varying amounts of carbon to form cast iron, wrought iron and steel, all of which corrode easily in damp conditions. Thus, they should be cleaned with methylated spirit rather than with water.

Corrosion on iron forms as a reddish-brown rust which, if unchecked, eats through the metal and destroys the object. Rust spots that have barely penetrated the surface can be removed with very fine steel wool or the abrasive side of a dish-washing sponge, and a few drops of household oil as a lubricant.

Check that corrosion is not hiding engraved decoration or inlay, which may be present on steel; if it is, rub it gently. If this is ineffective or if rust is more advanced, consult a conservator rather than proceed to harsher methods. After successful cleaning, iron and steel can be protected by waxing or oiling.

Zinc, Aluminum and Chromium

Zinc, aluminum and chromium are three other metals of which collector's objects are frequently made.

In Indian Bidri ware, which consists of bright brass or silver decoration inlaid into an artificially blackened zinc alloy, the zinc is reasonably stable; if it starts to corrode, when the surface develops a white powder, the advice of a conservator must be sought. Otherwise the silver or brass can be cleaned as described earlier.

Aluminum, though also reasonably stable, can develop a white powdery corrosion that should be brushed off before it pits the surface. Being soft, aluminum bends and scratches easily. Wash it in methylated spirit.

Chromium is a hard metal that is usually plated onto other metals. Although it does not corrode, it can suffer from peeling and pimpling. There is no remedy for this. Pimples should not be flattened or removed as this will puncture the film of chrome and encourage corrosion to form on the base metal. To ensure that no moisture penetrates beneath the chrome, avoid washing with water. A proprietary chrome cleaner or methylated spirit for the removal of dirt is all that should be necessary.

ARMS AND ARMOR

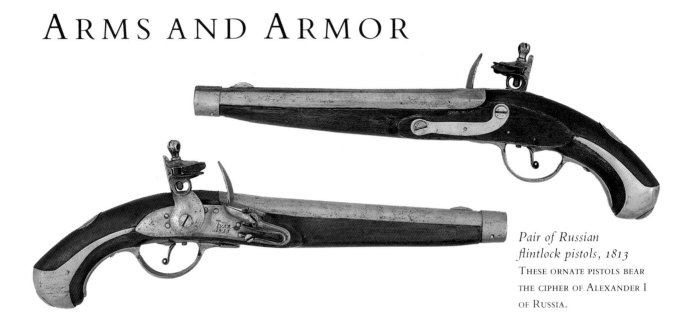

Pair of Russian flintlock pistols, 1813
THESE ORNATE PISTOLS BEAR
THE CIPHER OF ALEXANDER I
OF RUSSIA.

As soon as a new piece enters a collection, whether it be an edged weapon, firearm, armor, or piece of militaria, it is advisable to give it a close examination. To be safe, whenever handling a metal antique, clean, thin cotton gloves should be worn, even if your hands are naturally dry. Human sweat is a powerful corrosive, and many a sword blade or gun barrel bears a red fingerprint left by a previous careless handler. The gloves may seem rather over-cautious, but this simple precautionary measure could save hours of cleaning, and possibly prevent irreparable damage. In particular, Japanese sword blades should *never* be touched with bare hands as their surface is particularly susceptible to rust.

At this stage it is important to see the object as a collection of parts. Look at each component carefully for anything that is not quite right, such as spots of rust, scratches, dents, grease, small areas of missing wood, cracks, looseness, and missing screws. Check if the various parts appear to have suffered the same degree of wear; possibly one piece looks fresher, as if it were added later. See if the parts fit together neatly and closely. Check for any signs of previous restoration or over-cleaning – the presence of either may reduce a piece's value.

PRIMARY TESTS

If the item at hand is an antique firearm, it is vitally important to check that the weapon is not loaded and that the barrel does not still hold a charge. Gunpowder retains its potency for an astonishingly long time, and even a small amount should be treated with caution.

The test is simple and requires a piece of wooden doweling at least as long as the barrel. Carefully push one end of the rod down the barrel until it can go no further. Mark the rod at the muzzle and then withdraw the stick and place it alongside the outside of the barrel. If the barrel and length of doweling match, then the barrel may be presumed to be empty. If there is an appreciable space between the end of the stick and the end of the barrel, take care, for it could mean that an old load is still in place. The ball and powder can be drawn, but it is probably safer and simpler to get a gunsmith or an experienced dealer to do this. In the case of a percussion revolver, a visual check of the cylinders is usually sufficient.

Another important step when examining a firearm is to test the action of the lock mechanism. Springs may snap or metal chip or even break if this is done carelessly. In the case of a flintlock weapon, the curved arm – the cock – holding the flint should be gripped firmly and gently pulled back. With a percussion weapon, the hammer should be similarly gripped and pulled back.

There will normally be one click when the cock or hammer is more or less upright, but continue pulling gently until a second click is heard. If the action is functioning correctly, the cock or hammer should lock in this position, but it is important not to release your grip until you ensure that this locking action is certain. Grip the cock or hammer again and squeeze the trigger; if the action is working it will start to swing forward, but will be restrained by your grip. Allow it to move forward slowly until it stops at the end of its traverse.

If the action follows the above steps, then it is reasonable to assume that the lock is functioning correctly; if not, there is probably a fault in the mechanism that will need to be checked. This procedure should be followed every time the lock is operated, which should only be done occasionally. Failure to follow these simple precautions will eventually cause damage to the lock and firearm.

RECORDING

During this close examination it is a good idea to note the details and record the firearm's condition. Method is important, and a set program is recommended.

With an antique firearm look at the barrel first, then the lock and metal fittings. Look for rust and signs of wear, and check whether any engraving or decoration has been "refreshed." Next, examine the wooden body or stock. Check for scratches, cracks, and signs of any repairs or restoration. If the weapon is cased, as many firearms were in the late eighteenth century and much of the nineteenth century, look at the accessories, which should ideally match the weapon in date and type.

The usual procedure for edged weapons is to examine the blade for any marks, since many cutlers signed their products. Note any rusting, laminating, or flaking, all of which can occur on old metal. Look at the edges of the blade for nicks; sadly, some swords or daggers may have been playthings and the blade may well have been nicked. These nicks can be removed, or at least minimized, by a skilled conservator. The hilt needs to be examined in detail, for there may be cracked bars or repairs.

Individual pieces of armor are usually more of a complete entity, but it is essential to examine both the back and front of the various plates. Look for rust and dirt, as well as construction marks, such as small nicks in the edge of the plates or a few short, incised lines. These could be useful in identifying and authenticating the piece, since the same marks will normally be found on the larger elements if the piece is homogeneous. If the inside surface of the plates is very smooth, this could also indicate that the piece is a later copy. The weight is relevant; if a piece feels very heavy or very light, this may also be a sign that it is not original but a later copy. Another useful pointer is the presence of hammer marks left by the armorer.

Militaria embraces such an enormous range of objects, including medals, uniforms, books, and ephemera, that it is not easy to set out general rules. Moths are obvious enemies of uniforms, and any signs of activity (the visible presence of moth larvae) should be checked (see page 156). Badges need to be examined particularly closely for authenticity, as there are many modern copies.

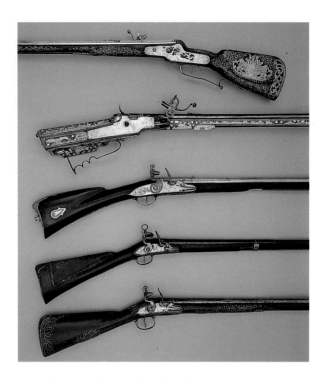

Fine firearms of the 17th and 18th centuries
TOP TO BOTTOM: GERMAN WHEEL-LOCK SPORTING RIFLE AND A SIMILAR EXAMPLE; AIRGUN WITH BARREL RESERVOIR; SPANISH SPORTING GUN; GERMAN FLINTLOCK FOWLING PIECE.

Italian edged weapons
LATE 16TH-CENTURY STAFF WEAPON (LEFT) AND SWEPT HILT RAPIER, *c.*1630, ITS BLADE INSCRIBED "FEDERICO PICININO."

Conservation

After the examination, the next step is to decide whether an object is in need of immediate conservation.

RUST

The greatest enemy to most arms and armor is rust. Undetected active spots can eat away the surface, destroying inscriptions and decorations.

If the rusting is minor it may be possible to remove it, but this must be done very carefully and slowly. Holding the piece firmly, a small medical scalpel or a thin brass rod with a slight point should be used to scrape off the rust, piece by piece. If the rusting is in or near any decoration, extra care is called for. Attempts to remove the rust may well cause damage to the decoration, but the rust must be eradicated. To that end, expert guidance may be needed.

If the rust is severe, it may be loosened by an application of oil left on the piece for a while to soak in. Chemical rust removers should never be used on antique arms and armor. Steel wool (preferably fine-grade) may be used, with extreme care, to tackle bad spots.

After the rust has been removed, a very fine polish, such as a mild preparation used for chrome fittings, can be used to give a final gentle rub. Once the surface is cleared of rust, a wipe with a mild solvent will help remove any dust, dirt, or grease. When the surface is thoroughly dry, a thin coating of wax should be applied. Clear lacquer, formerly a popular treatment, can discolor and crack, allowing damp to penetrate below the surface and attack the metal. Experts today tend to favor a microcrystalline wax instead, which can be applied to any metal surface.

WOOD

Woodwork generally requires little more than cleaning with a soft cloth or brush and then waxing, but if woodworm is present, advice should be sought. Inlay such as silver may be polished with one of the "softer" polishing materials, such as impregnated wadding, which can also be safely used on silver hilts, as well as brass and gold. In order to prevent damage to the wood, all polish must be thoroughly cleaned off with a soft cloth.

LEATHER

There is no truly effective method of dealing with old, cracking, and powdery leather. Old-fashioned saddle soap is a good treatment, but special preparations used by professional conservators may be preferable for more seriously deteriorated objects that are in danger of disintegrating completely if not treated.

One simple precaution should always be observed when unsheathing a sword, the scabbard of which is commonly made of leather. The weapon and scabbard should be held vertically, with the point down, so that there is no tendency for the scabbard to bend and perhaps crack as the blade is pulled out. It is vital that this procedure be followed, as much for the well-being of the handler as for the object. The exception to this rule are Japanese swords, which must be unsheathed with extreme care, always with the sharp edge of the blade uppermost.

SPECIAL PROBLEMS

The above procedures will be sufficient for most edged weapons and firearms, but there may be occasions when cleaning is less straightforward, such as in difficult-to-reach areas. With armor there may be overlapping plates where the lower plate, partly covered, can be seen to be in need of cleaning. No attempt should be made to remove rivets to separate the plates – that is the job of a skilled craftsman. An amateur, however, can carefully clean away any accessible dust and dirt and apply oil or wax. Extra care must be taken when trying to part plates for cleaning, since the leather that connects plates is often in poor condition and may well split or snap.

Restoration

One of the most difficult decisions faced by any serious collector is whether or not to have a firearm or other weapon restored. The arguments for and against have been thrashed back and forth, but decisions must be made on an individual basis, according to the specific condition and quality of the object in question.

If restoration is deemed necessary, a good general rule is that the work should be obvious at a range of six inches but not at six feet. The skill required to produce work of this standard is very high, and such tasks should not be attempted by the average collector.

REPLACING PARTS

In certain instances, however, it is possible for some simple restoration to be undertaken by the owner. If, for example, the ramrod or cock is missing from a flintlock pistol, replacement pieces are now readily available from a number of specialized suppliers. In general, there is little objection to such action, for it helps give a more complete idea of the object as it was originally made.

If replacing a part requires the use of a tool, it is essential to ensure that, when being used, it will cause no harm to the antique. If a screw is to be tightened or removed, see that the blade of the screwdriver is a good fit for the head of the screw. Too often a pistol is seen with a long scratch produced by a slipping screwdriver. Stubborn screws can often be loosened by various techniques, but if improperly handled these can cause damage, so in most cases expert advice is recommended.

Display and Storage

When the object has been examined, cleaned and, if necessary, restored, display must be considered. Ideally, the item should be in a stable environment with minimum variations in humidity and temperature. Generally, such conditions are beyond the scope of the normal dwelling, but the aim should be to avoid extremes (see page 181).

Dust and other pollutants should be avoided. A close-fitting glass case is ideal for exhibiting smaller pieces. Swords and longer weapons may be displayed on walls,

German Maximilian armor, c.1500–10
THIS ARMOR HAS BEEN THOROUGHLY CLEANED AND WAXED, AND ITS PERISHED LEATHER STRAPS HAVE BEEN REPLACED TO FACILITATE REASSEMBLY. (ABOVE)

15th-century Milanese sallet
THIS STYLE OF HELMET WAS WORN BY BOTH CAVALRY AND INFANTRY. HELMETS OF THIS DATE ARE RARE, AND FREQUENTLY SUFFER FROM SEVERE RUSTING. (ABOVE RIGHT)

but consider carefully the means of suspension. If an object is placed on a bracket, the points of contact should be covered by a "neutral" material (such as untreated cotton) to prevent damage. It is also important to ensure that no undue stress is placed on any part of the object.

If items are to be stored, they should be cleaned and then wrapped in acid-free tissue paper, which will not react with any part of the object. If stored in boxes or chests, these should be rigid and, ideally, inert and acid-free.

Coins and Medals

Second only to stamps, coins and medals are the most widely collected type of artifact. Their storage, however, is not straightforward, and the selection of a safe storage system for coins and medals is of fundamental importance for the welfare of any collection.

Composition

Coins have traditionally been made from three metals and their alloys: gold, silver, and copper. Gold was sometimes debased by the addition of silver and/or copper, and silver by the addition of copper. Copper, on the other hand, was usually alloyed with tin and/or zinc. These copper-alloy coins are traditionally called "bronzes" by numismatists, irrespective of what the alloying metals may be. In more recent times other metals have been employed – iron, zinc, aluminum, and cupronickel – and even plastics and porcelain have been used to make tokens.

Gold and copper are the only metals which do not have a silver-white appearance when pure. They are easily recognized by their well-known yellow and brownish-red colors, respectively. Alloys of copper, however, are often yellow, and may be confused with gold. Similarly, it is possible to confuse silver with other metals, but these were not used for coinage before the present century. If coins have been buried, it is normally easy to distinguish them: silver will usually have a mauve or gray patina, and that of copper will be green or brown. Under certain burial conditions, however, both silver and copper will go black, and base silver may turn green.

Ancient forgeries are not uncommon, often consisting of copper cores which have been plated with gold or silver. These are intentionally collected by some people.

Storage

All coins and medals, except those of relatively pure gold, are likely to deteriorate if stored in unfavorable conditions, such as damp or polluted atmospheres. Dampness is particularly hazardous for iron and for coins which have been buried, as these may be covered with unstable corrosion products. In some cases, these corrosion layers will contain chemicals, absorbed from the soil, which cause corrosion to continue in the presence of moisture. Storage at less than 40% relative humidity is usually recommended to prevent further deterioration.

One of the most familiar manifestations of a damp environment is the appearance of "bronze disease" on coins made of copper or any of its alloys. Bronze disease, the appearance of bright-green, powdery spots on the surface of the coin as the result of a virulent corrosion process, can destroy the whole coin if remedial action is not taken, such as lowering the relative humidity in the storage area, or having the coin professionally conserved.

The polluted atmosphere, which is mainly the result of the burning of fossil fuel, is almost impossible to avoid. However, collectors can unwittingly exacerbate the situation for their coins by exposing them to the products of modern industry, some of which emit into the atmosphere traces of aggressive gases harmful to metals. For example, the current spate of corrosion growths on lead and zinc artifacts is due to the ever-increasing emissions of formaldehyde into the air from some modern plastics used in the manufacture of numerous everyday objects, including furniture. The zinc and lead become covered with white crystals of zinc or lead formate. Lead is also in great danger from minute traces of organic acids in the atmosphere (such as vinegar vapor), which cause a rapid formation of crystals of lead carbonate on the surface of this metal. This corrosion process is very difficult to stop. Museum conservators have tried various treatments, but the only foolproof one is storage in a dry atmosphere.

Copper, and especially silver, tarnish by reaction with hydrogen sulfide. This pollutant, given off by decaying animal matter, is a natural component of the atmosphere, but it and similarly dangerous sulfur-containing organic compounds are also emitted by some textiles, paints, and other household materials.

ENVELOPES

The simplest storage system for coins is to keep them inside paper or plastic envelopes contained in cardboard, plastic, wooden, or metal boxes. Traditionally, archives of coins found on excavations have been stored in 2-in square manila envelopes in long, narrow cardboard boxes. Unfortunately, the paper and cardboard are usually made from inferior, cheap paper pulp, which absorbs acidic gases from the atmosphere and becomes very brittle. Hence, after a few years, the envelopes will split.

In recent years, paper envelopes have often been replaced by transparent plastic ones, but these are often made of polyvinyl chloride (PVC), which can cause coins to corrode. Plastics normally recommended for the storage of coins are polystyrene, polymethyl methacrylate, polyethylene, and polyester. The last two plastics are available as flexible transparent films.

Unless small, purpose-made polyester envelopes are available, it is safest to stick to paper – but insist on acid-free envelopes made of archival-quality paper. These should be stored in polyethylene, polystyrene, or metal boxes. Long, thin (2-in square) polystyrene boxes made for the storage of transparencies are ideally suited for the storage of coins in small envelopes, although specially designed polystyrene boxes are also available.

ALBUMS

The second approach to coin storage is to use albums; these are invariably made of plastic, and often of polyvinyl chloride (PVC), which is not recommended. The safest materials are polyethylene and polyester, which are available as album leaves, each page having a number of individual pockets. It is also important to use an album binder made of safe materials. A number of firms make archivally safe transparency storage systems (that is, conforming to museum standards for long-term storage), which may be adapted for coins. The main problem with album pages is that it is difficult to get the coins out of the pockets for inspection and study; in addition many of the pages have open-topped pockets, so albums must be stored and transported vertically. Furthermore, when the album is lying open, coins may slide out of their pockets when efforts are being made to retrieve another one.

Storage of coins in envelopes
THE BROWN PAPER, CARDBOARD, AND POLYVINYL CHLORIDE SYSTEM IS NOT RECOMMENDED FOR THE STORAGE OF COINS AND MEDALS. MUCH SAFER TO USE IN THE LONG TERM ARE ACID-FREE WHITE PAPER ENVELOPES AND POLYSTYRENE BOXES.

An interesting variation on the album system is to use the kind of plastic transparency holders which are designed to be stored in a filing cabinet. These hang from metal rods and usually hold thirty slides/coins. Archival-quality holders are available in polyester, and a further benefit of this system is that they can be stored in a lockable filing cabinet.

Corroded coins
TYPICAL EXAMPLES OF BRONZE DISEASE ARE EVIDENT ON THIS EARLY ISLAMIC BRONZE COIN (TOP LEFT), AND BASE SILVER TETRADRACHM OF ELYMAIS (TOP RIGHT). THE SASANIAN SILVER DRACHM (BOTTOM LEFT) IS HEAVILY TARNISHED, AND THE ZINC "EMERGENCY" COIN, MADE DURING WORLD WAR II, IS NOW COVERED IN ZINC FORMATE.

*Storage in an antique
mahogany cabinet*
MAHOGANY COIN CABINETS,
MADE WITH TRADITIONAL
CABINET-MAKER'S MATERIALS,
ARE A VERY ATTRACTIVE AND
SAFE WAY TO STORE COINS
AND MEDALS. "SYNTHETIC"
WOODEN CABINETS, SUCH AS
THOSE MADE FROM
HARDBOARD, SHOULD BE
AVOIDED AS SOME SYNTHETIC
ADHESIVES USED IN THEIR
MANUFACTURE MAY CAUSE
CORROSION.

CABINETS

Most collectors prefer special coin cabinets which have shallow drawers with preformed recesses for individual coins and medals. Traditionally, these were made of wood – mahogany was preferred – with brass fittings, and such cabinets are not harmful to coins. Nowadays, however, mahogany is prohibitively expensive, and some manufacturers use other woods, especially "synthetic" (compressed wood and plant fiber) materials like fiberboard, hardboard, chipboard, and plywood. These should be avoided because they contain synthetic adhesives which may contaminate the atmosphere inside the cabinet, leading to corrosion of the coins.

Steel cabinets are a possible substitute for wooden ones as they minimize the corrosion risk and maximize the security of a collection. They are especially recommended for medal collections, as many medals are made of lead, which is extremely susceptible to the effects of the immediate environment, particularly acid gases emitted by wood. Lead, however, is a soft metal, so it is particularly important to avoid knocking the medals against the cabinet, and to provide a soft lining material inside the drawers. Felt is not suitable since it is often made from recycled wool that contains sulfur and causes tarnishing. As an alternative, use a soft, looped-nylon fabric, which will not fray, or polyethylene foam, which comes in thin sheets; both are available in various colors. Highly recommended are polystyrene cabinets with trays, which are much safer for coins and have the added advantage of being far less expensive than cabinets made of wood or steel.

TICKETS

Polystyrene cabinets have square recesses in their plastic trays. This means that the card tickets can be square rather than round, and are therefore easier to use because they won't rotate in the recess like a round ticket in a round hole. These tickets should be of acid-free white or colored card. Under no circumstances should coins either be written upon or have any kind of labeling attached to them.

TESTING MATERIALS

Testing the materials to be used in purpose-made coin cabinets is a job for a scientific laboratory, involving sealing up samples of the materials to be tested in clean laboratory flasks with clean test pieces of several metals. It is surprising how many samples of textiles, "synthetic" woods, paints, and modern adhesives have caused corrosion of copper and/or silver and/or lead, the three metals normally used in the tests.

Display

The same rules regarding storage apply to materials used in the display of coins and medals. Coins and medals usually require a mount to hold them at the best viewing angle, and the recommended material for these is polymethyl methacrylate sheet, commonly known as Plexiglas. Coins should never be attached to a backboard with metal pins, as these may cause the coin to corrode. If pinning is inevitable because the coins must be displayed vertically, then the metal pins must be sheathed with an inert plastic tube, such as catheter tubing.

Cleaning and Conservation

Usually the cleaning of coins and medals is best left to a qualified conservator. Before it is even attempted, however, the question of whether to clean must be addressed. Soils and atmospheric dust can always be cleaned from coins and medals with a soft, pure cotton cloth or a brush with very soft bristles, but the removal of corrosion products is more problematic because of the issue of patina. In the case of bronzes, few collectors would remove a smooth green or brown patina as this is usually seen as desirable. An excavator is generally less circumspect; if the patina prevents the identification of a coin crucial for the dating of a level, the coin will usually be cleaned, irrespective of the aesthetic result.

Silver coins which have developed a smooth black or faintly blue tarnish are also often seen as having a desirable patina, although the legibility of the coin can often be improved by cleaning. Silver coins from excavations are usually covered with a smooth mauvish layer of silver chloride, which may be felt to enhance the appearance of the coin. Many corroded coins will, however, be improved in both legibility and appearance by cleaning, which is *always* a job for a trained conservator.

REMOVING CORROSION

There are two schools of thought among conservators on methods of corrosion removal. One approves only of physical removal of corrosion products using fine chisels and scalpels while viewing the coin under a microscope at a magnification of ×5 to ×20. The other prefers the use of chemicals to dissolve the corrosion products, followed in the case of bronze, and sometimes silver, by the use of a chemical coloring agent to repatinate the coin with a very thin, even layer appropriate in color to the metal.

The argument against physical cleaning is that it is too easy to clean away details or scratch the coin, while the argument against chemicals is that if the coin is badly corroded, it might dissolve. Chemical patination is also viewed as ethically unacceptable by some conservators. Discuss both approaches with a chosen conservator first.

SIMPLE CLEANING

Silver often responds well to careful brushing with a soft toothbrush and a pure bathroom soap, and heavy tarnish can be removed by immersing the coin *briefly* in a household reagent for cleaning tarnish from silverware, followed by a thorough rinsing under running water. Do not use a household silver polish to remove tarnish, as this will make the surface of the coin very shiny. Careful

Byzantine bronze coins
CHEMICAL CLEANING AND TONING BY A CONSERVATOR HAVE REMOVED THE CORROSION FROM THE COIN ON THE RIGHT.

application of tarnish remover to the surface of the coin with a cotton-tipped swab will remove tarnish from the highlights and leave it in the recesses, thus creating an artificial contrast that affords improved legibility.

Little can be done to corroded bronze coins without the risk of permanent damage. The use of a soft-bristled brush to remove mud and dirt is all that may be suggested.

Good gold coins need no treatment, while those of base gold can usually be treated like silver. Coins made of modern metals – zinc, iron, aluminum, and cupronickel – have not usually been buried and are therefore normally only dirty. Washing with water containing a few drops of a neutral (non-ionic) detergent is usually sufficient for these, followed by a thorough rinsing under running water for thirty seconds and drying with a soft cloth.

The simple methods given here are widely used in museums, but it is always wise to seek professional advice before cleaning coins of any value.

PROTECTIVE COATING

The last stage of the conservation process is to apply a protective coating. Coins which have been chemically cleaned will respond well to a coating of a dilute nitrocellulose lacquer, applied carefully with a small paintbrush. If the lacquer gives the coins a rather shiny appearance, it should be diluted with the appropriate solvent before use. When the lacquer is quite dry, the coin may be brushed with a toothbrush which has first been rubbed over a block of paraffin wax. Other coins normally need no surface treatment, although an application of the waxed toothbrush may produce a pleasing effect.

JEWELRY; OBJECTS OF VERTU

The possession of a jewel can symbolize many attributes and emotions, including admiration, love, wealth, and power. The jewel itself may even be believed to hold magical properties, but whatever the main factor behind its ownership, above all it has been created to be worn. The human form provides the perfect setting for a variety of adornments; indeed, throughout the ages jewelers have used the body – from the top of the head to the tip of the toe – as the canvas for their compositions.

The term "vertu" applies to objects with some original practical use, such as snuffboxes and seals, whose craftsmanship has become their *raison d'être*. On the whole, objects of vertu are created from the same materials as most jewels, occasionally by the same craftsmen.

Gems

For a gemstone to be deemed sufficiently desirable to be used in jewelry it must possess three main attributes: beauty, durability, and rarity. The beauty of a gem is chiefly in its color or, in the case of a white diamond, its lack of color, enhanced by the optical effects of light that produce its unmatched brilliancy, luster, and "fire." Diamond-cutters, or lapidaries in the case of all other stones, are responsible for skilfully uncovering this beauty and displaying it to its fullest extent by using their broad knowledge of the effects of light on gem materials.

The durability of a gem depends on its hardness and toughness. In 1822, hardness was defined by Friedrich Mohs (1773–1839), a German mineralogist, as a material's ability to resist abrasion from another substance drawn over its surface. He drew up a table of common minerals whose hardness ranged from 1, the softest, to 10, the hardest. For both the jeweler and the owner of the jewel, knowledge of these numbers on the Mohs scale may prove vital. The hardness of gemstones must be sufficient to enable them to be used in jewelry, but if they are soft, appropriate precautions must be taken. Toughness means resistance to chipping, cracking, or breaking. The possession of "cleavage" in a crystalline mineral can sometimes be an asset for the cutter as it permits the stone to be split along certain definite directions and give a more or less smooth surface, but it is usually a hindrance. During cutting, the stone may become flawed or break along these directions unintentionally. Naturally, these hazards should be borne in mind by the wearer of such gems.

Rarity is perhaps the key attribute to both the commercial and intrinsic value of a gemstone. The mineral itself may not be scarce but fine gem-quality specimens may be. While owners of jewels can have little influence on the rarity of gems, they can play an enormous part in maintaining their beauty and durability.

Minerals

The majority of gemstones are minerals, of which the diamond is the hardest (10 on the Mohs scale). However, as with all gem materials, each individual stone has its own degree of hardness, a fact that is frequently overlooked when wearing diamond jewelry, or indeed any other gems. The inadvertent rubbing of a diamond bracelet over the surface of a diamond ring would doubtless cause one of the stones to scratch the other, or if rings are worn together on the same finger the facets of the individual stones may rub together and cause abrasions. The attractiveness of a gemstone can be marred by these scratches as they ruin the polish of the facets, from which light is reflected and refracted. Although a hard material, a diamond also possesses perfect cleavage in four directions. Thankfully, a diamond rarely cleaves during normal wear, but care should be taken not to knock the stone as it may chip or, even more devastatingly, split in two.

The rich red ruby and the dramatic blue sapphire are varieties of the mineral corundum; their different colors are due to chemical impurities within the mineral, which is naturally colorless. Rubies and sapphires are hard stones (9), but have a tendency to brittleness and can develop or extend cracks and internal fissures if they are dropped on a hard surface or hit sharply.

The emerald is the green gem variety of the mineral beryl, whose other popular variety is the aquamarine. Again, a foreign element gives the emerald its striking hue. The emerald is fairly hard ($7\frac{1}{2}$) but it has a tendency to brittleness and is rarely free from inclusions, some of which may come up through the surface of the stone. The characteristic visual effect of emerald inclusions is called "*jardin*," and can prove disastrous to the stone's life: part of the stone can break away if the slightest knock occurs near these inclusions.

Another attractive gem with a good degree of hardness (8) is the topaz, the warm, sherry-colored variety being the most highly prized. Its one major failing is its very easy

Lady Agnew of
Locknaw, *John Singer
Sargent*, c.1892–3
JEWELRY IS ALWAYS CREATED
TO BE WORN, AS SO
BEAUTIFULLY ILLUSTRATED
HERE. THE PENDANT WORN
BY THE SITTER APPEARS TO BE
SET WITH AN AQUAMARINE
WITHIN A BORDER OF
TURQUOISE BLUE FLOWERS.
(LEFT)

*Section of an early
20th-century turquoise-
fringed necklace*
MANY STONES IN THIS
NECKLACE HAVE FADED OR
ALTERED IN COLOR, A
PHENOMENON WHICH IS
THOUGHT TO BE DUE TO
DEHYDRATION. (ABOVE)

cleavage – the slightest knock may cause internal fissures or even break the stone in two.

Zircon is also relatively hard ($7-7\frac{1}{2}$) but prone to abrasion, which, naturally, is an added hazard. Severe problems may occur with heat-treated zircons, which can be either colorless, blue, or yellow. Various gemstones are subjected to heat treatment, which can improve or alter their color or even improve the appearance of certain inclusions. However, zircons can be damaged by ultra-violet light rays, the type of light emitted by a sun lamp, causing a treated white zircon to revert back to its original brown color. Even very strong sunlight may cause heat-treated stones to revert to their original color.

The green peridot, a favorite with the Edwardians, has a hardness which varies between $6\frac{1}{2}$ and 7. This is relatively soft for a gemstone and renders it vulnerable to damage by abrasion. It also possesses distinct cleavage.

Another soft gemstone is the opal ($5-6\frac{1}{2}$), a hardened gel formed from silica and water – a relatively simple formula that can produce a stunning material. The gem varieties prevalent in jewelry are white, black, water, and fire opals. Whereas the fire opal may be a distinctive orange-red, it is also the least likely variety to show the wonderful play of color for which the gem-quality specimens are famed.

The black opal, a twentieth-century Australian discovery, is the most valuable variety, with its spectacular flashes of green, blue, red, or yellow seen against a background of dark gray or black. Sadly, with this gemstone beauty has its price. Not only is the opal soft, but it is also porous, so contact with liquids should be avoided. It still contains varying amounts of water and will dehydrate if heated or contract in extremely cold weather. Leaving an opal for any length of time in direct sunlight may cause it to crack, and wearing one while defrosting a refrigerator may also cause damage to it.

The soft (slightly less than 6), porous turquoise shares many of the hazards pertaining to opals. The fading of its color, or the alteration from a blue to a green shade, is thought to be due to dehydration. Stones are sometimes waxed or oiled professionally to improve their appearance and color stability, but this coating can be affected by perspiration, cosmetics, or dirt.

Lapis lazuli is frequently used in objects of vertu or is set in signet rings. This gemstone, which is renowned for its vibrant blue color, is fairly soft ($5\frac{1}{2}$). Lapis often glitters with golden spots, which are iron pyrites crystals. This latter mineral was popular during the eighteenth century, when it was often (wrongly) termed marcasite, a mineral with the same chemical composition but from a different crystal system. "Fool's gold," as iron pyrites is often called, sparkles to great effect, and although its hardness is only between 6 and $6\frac{1}{2}$, it is fairly durable. Its main drawback is its fibrous nature, which renders the stone somewhat brittle and prone to cracking if handled roughly. An advantage to using iron pyrites in the eighteenth century was that it did not rust, as could the cut-steel jewels of the same period. Steel, which is an alloy of iron and carbon, was cut and faceted in the same way as a gem, and in this form looked most effective, particularly when mounted in a variety of jewels or objects.

Quartz is the generic name given to the most common and largest group of minerals. The crystalline variety of quartz includes stones such as rock crystal, rose quartz, citrine, smoky quartz, cat's eye, tiger's eye, and amethyst. The stones are of average hardness (7) and do not on the whole possess any hidden hazards. Citrine and amethyst are, however, very susceptible to heat, which can cause their color to change. Usually, a relatively high temperature is required to produce this effect, but prolonged exposure to sunlight may alter the color.

The cryptocrystalline quartz is usually referred to as chalcedony or, if banded in formation, agate. The varieties include cornelian, sard, chrysoprase, bloodstone, moss agate, onyx, sardonyx, and jasper. These are usually the

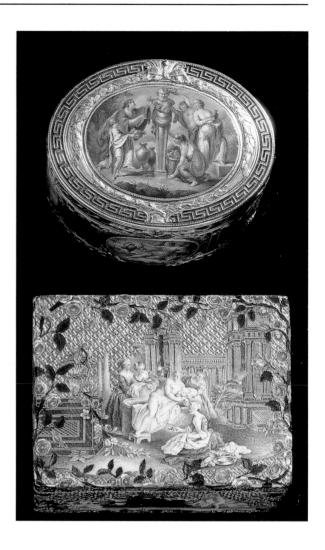

so-called "hardstones," which are used for many objects of vertu, cameos, or intaglios. All chalcedonies can be stained to produce a variety of colors – including the black onyx, which is nearly always stained chalcedony. Usually this staining or dyeing is permanent, but occasionally it may react with certain chemicals. For instance, the blue dye on jasper, stained to imitate lapis lazuli and usually referred to as "Swiss lapis," has been known to wear off because of a reaction with the acid chemicals present in some people's skin or in cosmetics, scents, and hair sprays.

Organic Gem Materials

The most highly prized organic gem material is undoubtedly the pearl. Produced in molluscs, this gem is admired for its exquisite luster, called the "orient" of pearl. Pearls are composed of calcium carbonate, organic conchiolin, and water, and this mixture, or nacre, is arranged in

Other Materials

The majority of other materials used in jewelry are relatively soft – nearly all well under the desired figure of 7 on the scale of hardness – and therefore prone to abrasion. Amber and jet are extremely soft, being slightly above 2 and $2\frac{1}{2}$, respectively. Ivory ($2\frac{1}{4}$–$2\frac{3}{4}$) also has a tendency to be highly absorbent, enabling scents and acids and oil from the human skin to discolor it (see page 178). Prolonged bouts of sunlight will both bleach and crack it. Tortoise-shell ($2\frac{1}{2}$), too, should be kept away from heat and moisture in order to prevent damage.

Although jewels of cut steel and Berlin ironwork can be considered hard materials, they can deteriorate from the effects of moisture and pollutants in the atmosphere. Collections of cut-steel jewelry have often been embedded in boxes of chalk powder, no doubt intended to absorb some of the fatal moisture.

Man has produced a number of excellent materials that are highly popular with jewelers, including paste and other glasses, porcelain, and plastic. All are relatively soft and prone to abrasion, and some are brittle.

The Snuffbox

During the *ancien régime*, when the craze for taking snuff swept Europe, the snuffbox was a symbol of status, wealth, and discernment – as well as a receptacle for powdered tobacco. Inspired by the constant demand for novelty, goldsmiths created boxes of diverse forms. This quintessential object of vertu ranged from the simple, unadorned container to elaborate confections in which materials such as shells, hardstones, or lacquer were combined with mounts that were variously chased, engraved and/or enhanced with enamel and precious gems.

HANDLING

Since the snuffbox was made to be used, considerable attention was given to its feel and balance in the hand, as well as its efficacy in protecting the snuff from the air. The etiquette of snuff-taking required the box to be held and opened in one hand, leaving the other free to take the pinch of snuff. This tested the skill of the hinge-maker, who needed to strike the right balance between a tight fit and a fluid opening. Careless attempts to open the box in the traditional manner would almost certainly upset the alignment of the hinge and possibly damage the box. It is advisable to hold the box firmly in one hand and to ease the lid with the other, taking care to apply the pressure directly opposite the hinge.

Birmingham bird- and animal-head bonbonnières, c.1765
THIS TYPE OF PAINTED ENAMEL IS EASILY SCUFFED BY COMPARABLE OR HARDER SURFACES. (ABOVE)

18th-century French (top) and German gold snuffboxes
THE *BASSE-TAILLE* ENAMEL OF THESE BOXES IS PRONE TO CHIPPING AND, IF HELD IN AN OVER-HOT HAND, FLAKING. (OPPOSITE)

concentric layers. Cultured pearls are produced by inserting a mother-of-pearl bead into the mollusc and thereby inducing the mollusc to coat the bead with nacre. Both natural and cultured pearls are quite tough, yet should be handled carefully as the nacre can easily scratch and they can also lose their luster and crack. These results are usually due to the conchiolin in the pearl drying out in very dry atmospheres, or the calcium carbonate being dissolved away by certain acids (such as those which can be in perspiration or natural skin oils). They can also be damaged by chemicals in scent, hair sprays, and other cosmetics. These chemicals can also penetrate into the drill hole and thus enter into the gem's concentric layers. A build-up of chemicals not only dulls a pearl, but will break down its structure, eventually causing it to dissolve.

Other organic gem materials which are often carved as jewels are coral and shell. They are both very soft ($3\frac{1}{2}$) and brittle, and therefore require the gentlest care.

ENAMELING

Many snuffboxes feature enameled decoration. Enamel, a vitreous coating fused to a metallic base, is usually made from soft glass or sand, soda or potash, and red lead that have been melted to make "frit." This is ground to a fine powder, applied to the metal body – sometimes with a bonding agent such as oil of spike lavender – and then fired in a kiln at a very high temperature. The transparent frit can be colored with a small percentage of metallic oxide or made opaque by adding tin oxide. Several layers of enamel and subsequent firings are needed to achieve an appropriate effect. Subtle opalescent effects, much favored by the Russian goldsmith Peter Carl Fabergé (1846–1920), are made by varying the tones of each fired layer.

box. Sometimes chased laurel-leaf borders are enhanced with translucent green and interspersed with domed drops of enamel worked to simulate pearls. While all enamel is delicate, the pearl-like variety is the most vulnerable and rarely is such a box found totally free from enamel loss. Any enameled surface subject to a blow by a hard object or, worse still, dropped, will chip and shatter; abrasion by substances harder than the vitreous body will also cause scuffing and scratching. Close scrutiny with the aid of a loupe in a strong light should reveal any damage, as well as previous attempts at restoration. Lack of symmetry of design is a quick indicator of major damage, while a loss or chip will catch the light when the box is turned about. Hairline cracks are often visible due to the dirt that has

Display of 19th- and 20th-century jewelry
BLACK VELVET STANDS, AVAILABLE FROM JEWELERS, DISPLAY THESE OBJECTS TO THEIR BEST ADVANTAGE. THE STANDS SHOULD BE COVERED WITH MATERIALS THAT ARE NOT ABRASIVE AND CONTAIN NO HARMFUL CHEMICALS, SUCH AS PURE COTTON, VELVET OR SATIN. TO PROVIDE THE MAXIMUM AMOUNT OF PROTECTION, THE STANDS SHOULD BE PLACED IN A SEALED, GLAZED VITRINE.

Isolated areas of enamel can be applied in different ways: *champlevé*, contained within fields excavated from the body; *basse-taille*, in which the excavated ground is engraved with decoration; or *cloisonné*, where ribbon-like metal strips applied edgewise divide the different colors. Alternatively, a surface can be totally covered, as found on the copper-bodied Battersea and Staffordshire wares, or partly enameled, often in translucent colors over an engine-turned ground, this method being perfected by mid-eighteenth-century French goldsmiths. Another variant is painting on enamel (usually opaque) in metallic oxides, which are then fired.

As goldsmiths sought new levels of sophistication, different combinations of enamel work were used on one

accumulated in them. Bright light will also reveal, by showing differences of tone and refractability, most restoration work, particularly in translucent enamel. Quite often a difference of texture can be felt as well, thus confirming the visual judgement.

Handling and Wearing

There are many types of body adornment, from toe rings to tiaras, and all require special attention. When wearing a jewel check that any fittings are secure, hinges are in good order, and links are not wearing thin; these problems can often be remedied by a jeweler. Clip fastenings for earrings are a twentieth-century invention – prior to the

1930s all earrings were designed for pierced ears. Naturally, clips are not always as secure or as comfortable as the
pierced fittings, so it may prove worthwhile to have the
clips converted to posts if you have pierced ears (it may
also prevent the loss of a favorite piece).

Bracelets are highly vulnerable jewels, as they are prone
to bumps and scrapes (also the case with rings and
cufflinks); extreme care should be taken when wearing
them to avoid unnecessary knocks. Pendants should be
worn on a chain or necklet strong enough to hold them,
and a low, hanging pendant should not swing against any
other surfaces or get trapped or tangled in another object.
This also applies to *sautoirs*, long chain necklaces popular
in the early twentieth century.

The material on which a brooch or clip is worn is an
important consideration. Pushing a delicate pin through a
heavy fabric can weaken the fitting, which may immediately or eventually break. Conversely, heavy brooches or
clips, such as those produced in the 1940s, should not be
worn on light fabrics as they may either not lie flat or may
damage the clothing. Also, a spray of scent or hair spray
aimed in the wrong direction may do actual damage to the
jewel and, in some cases, temporarily dull the polished
surface of the gemstone.

Display and Storage

A sealed, glazed vitrine, placed away from strong
sunlight, is ideal for displaying jewels and objects of vertu.
Such a case will also keep out any dust or moisture. If the
vitrine is to be lit, fiber-optic lighting should be considered. This form of "cold light" separates the heat from
the light, thereby ensuring, along with controlled humidity, an even environment, which is necessary to maintain
the stability of different materials (see page 180).

A wide variety of stands that will display jewels to
their best advantage can usually be purchased through a
jeweler. A large selection of storage cases and boxes is also
available on the market. Both the stands and cases should
be covered or lined with materials that are neither abrasive
nor contain any harmful chemicals; pure cotton velvet and
satin are suitable. It is also possible to have cases specially
made to fit a particular jewel; these should neither cramp a
piece nor distort it by not providing the correct support.
Although jewelry boxes are generally considered the
safest place to store most jewels, more compact jewelry
rolls are ideal for encasing chains or bead necklaces.

Most objects of vertu were originally retailed in
purpose-made, plush-lined shagreen, fishskin or leather
cases. These cases have rarely survived, but those that
do remain provide an indication of the degree of
protection that was then thought to be necessary: the box
isolated the object, enclosed it tightly in a firm support,
and kept it safe from knocks from other boxes. Such
care is equally applicable today.

Cleaning

Thorough cleaning should only be carried out by a
professional, but there are a few basic, safe methods of
caring for jewels and jeweled objects at home. As stated
above, for the true beauty of a gemstone to be shown off it
needs to reflect and refract as much light as possible, and
this will be hampered by any dirt or dust covering its

polished surfaces. Indeed, diamonds have a tendency to attract grease. This is not a helpful property when it comes to wearing them, because any grease-containing substance, such as soap and facial and body creams, will leave a thin coating of grease on the diamond. This layer will not only decrease the brilliance of the stone but will also serve to attract even more dust and dirt.

Before attempting to clean any piece certain factors must be taken into consideration. First, it must be ascertained whether or not the material is porous, since a cleansing method requiring the use of a liquid could prove disastrous. Thought must also be given to the setting. Prior to the nineteenth century stones were mounted in closed settings, which only allowed the surface or front of the stone to be open to light. The setting at the back of the material could be covered with a thin foil, produced in a variety of colors, which improved the color of the stone or indeed gave color to a colorless gem. When cleaning or wearing such jewels, no moisture should be allowed to enter into the back of the setting as the foil will become either dull or discolored, and thereby ruined. This is also the case for any similarly set jewels without foil, for a film of water behind the stone will dull its brilliance. Many antique jewels contain small glazed miniatures or hair compartments often used for memorial purposes. Again, they have been sealed to prevent dirt entering them, and any moisture will prove disastrous to the painting or the lock of hair encased. Any strung beads should not be immersed in liquid as this may well result in the string rotting over a period of time.

Having ascertained that a jewel will not be harmed by moisture, the safest method for cleaning the piece is with the simplest materials: a soft toothbrush, lukewarm water and a few drops of a mild liquid detergent. A small jar should be filled with the liquids and then the jewel carefully dipped in and left to soak. The toothbrush is useful for searching out any dirt behind the claws. Naturally, this operation should not be carried out near a sink with an open plughole. It is possible to buy specially designed washing jars with a mesh basket to hold the jewel suspended in the water. They simplify the process and, should any stones happen to come out of their settings during the cleaning, they will be held safely in the mesh.

After a rinse in clean water, the jewel should be allowed to dry naturally, preferably on clean, acid-free absorbent paper; any undue rubbing with the wrong cloth might cause the cloth to catch onto the piece and subsequently loosen the claws. Excessive heating can also cause harm. Pearls and porous materials such as turquoise can be cleaned with a jeweler's cloth, which is usually made from either pure cotton or chamois. These cloths can also be used to give the final polish to the washed jewels. The above-mentioned processes should also clean the metals around the gemstones. However, jewels should be taken on a regular basis to a jeweler, who has more sophisticated equipment to carry out a thorough cleaning job.

A gold box enhanced with applied decoration in different colored gold (achieved by combining other metals with gold, such as copper to make red gold or silver to give green gold) can tarnish. If this is only superficial, judicious use of a jeweler's cloth will restore the brilliance. However, constant polishing will flatten any chased or engraved highlights, and applied decoration, if beginning to lift, could be torn off. The danger is even more acute in the case of silver-gilt or gilt-metal boxes, as polishing may result in removing the surface layer of the metal. Abrasive cleaners can be harmful and should not be used.

More profound cleaning and polishing must be done by a professional conservator who is fully aware of the nature of the materials used. The same applies for any restoration that may be needed. Provided common sense is used, general care of snuffboxes and other objects of vertu is

neither expensive nor problematic. They should never be allowed to rub against one another, and the environment in which they are kept should be stable (see page 180). In some cases water can cause more damage than anticipated: for instance, if water is used to clean a Staffordshire enamel, it can seep in through hairline cracks and result in the flaking off of a large piece. An erroneous assumption about the nature of the surface can end in disaster if an inappropriate cleaning method is used.

The Role of the Jeweler

Apart from the regular cleaning and checking of jewels and objects of vertu, there are other invaluable services that a jeweler can provide. Although some jewelers act purely as retailers, they should have access to the skilled craftsmen who can repair or conserve pieces.

Gemstones that are badly scratched or chipped can often be repolished or, in some cases, recut. A jeweler will know whether it is possible to carry out either of these remedies without causing further damage to the jewel, or in the latter case, if the inevitable reduction in the size of the gemstone is warranted. This highly skilled job can be very expensive as well as hazardous. However, a competent jeweler will be able to advise as to whether or not it is worth the cost and the risk. The stone will lose weight but a highly superior gem, lacking in any abrasions and possessing far more beauty and life, may be the result.

Jewelers may be able to recast a broken section of a jewel, repair broken links and claws, or refoil a setting. They will also be aware of any pitfalls, such as destroying or obliterating a maker's mark, while carrying out a repair. When it comes to restoring an ancient or antique jewel, an expert may be able to advise on how much or how little can be done without harming its intrinsic value.

Both natural and cultured pearls should be cleaned and restrung on a regular basis; if worn fairly often, this should be about every six months. The best way of restringing pearls is to make a knot between each bead; this will prevent the pearls from rubbing together and damaging each other. The knots will also ensure that only one pearl is lost, not many, should the silk thread break. If the surface of a natural pearl is badly cracked or discolored, the pearl can be "skinned." Skinning is a hazardous and costly operation, and there are very few specialists who can embark on such a drastic course of action.

Enamel loss on snuffboxes can be restored either by the use of "cold enameling," using resins and either natural or synthetic pigments, or by refiring. The latter, which requires great precision judgement about the relative firing levels of the different enamels, is the riskiest, although if successful most effective, method. A skilled goldsmith should be able to remake a hinge or reset a part that has become loose or detached.

Section of a gold and enamel bracelet, Bapst and Falize, c.1890
A HIGHLY SKILLED JEWELER WOULD BE ABLE TO RESTORE THE MISSING GOLD DECORATION, APPARENT FROM BOTH THE BACK AND FRONT OF THE PIECE, BY RECASTING THIS SECTION. (LEFT AND BELOW)

Pair of late 19th-century diamond star brooches
THE BROOCH ON THE RIGHT, LIGHTLY CLEANED WITH A SOFT TOOTHBRUSH IN A MIXTURE OF MILD DETERGENT AND WATER, CONTRASTS FAVORABLY WITH THE UNCLEANED. (OPPOSITE)

CLOCKS AND WATCHES

 Clocks, watches and music boxes are complex instruments which will continue to function effectively as long as they are treated with consideration. While everyday handling and winding can be safely and easily undertaken by the layperson, and the instrument fully wound and set without fear of damage, attention to the movement must be regarded largely as the province of the specialized restorer.

Not only should oiling, cleaning and general overhauling of the movement be undertaken by a professional restorer, it should also be carried out as regular maintenance to a working piece rather than as a remedy for trouble which has already caused the mechanism to break down. In the event of a clock, watch or music box having suffered neglect, breakage or wear, restoration will almost always return it to full working order. Conservation ethics demand that, as far as possible, the original materials are maintained, but if the clock or watch is to be functional it is often inevitable that some parts will have to be replaced.

Automata are not as easy to maintain. Their mechanisms are often crudely constructed and not made in such a way that they can be taken apart easily. Involving a variety of materials, some automata are also likely to need the attention of several specialized restorers.

French Empire mantel clock, c.1815
THIS CASE HAS BEEN DECORATED USING THE NOW EXTINCT ART OF MERCURIAL GILDING. THE SURFACE OF ORMOLU COULD EASILY BE IRREPARABLY DAMAGED BY THE USE OF SUCH APPLICATIONS AS METAL POLISH, AND SO IT IS ESSENTIAL THAT CAREFUL CONSERVATION TECHNIQUES ARE EMPLOYED WHEN CLEANING SIMILAR ITEMS.

CLOCKS

Clocks are not only pieces of furniture but also complex machines constructed from a variety of materials, and which must work continuously. They therefore present more problems of day-to-day maintenance and care than do most decorative-art objects. However, observing a few basic rules, and knowing when to refer to expert help, will ensure that valuable timepieces are protected against Time itself.

Basic Care and Maintenance

SITING
Clocks should be kept away from extremes of temperature and humidity. Direct sunlight should be avoided, as should the dusty air above open fires. Clocks will only perform well when solidly supported: a mantel clock needs all feet touching the surface to prevent rocking; a wall clock needs a strong screw for support and, ideally, a second securing screw to prevent it from shifting. It is important to screw a longcase clock to the wall – a single screw placed a little lower than the top of the trunk door is sufficient. To ensure the clock is vertical, place a predrilled block of wood between the backboard and the wall, and screw through this. A large washer should be placed between the screw head and the backboard.

WINDING AND SETTING
When winding a clock, hold the case firmly and use a snug-fitting unworn key. When introducing the key, take care not to knock the dial or it may become marked or damaged. While you should not use excessive force when winding, neither should you be too diffident. The concept of "overwinding" is basically a myth; the clock will tell you when it is fully wound, and it is quite a feat of strength to break a mainspring. An eight-day English fusee clock will take about sixteen full turns to be fully wound, and incorporates an automatic stop mechanism. A French spring-driven clock will require only three to four full turns to keep it running for a week. To wind a thirty-hour longcase or lantern clock, pull down on the appropriate chain or rope (only one will move freely) until the weight reaches the top; it is advisable to support the weight as it rises with your other hand. An eight-day longcase clock should be wound until the pulleys reach the board supporting the movement. Establishing a regular winding day will save a lot of inconvenience. It is also advisable to stop clocks by stopping the pendulum if you are going away for more than its period of duration.

Hands must only be turned clockwise and not forced if resistance is met. If your clock strikes or chimes, pause to allow it to do so at each time it is meant to.

Regulation of pendulums
The approximate change in rate (in minutes per day) for an adjustment of one complete turn of the rating nut is, from left to right: Longcase clock pendulum: ½min; English wall clock or bracket clock pendulum: 2mins; English mantel or bracket clock pendulum: 2mins; French clock pendulum: 3mins; Verge clock pendulum (where the bob is screwed up and down the rod): 1½mins.

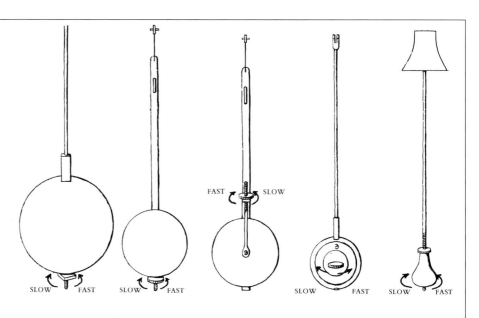

REGULATION

A pendulum clock that gains or loses can be regulated by altering the length of the pendulum – the longer the pendulum, the slower the clock. This is usually done by turning the nut on the threaded rod which supports the bob (the weight at the bottom of the pendulum).

Most French clocks have a simple system for regulation that involves the turning of a small squared rod that projects through the dial above the XII. This should be turned clockwise to gain and counterclockwise to lose. If the pendulum is suspended by a silk thread, the regulating effect of one complete turn of the rod will be considerable – ten to fifteen minutes gained or lost a day. However, later French clocks with the pendulum hanging by a steel spring will have their rate altered by about one minute per day to each complete turn of the rod.

Clocks without pendulums are usually controlled by an oscillating wheel (the balance wheel) in conjunction with a fine spiral spring, the balance spring (commonly called the hairspring). These and associated parts are often mounted on a rectangular plate called the platform, which in carriage clocks, for example, can be seen through the top glass. To regulate such clocks a small lever is used. This will be found on the platform, and in the case of carriage clocks will extend over the top of the back of the movement. The letters "S" and "F" (slow and fast) or "R" and "A" (*retard* and *avance*) are marked on either side. This lever may be moved very slightly in the appropriate direction; a small nudge makes a difference of about three minutes per week. If a clock is clean and in good mechanical order, surprisingly accurate time-keeping can be achieved from fairly humble pieces. Accuracy to within one minute a week can be expected from most mantel clocks, and weight-driven longcase clocks should be accurate to within thirty seconds a week.

TRANSPORTING

Before transporting a pendulum clock it is essential to remove the pendulum or to clamp it to the movement. Once the pendulum has been removed, the clock may start to tick at a much faster rate. Prevent this by carefully inserting a wedge of tissue paper between the backplate and the rod, or "crutch" (the steel or brass wire hanging from the back of the movement, with a fork or loop through which the pendulum passes). Some English bracket and mantel clocks incorporate a block and clamping thumbscrew which secure the pendulum for travel while still in place; the block can clearly be seen behind the pendulum rod about halfway down. When this thumbscrew is later removed, it should be kept safe in

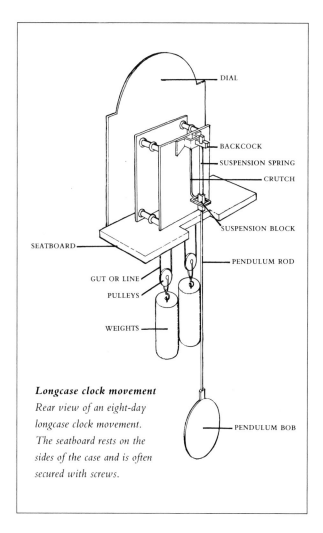

Longcase clock movement
Rear view of an eight-day longcase clock movement. The seatboard rests on the sides of the case and is often secured with screws.

Labels: DIAL, BACKCOCK, SUSPENSION SPRING, CRUTCH, SUSPENSION BLOCK, PENDULUM ROD, PENDULUM BOB, SEATBOARD, GUT OR LINE, PULLEYS, WEIGHTS

the spare hole at the edge of the backplate or in one of the brass straps connecting the movement to the case.

To dismantle a longcase clock, remove the hood by lifting it forwards, or upwards in some very early clocks. Next, remove the pendulum and unhook the weights, preferably with someone else holding the edge of the dial at the same time. Ideally, weights should be taken off only when the clock has run down completely otherwise the line may get tangled in the movement. The line should then be coiled neatly. Next the movement, dial and seatboard, which are all attached to each other, can be lifted from the case; screws securing the seatboard to the side of the case may have to be removed. All these parts can now be transported separately. Particularly fragile and vulnerable are the hands, the crutch, and the pendulum suspension spring. The latter can be well protected by slipping a length of plastic tubing over it which fits snugly around the suspension block.

Detail of English marble and ormolu clock, c.1805
ALTHOUGH THE ORMOLU MOUNTS ARE COVERED IN DIRT, THE WORK OF THE CONSERVATOR HAS BEEN LIMITED TO THE MOVEMENT. THE CRITERION FOR THIS DECISION WAS THE OWNER'S DESIRE TO RETAIN THE CLOCK'S FAMILIAR, CHARACTERFUL APPEARANCE, GIVEN THAT THE DIRT WAS NOT CAUSING ANY DAMAGE TO THE OBJECT.

To set up a clock, follow the dismantling procedure in reverse (see below). At this stage, it might be useful to mention the technique of putting a clock "in beat." Simply speaking, this is the business of equalizing the time between the "ticks" and the "tocks." This is properly effected by bending the crutch slightly in a plane parallel to that of the dial. This should only be done by those who have some experience of the procedure.

To set up a longcase clock, the case should first be secured to the wall as described earlier. The movement and seatboard should be placed on the sides of the case, the weights hung on the pulleys (you will have to wind some gut onto the barrel before you can do this, providing tension with a hand to prevent tangling), and the pendulum hung on the backcock. Ensure that the crutch is not rubbing the backboard, that the suspension block is not resting on either end of the loop of the crutch, and that the pendulum bob does not rub against the back of the case. The hood can now be replaced.

ROUTINE CLEANING

Crystals may be cleaned with any household cleaner suitable for glass, though be careful not to allow it to come into contact with any other part of the clock, and wooden cases can be waxed (taking care not to snag any loose pieces of veneer with the cloth). All metal parts, however, such as mounts, cases, dials, movements and pendulums, should be left well alone. On no account should metal polish be allowed anywhere near a clock; it can leave nasty

residues, affect any wood it contacts, remove gilding and the silvering on brass, blur the crispness of engraving, impair the mechanism if it seeps inside, and damage ormolu irreparably. Needless to say, the oiling, cleaning and general overhaul of the movement should always be entrusted to a clock conservator.

Restoration

Restorers are now tending to adopt a far more conservative approach towards their work, and will strive to preserve, whenever appropriate, those signs of age which carry so much of the history of a piece. Great damage can be caused by insensitive restorers, to movements in particular. They may discard or alter parts unnecessarily because they do not completely understand their function, and they may even indulge in the severe and unacceptable practice of buffing parts with abrasives and a motor-driven wheel. Buffing will destroy an original surface finish, round off all crisp edges and corners, and efface the definition of any engraving.

Patinas built up over years on brass mounts, for instance, can look attractive and add character to the piece. A fine original surface on a wooden case can never be imitated entirely successfully. Mercury gilding, where present, should *always* be preserved, even if partly worn away. Movements have been particularly subject to alterations and "improvements" over the years, though in many cases these can happily be left and regarded as part of

Movement from English striking tavern clock, c.1770
DIRT HAS BEEN REMOVED FROM THE MOVEMENT, BUT SOME PITTING FROM CORROSION REMAINS (RIGHT). NON-ABRASIVE CHEMICALS ENSURED THAT AS LITTLE AS POSSIBLE OF THE ORIGINAL MATERIAL WAS LOST THROUGH CLEANING. A NEW PAIR OF HANDS HAS BEEN MADE IN KEEPING WITH THE CLOCK'S PERIOD.

the clock's history. Increasingly, it is the case that restorers will try to avoid "over-restoration" and any unnecessary interference with the clock.

Much of a restorer's work is invisible, but the following checkpoints should tell you if a job has been well done: the restored clock should keep time according to its capabilities (which should certainly be within a couple of minutes a week); it should strike when the minute hand is directly at twelve; hands should offer a reasonable amount of resistance when being set, without being stiff; crystals should be clean and, in the case of carriage clocks, should not rattle; the ends of the winding squares onto which the key fits should be polished and should wind up smoothly; pins should be well finished; and the movement should not show fingerprints. There are other, less obvious, signs of good-quality work, and some of these involve the escapement. This is the part which allows the wheels to run down at a regular rate controlled by the pendulum or balance wheel, and which also transmits energy to keep the pendulum or balance wheel running. Careful adjustment of the escapement is essential to the good running of a clock, and leads to what clock experts refer to as "a good action" – in other words, a healthy arc of pendulum swing or a frisky oscillation of the balance wheel. You may well find that the tick of a pendulum clock is quieter after an overhaul; this is a good indication that the escapement is working sweetly and efficiently. The final sign of a good restorer is that all work should be guaranteed for one year, without question or quibble.

PROFESSIONAL MAINTENANCE

The movement should be regularly cleaned and overhauled, and should certainly be inspected every five years by a professional. A carriage clock, which has a platform escapement using a balance wheel and spring, will require attention more frequently than a longcase clock because the thickening or drying out of the oil will affect its much smaller and more delicate parts sooner. In such cases, the timekeeping will be impaired so the clock will, in effect, tell you when it needs to be cleaned.

Do not make the mistake of waiting until the clock stops and refuses to be revived before having it fully overhauled. A good restorer will, of course, be able to advise you as to when a clock needs attention, but there are signs which may or may not be obvious to you, for instance, intermittent problems with the clock's performance, such as bad timekeeping. Watch out for frayed or worn gut and rope lines. If moldings or veneers start to come loose from a wooden case, the glue is breaking down and the work of a case restorer is needed.

Clock Maintenance Procedures

The layperson generally knows little or nothing about the inner workings of a clock movement, so the restorer's job will always remain something of a mystery. But it will undoubtedly be helpful for every clock owner to learn something about the basic processes of professional clock maintenance.

Firstly, the clock is inspected for wear, faulty parts and incorrect setting-up. The clock is then dismantled, and all pivots (the reduced ends of the arbors or spindles which rotate in the bearings of the plates) are redefined, if necessary, and polished. Those bearings which are excessively worn have to be rebushed. This process involves enlarging the bearing hole still further, and inserting a brass sleeve which will take up wear. Pinions (small steel wheels) are polished as necessary, and the escapement is then attended to by the removal of any wear and by building up the material again to make it run efficiently.

Parts that are broken or in danger of breaking are repaired, and previous poor repairs are made good. Missing parts must be made in replica. Screw heads and hands are polished or reblued (see below). All parts are cleaned with chemicals, and the clock is finally reassembled, using new gut or lines if necessary, and thoroughly tested.

LUBRICATION

The lubrication of a clock should only be undertaken by an expert, who will use the right oil and know where it should be applied. Clock oil has been developed for the purpose and has a number of specific properties. It tends not to dry out as quickly as ordinary oils, and stays where it is put, whereas the use of incorrect oils can cause many problems, including corrosion. A visit by a restorer every three years or so just to lubricate a clock could well increase the time between full overhauls.

DIALS

Dials can be restored and cleaned; this is justified even according to current conservation ethics by the fact that it makes the dial easier to read.

Resilvering involves electrolytic exchange, whereby a silver compound is rubbed onto the brass and a very thin layer of silver is deposited on the surface. Careful preparation of the surface is crucial to this process in order to avoid removing any more material than is absolutely necessary. Some restorers may prepare the surface by spinning the dial on a machine and using coarse abrasive paper. This not only leads to a brash, unattractive appearance, it also removes the fine lines of engraving. Good results can, in fact, be achieved by applying the silvering powder directly onto the existing silver, thus producing a less harsh finish and preserving the original material. Brass plates and spandrels (corner pieces) are carefully cleaned and then lacquered to prevent tarnishing and give a richness of color, but buffing should be avoided. Similarly, gilded dial plates and spandrels are washed but otherwise left alone.

With painted dials, the ground paint of the dial should be repainted wherever possible, though if areas of paint are flaking off the unsound areas should be consolidated. A crazing of the surface due to paint shrinkage should be tolerated as it adds character to the dial. Numerals should be replaced in the appropriate style and scale, and signatures may be very slightly retouched by hand, but never by the use of transfer lettering. Wooden dials may have become cracked over time, resulting in damage to the gesso and paint surface. In this case, the dial restorer will repair the wooden plate, fill in the missing gesso, and repaint. If an enamel dial has been smashed, has chunks missing, or is badly chipped around the winding holes, the clock restorer will need to call upon the services of a ceramics restorer, who can imitate the very particular white of an enamel dial. Only in extreme cases of disrepair should this conservator have to cover the original enamel surface completely. The ceramics restorer can also deal with porcelain dials in the same way.

HANDS

The hands of a clock are also subject to damage and inappropriate replacement. Broken hands may have been repaired in the past by having plates riveted or soldered onto the back. These can be removed and the hands can be repaired more neatly using a hard solder joint. Because the dial and hands are generally the focal point of a clock, they will have been designed to be viewed as a whole, and replacement hands that have either been poorly executed or are out of character can spoil the look of the whole clock. A good restorer will be able to draw on his experience and archives to reproduce a set of hands in full sympathy with a dial. Though a time-consuming job, the creation and fitting of an appropriate set of hands can make all the difference to a clock's appearance.

Steel hands have often been blued, a process involving the heating of the steel so that it develops an oxide layer, which reflects light with a rich blue color. Rebluing by a conservator will not only improve the appearance of the steel hands considerably, but it will also provide valuable protection against corrosion.

CLOCK CASES

The conservation and restoration of clock cases present particular problems because of the range of materials and methods of construction used. Woodwork is best dealt with by a competent furniture restorer who is well versed in clock cases. Missing brass mounts and finials can be reproduced by making a rubber mold from an existing example and casting another by means of the lost-wax

English 18th-century longcase clock dials

THE DIAL ON THE RIGHT HAS BEEN RESILVERED AND CLEANED, AND ITS STEEL HANDS REBLUED. (RIGHT)

French Empire mantel clock, c.1815

THIS ELEGANT CLOCK, SIGNED "KINABLE" ON THE ENAMEL DIAL, RETAINS ITS ORIGINAL MERCURY GILDING, WHICH HAS BEEN RESTORED TO ITS BRIGHT STATE BY CAREFUL CLEANING. (BELOW)

process. The piece is then finished, chased, and colored or gilded to match the original. It is important to replace any broken crystals, for they provide protection against scratches and the atmosphere. Missing or decayed silks behind frets should be replaced for the same reason.

It should be remembered that the colors originally used were much brighter than the timid hues that tend to be in use nowadays. For example, a bright yellow silk behind the frets of a black ebonized case can look surprisingly effective and dramatic.

The cleaning of metal cases must also be undertaken only by experts. The beautiful matte mercury gilding with burnished highlights at which the French excelled can easily be ruined by careless treatment. A French Empire ormolu clock case breaks down into a surprising number of components, and even a relatively simple mantel clock incorporating a couple of figures might well consist of fifty separate parts. The satisfactory cleaning of such cases requires that they be taken apart completely and reassembled after careful washing. This is a lengthy job and often involves the making of new screws, nuts and pieces of studding where threads have worn.

Boulle cases (tortoiseshell inlaid with brass) are particularly prone to decay, as the brass inlay lifts when the old glue breaks down or when the ground-work expands or contracts due to atmospheric changes. Boulle cases should be dusted only with a soft brush and not a cloth. Any pieces that fall off should be saved to be re-attached when the case is eventually restored. Tortoiseshell is now an illegal import, but synthetic substitutes are available which will succeed in fooling the eye, if not the expert. Boulle restoration is extremely time-consuming and expensive, often to the extent that it is simply not economically viable for clocks.

Particular Problems of Certain Clocks

Though many of the rules of clock care are common to most types, certain clocks need special treatment. Regulator clocks (longcase or wall clocks designed for great accuracy) have particularly delicate escapements, so the crutch must always be secured carefully when the movement is transported. Regulators often incorporate heavy mercury-filled pendulums. Great care must be taken not to spill the mercury, which produces poisonous vapors; the brass cap of the jar is not designed as a seal. High-precision boxed marine chronometers are even more delicate and, again, only expert help should be sought when they need to be moved.

Skeleton clocks should always be protected by a glass dome, and a replacement must be found if one is broken or missing. Because the movement of these clocks is always on show, it is more important than ever to ensure that the restorer will not use any motorized buffing techniques that will destroy the definition of the metalwork.

Cheaper mass-produced clocks, such as those from the United States and Germany (particularly the Black Forest), take just as long to repair as do higher-quality pieces, and owners must always be prepared for the fact that the cost of repair and restoration may not necessarily bear any relation at all to the value of a piece. Nevertheless, many of these clocks are becoming collectable items, and they should be maintained in good repair.

The frames of Black Forest clocks are made of wood and, in the case of weight-driven wall clocks, may deform because of the pull of the weights, thus stopping the clock. The frame must then be totally rebuilt.

The bellows of early cuckoo clocks are prone to perishing. It is important that these should be re-covered rather than replaced by a modern pipe-and-bellows assembly, because the soft tone of the originals simply cannot be matched. The wooden cuckoo itself is similarly prone to decay, but always opt for restoration rather than replacement with a plastic stand-in.

Finally, musical clocks are all too often subject to abuse at the hands of a tone-deaf repairer, though luckily this is not irrevocable since their original melodies may be discovered and recreated by an expert. Interestingly, musical clocks have been made ever since Medieval times, and until the advent of the music box they were the only form of mechanized music. If the piece is in its original condition and in good mechanical order, the music will sound just as it was when played by the maker and the first owner, thus making it all the more valuable and important as an historical piece.

18th-century boulle bracket timepiece
THIS WELL-PRESERVED LOUIS XV CLOCK HAS A 12-PIECE DIAL SIGNED *PELLETIER A PARIS* AND A CASE MADE OF TORTOISESHELL INLAID WITH SCROLLING BRASS OUTLINED WITH GILT-BRONZE MOUNTS. THE PIECE HAS A QUARTER-REPEATING MECHANISM WHICH, WHEN THE CORD IS PULLED, TELLS THE TIME BY STRIKING BELLS. THIS WAS A PARTICULARLY USEFUL FUNCTION BEFORE THE ADVENT OF ELECTRIC LIGHTING.

WATCHES

People expect a lot from watches – that they should keep going while being subjected to enormous variation in terms of position, motion and temperature. Certainly, it can be infuriating when they fail, but often this is more the fault of the owner than the watch.

If watches are not to be worn or carried, you might like to display them in showcases. Pocket watches can be displayed on old watch stands, and special Plexiglas stands are available for wristwatches. Unused watches should be wrapped in acid-free tissue paper, not cotton wool, and stored in a strong box. Watches used to be fitted with crystals made of real glass until the Second World War, when "unbreakable" plastic became the norm. Although much more durable than real glass, plastic is more easily scratched. Therefore, ideally crystals should be replaced with what would have been the original material.

Pocket Watches

Because of changing fashions, chiefly the decline of the vest, pocket watches are seldom worn nowadays. An obvious point, but one which nevertheless needs stating, is that pocket watches must be secured to clothing to prevent loss or damage through dropping. Therefore, chains and their fittings must be sound, and the loop at the pendant should be unworn and securely fixed to the watch. As ever, it is important to use a well-fitting unworn key with key-wind watches. Surprisingly, two different-sized keys may be required for the two functions of hand-setting and winding. Particular care should be taken when winding watches with white enamel dials since these are easily chipped. With some pendant-wind watches (those wound with a button), owners are sometimes unaware that the hand-setting mode is brought into play by depressing a thumbnail piece in the band of the case. When opening the backs of cases, a sharp knife should never be used. If a fingernail is not sufficient then the tip of a blunt knife should be inserted very gently and given a slight twist. This should always be done in such a manner as to avoid scratching the case, and only in instances where the back is hinged.

If crystals break or are lost, replace them immediately. Even if the watch is not being worn, the hands and dial may still be damaged. Special care should be taken with the inner crystals of hunter watches (those with a lid over the crystal), as these are extremely thin. To save wear, a particular problem with gold cases, the catch of a hunter watch should be depressed before the cover is closed.

It is not advisable for owners to regulate a watch (adjust it to make it keep good time); a quick visit to a reputable watch repairer could save possible damage. If owners insist on opening the case to admire the movement, they should take care not to touch the movement, dial or hands. Look out for signs of deterioration to cases, especially enamel or repoussé cases. Lids, catches and hinges must be sound in order for the watch to snap securely shut. If problems arise, always refer the watch to an expert. If a pocket watch is carried on the person, it is advisable to protect it within a leather or suede bag.

"Graves" watch, Patek Philippe
THIS WORLD-FAMOUS POCKET WATCH MADE IN SWITZERLAND BETWEEN 1928 AND 1933 WAS, UNTIL RECENTLY, THE MOST COMPLICATED PORTABLE TIMEPIECE IN THE WORLD. IT INCLUDES, AMONG ITS MANY FUNCTIONS, A CALENDAR WHICH TAKES INTO ACCOUNT LEAP YEARS AND THE DIFFERING LENGTHS OF THE MONTHS, A SOPHISTICATED CHIMING AND REPEATING MECHANISM, AND VARIOUS ASTRONOMICAL DIALS.

Display of watches and parts and tools used to make watch straps
THIS GROUP OF WATCHES INCLUDES TWO WITH PROTECTIVE LIDS OVER THE DIALS. THE WRISTWATCH, THIRD FROM THE LEFT, WHICH DATES FROM THE FIRST WORLD WAR, IS OF THE TYPE KNOWN AS A "HUNTER," WHILE THE POCKET WATCH, TOP LEFT, WHICH HAS A SMALL, GLAZED APERTURE IN THE LID ALLOWING THE HANDS TO BE READ WHILE THE LID REMAINS CLOSED, IS CALLED A "HALF–HUNTER."

Wristwatches

Over the last few years, enthusiasm for vintage wristwatches has grown enormously. It should be noted, however, that they need considerably more care and attention than do their younger quartz colleagues.

Manual watches should be wound once a day at a regular time. This should be done with the watch taken off the wrist, using both forefinger and thumb rather than just the forefinger under the button. The watch is fully wound when you are unable to wind any further; do not be too diffident about it. If an automatic (self-winding) watch has not been worn for a while, or if you lead a sedentary life, it will require manual winding. This should be done in the same way as for manual watches, though since you cannot tell when it is fully wound twenty winding strokes should be sufficient. A worn button will make winding difficult to control and should be replaced. When pulling out the button for hand-setting, use two fingernails between button and case, twisting the button slightly as you pull, particularly if the watch is old.

To keep the watch safe, the strap, bars and lugs should be kept in good condition. The strap must fit well between the lugs to prevent the bars from springing out. A watch should not be worn too tightly as this puts undue strain on the lugs and case. It is best to take your watch off at night, when participating in sports, and during any activity where it may be subjected to extremes of humidity.

It was only during the Second World War that antimagnetic alloys began to be used in watch construction. If a watch is behaving erratically, it may be because it has become magnetized. Areas of high electric or magnetic fields, such as the backs of televisions, should be avoided. Even proximity to the strong, door-closing magnets of cupboards can cause problems.

The frequency of overhauls depends on various factors, such as the condition of the case and the size of the watch, but as a general rule once every two years should be sufficient. Apart from problems caused by dirt getting into the watch, the oil becomes thicker and less efficient. An overhaul will involve stripping the watch completely, replacing faulty parts, cleaning the parts by machine, and reassembly. The watch can then be adjusted for time-keeping. Waterproof watches, in addition, need to have their seals changed, and are tested in a special pressurizing machine. Crystals can also be changed.

Regulation can be a complicated matter. The watchmaker's timing machine, which gives a direct print-out of the watch's performance, greatly facilitates the process, and is used to correct consistent gain or loss.

MUSIC BOXES

Music boxes produce music by means of a pinned cylinder or a steel disk whose projections pluck the teeth of a steel comb. They range enormously in size and type, from early delicate movements contained in snuff-boxes, to large cabinets housing elaborate mechanisms playing on drums, bells, and even organs. Although not in frequent use and appearing to have comparatively simple mechanisms, music boxes are very often found in surprisingly poor condition and in need of repair.

General Care

Many of the rules of music box care are the same as those for clocks. They should be kept in conditions which avoid extremes of humidity and temperature, and out of direct sunlight. Wooden cases can be waxed, though care should be taken not to catch any loose veneer or inlays which may be lifting. Only well-fitting keys should be used for key-wind boxes. Before transporting a music box, it should be at the end of the tune. If it is left in the middle of a tune, there is a risk of pins and comb being damaged as a result of the cylinder moving axially. When carrying a box, do not use the handles – they are often not to be trusted – but carry with your hands, supporting the base of the box. If the box was designed with an inner glazed lid and the glass is broken or missing, have it replaced. As well as protecting the movement, this glass will protect you if ever the governor (the fan-blade assembly which regulates the speed of the mechanism) should fail, causing the teeth to fly out. The disks from disk machines should only be played if in good condition; never play them if they are rusty, if the projections are bent, or if the drive holes at the edge are damaged or broken. Should any problems arise with the movement, seek expert help.

Operation

Springs should be wound until they will go no further; they are very strong and most unlikely to break. Originally, the spring barrel would almost certainly have incorporated an automatic stop mechanism, though in many cases this has been removed by lazy repairers who could not be troubled to maintain it. On early key-wind boxes the control levers and winding square are found behind the flap at the left-hand end. On later lever-wound boxes the levers are inside the box on the right.

To operate the box, the stop/start lever should be pushed towards *Start*, held there for a second or two, and then returned to *Stop*; this will allow one tune to play, after which the box will stop automatically. If you wish the box to play continually, the lever should be left in the *Start* position. The instant stop lever – found only on the earlier models – simply halts the fan blades of the governor, which allows you to stop the box in mid-tune. It is safer not to use it except for transportation, when it should be engaged at the end of a tune as an added precaution against damage to the mechanism. The purpose of the tune change/tune repeat lever needs no explanation. So long as the music box is in good condition and is treated appropriately, the frequency of its use should not be a cause for concern.

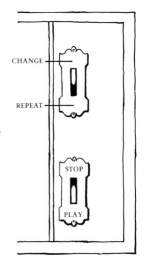

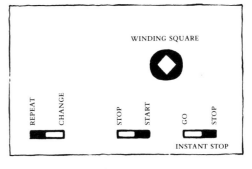

Music box controls
Right: Controls as seen to the right of the movement inside lever-wound boxes. Below: Controls as seen behind the flap at the left-hand end of key-wound boxes. On no account should any part of the movement, other than these controls and the winding lever or key, be interfered with. This could be dangerous and lead to extensive damage.

Restoration

The music box restorer should be able to provide a range of services, from a routine clean and overhaul to replacing a governor or repinning a cylinder. A general overhaul will involve dismantling the movement, and cleaning and polishing all parts, including the screw heads. Any faulty parts, typically the ratchets and springs, must be repaired or replaced. The wheels of the governor often become worn and have to be replaced.

away at the steel pins while the brass remains intact. Then the cylinder is cleaned and each new pin inserted, one by one, by hand. The cement is replaced and distributed evenly by spinning the cylinder while heating, and the pins are ground to the same length on a lathe.

The restorer sometimes comes across the problem of a chemical breakdown of the lead weights under the teeth, a condition known as "*maladie de plomb*." This is caused by the lead forming lead carbonate (because of the organic acids present in the wood of some cases), which then reacts

Detail of movement from a Swiss 10-air music box, c.1890

THIS MOVEMENT IS IN PERFECT WORKING ORDER, HAVING BEEN FULLY RESTORED. THE BED-PLATE HAS BEEN REPAINTED AND ALL PARTS CLEANED AND POLISHED. MUCH OF THE WORK OF THE MUSIC BOX RESTORER INVOLVES THE CAREFUL ADJUSTMENT OF THE COMB, TEETH, DAMPERS, CYLINDER AND PINS TO ACHIEVE THE BEST POSSIBLE MUSICAL RESULTS.

If the teeth or tooth tips are broken, or if the pins on the cylinder have become bent or broken, the movement may have suffered what is called a "run" (that is, when the cylinder turns extremely rapidly because the governor has become disconnected either through breakage or because screws have been undone with the spring wound). Teeth and tips can be replaced, but this is a highly delicate and specialized job which can be performed successfully by only a very few experts. When pins on the cylinder have become excessively bent or rusty, replacements are substituted in a time-consuming process known as "repinning." Firstly, the cement inside the cylinder, which anchors the pins and provides its rigidity, is removed by heating. The cylinder is then immersed in acid, which eats

with the carbon dioxide in the atmosphere. The condition requires the complete replacement of all the leads.

After cleaning and repairing, the music box needs to be "finished," in other words, tuned and adjusted to make the music sound as pleasing as possible. To achieve this, the worn tips of the teeth are ground so that they are all in line, and the comb's position is adjusted in relation to the cylinder; these are the measures which will help the music to play rhythmically. The small curved steel springs below the tooth tips, known as "dampers," are then adjusted to prevent grunts and squeaks. Finally, the comb is tuned, where necessary; this is done by removing material from the leads to make the note higher, or by filing the roots of the teeth to make the note lower.

AUTOMATA

Automata are figures whose concealed mechanisms, when activated, cause them to mimic the movements, and sometimes the sounds, of humans and other creatures. As with clocks and music boxes, automata should be kept away from direct sunlight and extremes of temperature and humidity. Watch for the presence of woodworm (new round holes and piles of wood powder are the tell-tale signs) and have them treated. Routine cleaning at home should extend only to careful light dusting with a soft brush. The cleaning of porcelain, wax, leather, painted gesso, or any other of the various materials found in automata should be left to the professional.

French musical automaton of a monkey fiddler, c.1870
THIS PIECE HAS BEEN EXTENSIVELY RESTORED (ABOVE) BY FOUR SPECIALISTS, WHOSE WORK INCLUDED THE COMPLETE OVERHAUL OF THE MOVEMENT, THE MAKING OF NEW HANDS, LIPS, VIOLIN BOW, TABLE, TABLECLOTH, FEET AND SHOES (ABOVE RIGHT). UNFORTUNATELY, THE ORIGINAL SILK CLOTHES HAD ALSO PERISHED AND REPLACEMENTS HAD TO BE MADE FROM SILK DATING FROM THE TIME OF MANUFACTURE. THE ORIGINAL BUTTONS AND BUCKLES HAVE BEEN RETAINED.

As with clocks, if a separate key is used for winding ensure that it fits snugly. If any parts become unattached from the piece they should be labeled immediately, saved, and given to the restorer to repair. If the piece stops working, it is not advisable to attempt to resuscitate it by agitating the figure's moving parts.

Judging by the condition of many automata, it seems unlikely that many were ever kept under domes or in cases. The clothes of the figures are often dirty or rotting; they should be restored by a textiles expert, who will try to retain as much as possible of the original material. The mechanisms are often of crude construction and made from poor-quality materials; furthermore, they were often designed in such a way that they cannot be taken apart. Nonetheless, much can be achieved through restoration – often involving several specialists.

SCIENTIFIC INSTRUMENTS

 Scientific instruments – devices central to astronomy, navigation, surveying, weather-forecasting, physics and mathematics – constitute a relatively specialized field. The ways in which they were made are complex, and the different materials involved in their construction and function each demand individual care.

Made predominantly of metal – usually brass and bronze and, to a lesser extent, silver – scientific instruments are subject to corrosion and most other problems associated with metals. But the range of scientific instruments also incorporates glass, wood, ivory, bone, shagreen and leather; each of these materials also demands special care. Conditions of storage and display must be adjusted to suit the sometimes opposing needs of metals and the materials with which they are combined. Globes are often particularly in need of protection against humidity and light as they are usually covered in paper and are likely to have been hand-colored with water-based pigments.

A notable aspect of many scientific instruments is the bronzing, lacquering or satin finish which was often applied – for functional rather than decorative reasons – to the metals of which they are made. These finishes, an integral part of scientific instruments, are all too often removed by unsuitable cleaning materials or insensitive techniques of restoration.

Frosino Volpaia gilt-brass nocturnal and quadrant, Florence, 1527 (below) and Leonhart Miller ivory diptych dial, Nuremberg, 1627 (above).

THESE TWO FINE AND WELL-PRESERVED OBJECTS ARE A TESTAMENT TO THE EXCEPTIONAL ACCOMPLISHMENT OF EARLY INSTRUMENT MAKERS. THEY ARE DISPLAYED ON AN ENGRAVED DUTCH MAP OF EUROPE BY BAPTISTA VAN DOETEEUM, *c.*1599.

Scientific instruments include a wide range of diverse objects: devices for observing the heavens, plotting the course of ships at sea, measuring the lie of the land, recording atmospheric conditions, and exploring the laws of physics and mathematics. The way in which they were made and the materials involved in their construction and function each demand particular care.

Types of Instruments

Scientific instruments fall into four main categories: astronomical; navigational; surveying; and drawing and calculating. The four groups comprise, respectively, telescopes, quadrants, astrolabes, planetariums and armillary spheres; globes, octants, sextants, chronometers and compasses; levels, theodolites and barometers; and drawing sets, including parallel rules, sectors, protractors and dividers. There are of course many more, devised for use in many other scientific disciplines.

Most collectable scientific instruments date from the eighteenth and nineteenth centuries. Many are masterpieces of craftsmanship, made out of metals, ivory, wood and other diverse materials.

Materials

The materials used in making earlier scientific instruments were mainly wood and ivory. These were gradually replaced by metals, chiefly the copper alloys brass and bronze, which are resistant to corrosion.

Of the woods, mahogany was the most widely employed. Boxwood was also favored, and many navigational instruments, later fashioned from metal, were first constructed from fruitwood. Boxwood, being fine-grained, could also be engraved and because of this was used for scales. Lignum vitae was used for such components as lens mounts in telescopes and microscopes. The cases of fine instruments were of mahogany, while those of more ordinary examples were of oak.

Ivory and bone, being much easier to work than metals, were used with gold and silver to make fine instruments, including early sundials. Ivory and bone were also utilized for scales on wooden instruments. Leather was sometimes employed to give a better grip on the outer cover of telescopes, and to make covers for small box sextants. Shagreen, reserved for very fine instruments, was used on microscopes and telescopes, and for the outer casing of some drawing instruments and pocket globes.

Glass, crucial to the function of optical instruments, was used for lenses, mirrors and colored filters on sextants.

Wooden octant, George Adams, London, 1753
OCTANTS ARE COMPOSITE OBJECTS AND CAN INVOLVE DIVERSE SKILLS TO CONSERVE AND REPAIR. THIS EXAMPLE COMPRISES A MAHOGANY FRAME, BOXWOOD LIMB, AND DIAGONAL SCALE WITH IVORY INSCRIPTION PLATE. THE MIRROR FRAMES, PEEPHOLE SIGHT AND GLASS-FILTER MOUNTS ARE MADE OF BRASS.

Certain types of planetariums consist of two hemispheres of thin glass painted with the constellations.

Copper alloys – notably brass and bronze – are the main metals used in the construction of scientific instruments. Superseding wood, they were the chosen materials for the frames of sextants and their bearings. Stressed brass was used for the tubes of telescopes. Fine pivots were made mostly of hardened steel, and screws and pins mostly of steel or a copper alloy such as brass. Aluminum appeared early in the twentieth century but, being light and soft, was effective only for castings and small parts.

Silver in scientific instruments was most commonly used for scales, and on sextants and theodolites. Since it is softer than copper alloys, silver can be engraved more easily and more accurately. The scales were made as a separate piece, and afterwards were pinned onto or inlaid into the brass or bronze frame. Complete drawing sets and other instruments made for display rather than daily use were sometimes fashioned from silver. Lead was rarely used, except as a weight in compasses.

Plastic was introduced in the late nineteenth century. Cellulose nitrate was used to make mass-produced scales and other pieces, while Bakelite, which can quite easily be mistaken for ebony or other hardwoods, was used in the manufacture of handles and covers.

Finishes

A distinctive aspect of the metal parts of scientific instruments is their finish. Finishing was carried out both to prevent reflection from the sun and to stave off corrosion, which was particularly likely to occur in the damp, salty conditions of life at sea.

Increasingly fine grades of abrasive, which were applied along the length of individual parts, produced a matte, satin-like finish, whereas polishing was used only where brightness was desirable, particularly on steelwork. Bronzing, whereby the metal was colored with chemicals, also prevented glare. Arsenic was employed to produce a dark gray metallic finish, and antimony a nut brown. Black lacquer, which was used to prevent reflection inside telescope tubing, was applied around the eyepieces and filters of telescopes, and on the bases of mirrors.

Since bronzing is easily scratched, a coat of translucent lacquer was applied to protect it. Lacquer also protected the instrument from corrosion, particularly on scales and other parts where engraving needed to be seen clearly. These surface finishes produced a very slight color change on the metal; the gray of bronzing when coated with yellowish lacquer resulted in a greenish finish, which is not to be confused with tarnish or corrosion.

Handling

Fingerprints are very corrosive to copper alloys and steel. When handling scientific instruments made of these metals, wear clean white cotton gloves or plastic surgical gloves. Rubber gloves are inadvisable since they may contain sulfides, which also corrode metals, and plastic gloves do not provide a firm grip.

Before handling an instrument, examine it for unattached parts, particularly those that may appear to be fixed, but, like the upper hemisphere on a planetarium, are merely balanced. Do not pick up an instrument by any thin, protruding part; where there is a handle, use it, and place the other hand beneath the instrument.

Cleaning

No cleaning other than careful dusting should be attempted by the layperson. A fine, soft camel-hair, sable or squirrel-hair brush, whose ferrule has been wound with tape to prevent scratching, can safely be used to remove most surface dirt and dust. Airbrushes with an integral bulb, like those designed to clean photographic lenses, are also suitable, particularly for cleaning glass parts.

On no account should water or detergents be used, while household cleaners containing ammonia and other alkalis will remove lacquer and bronzing and gradually erode satin finishes. Silver may be cleaned with small cotton-tipped swabs moistened with silver cleaner, but care should be taken to prevent any of the substance touching other surfaces. It is also vital that this cleaner be thoroughly rinsed off with small swabs dipped in distilled water, and then the area dried with cotton wool.

Thorough cleaning, possibly involving the dismantling of instruments, can be carried out by a conservator, who, with due care, may use a mild cleaning agent.

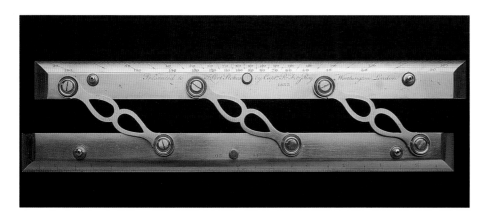

Parallel rule,
London, 1833
THE PARALLEL RULE WAS USED FOR CHART WORK (TO PLOT A COURSE) FROM 1584. CONSERVATION OF THE INSTRUMENT SHOWN WOULD BE RELATIVELY STRAIGHTFORWARD AS IT IS ENTIRELY OF NICKEL ALLOY.

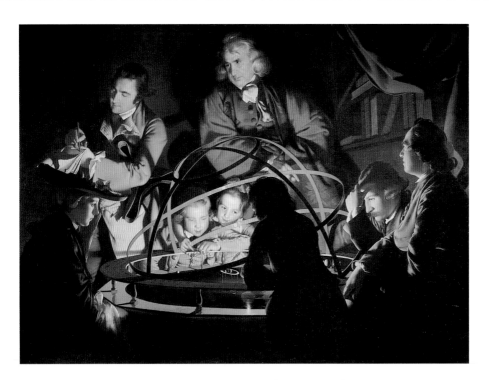

A Philosopher
giving that Lecture
on the Orrery ...,
*Joseph Wright of
Derby, exhibited 1766*
THE ORRERY IN THE PAINTING
IS A MECHANICAL MODEL
SHOWING THE MOVEMENT OF
THE SOLAR SYSTEM'S
HEAVENLY BODIES AROUND
THE SUN. ORIGINAL ORRERIES
WERE NOT SCIENTIFIC
INSTRUMENTS, BUT ORNATE
FURNISHING PIECES WITH
HIDDEN MACHINERY. THEIR
CONSERVATION CAN BE
COMPLEX, AS THE VARIOUS
MECHANICAL AND
DECORATIVE PARTS MAY
WARRANT SPECIALIZED
ATTENTION. (LEFT)

*Portuguese azimuth
compass, Manoci
Ferreira, 1780*
THE COMPASS IS MOUNTED IN
A POLISHED ROSEWOOD CASE,
THE BOWL COMPRISES BRASS
AND ROSEWOOD AND IS SET
ON SQUARE BRASS GIMBALS,
AND THE COMPASS CARD IS
OF PAPER AND CARD.
CONSERVATION TREATMENT
OF SUCH AN INSTRUMENT
COULD PROVE HIGHLY
PROBLEMATIC, SINCE IT
WOULD INVOLVE THE SKILLS
OF BOTH A PAPER
CONSERVATOR AND A METAL
AND WOOD CONSERVATOR.
(RIGHT)

Transportation

Pack all moving parts with acid-free tissue paper, followed by bubble wrap or foam rubber, and place the instrument in a strong carrying case with a solid base. Ordinary foam rubber may be used for packing, and wooden or cardboard boxes for transportation, but it is inadvisable that scientific instruments be wrapped or stored in them over any significant period of time since acids and sulfides in these materials may cause corrosion.

While aneroid barometers (which measure atmospheric pressure by means of evacuated bellows) can be transported in the same way as other scientific instruments, mercury barometers need special care. If the instrument is moved too quickly, the mercury may hit and shatter the tip of the glass tube in which it is held. Mercury can also spill from open-cistern barometers.

To transport a mercury barometer, always move it very gently and lay it at an angle of 30° from the horizontal on a 2in bed of foam, ensuring that the top is higher than the bottom. Tape it down with cotton document tape. As an extra precaution, it is advisable to place a tray beneath the bed of foam; if a spillage were to occur, this would ensure that the mercury could be retrieved. Note that the vapor given off by mercury is poisonous.

Storage and Display

Scientific instruments should be kept in a clean, dust-free atmosphere, if possible under a glass dome or in a glass or Plexiglas case. Light, however, has a detrimental effect on organic materials; to protect ivory, lacquer, ink, paint and paper, light levels should be below 150 lux, and sometimes as low as 50 lux, ideally with a UV filter fitted to the appliance. To suit both metals and organic materials such as ivory, the relative humidity should remain constant at 50–55% (see page 181).

Metals are vulnerable to sulfides, which occur naturally in the atmosphere and also in certain dyes. Sulfides are also present in felt, velvet, wool and silk; these materials are therefore unsuitable for displaying or storing scientific instruments. Cotton or nylon are considered to be safer substitutes for this purpose.

New oak, new mahogany and other new woods, as well as certain glues that are found in display and storage cases, also emit acetic acid. The acids present in ordinary cardboard attack metals as well. Although acid-free tissue wrapped around the instruments provides short-term protection, scientific instruments should not be stored in wood or cardboard for any extended period of time.

Damage

Bent, twisted or broken parts are likely to be the result of ill-use, accident or forcing. Over-tightening of screws can cause damage, too, as pressure is exerted on parts not designed to bear it. Broken or damaged screw heads betray the use of screwdrivers of the wrong shape or size for the screw. Slots on the heads of screws in scientific instruments are usually of the parallel type, and certain other specific types are also encountered. To avoid damage, it is therefore important for a conservator to use screwdrivers that exactly fit the screw heads.

Retapping of parts – where completely new holes have been made and modern screws inserted – creates serious damage and is likely to have been caused by ignorant or unsympathetic restoration.

In cases where they are unlacquered, or where lacquer has begun to deteriorate, the metal components of scientific instruments may suffer from corrosion. On copper alloys, a dark brown tarnish may form. If the piece is kept in favorable conditions, the tarnish will remain stable. In damp conditions, it will turn into verdigris, a bright green corrosion. Bronze corrosion or bronze disease – bright green powdery spots – is another consequence of over-damp conditions.

As has been mentioned above, fingerprints, which contain salt, sodium chloride, lactic acid, and amino and fatty acids, are highly corrosive. They can penetrate bronzed and lacquered surfaces to leave unsightly marks and corrosive substances. It is advisable to wear either clean white cotton gloves, which contain no harmful dyes, or plastic surgical gloves when handling scientific instruments, and especially when the damage caused by fingerprints would be irreversible, as on the metal speculum mirrors of telescopes.

Corrosion can also be caused by the degradation of the plastic components of scientific instruments. Cellulose nitrate has a tendency to break down, emitting nitric and acetic acids, which cause rapid and serious damage to copper alloys, aluminum and, occasionally, steel. It is not always obvious when any plastic used has started to degrade: a smell of vinegar or camphor and sweating on the plastic are early signs. Whenever possible, degrading plastic should be completely removed.

Ivory and wood, and the animal glues that bind them together, are susceptible both to dry and to damp atmospheres. In over-dry conditions, wood cracks, ivory warps and animal glues dry out. In over-damp environments, wood acquires mold, ivory again warps, and animal glues turn to a mushy consistency.

Globes

The first globes were made by the ancient Greeks, who theorized that the world was round. But it was not until the late fifteenth century – after a long intervening period when it was generally held the earth was flat – that globes began to be produced in large quantities. Some were made from metals that include silver and gold. Most antique globes are terrestrial (representing the earth), but celestial models showing the constellations were also made, such as the original Farnese globe of around 300 BC.

In around 1540 the classic method of making globes from papier-mâché shells evolved. These orbs are strong, light and often complex in structure, consisting of more than one material. The traditional sphere is made of a wooden "skeleton" inside a firm shell of papier-mâché coated in plaster that turns on an internal central pillar between the North and South Poles. At each end are external pivots attached to a vertical meridian ring that supports the central pillar. The whole sphere is then suspended within a horizon ring encircling the equator. The paper that covers the sphere was first printed flat as willow-leaf shapes (known as gores), which were cut out, dampened and pasted onto the sphere. On a good globe the registration of each piece is so exact that the joins are difficult to see. The gores were colored either by hand or by color-printing, and it is important to distinguish between the two methods when deciding on the correct conservation treatment to adopt, as the colors painted by hand are usually less stable.

HANDLING AND CLEANING

Natural moisture and grease from the hands will discolor the surface of an antique globe, so it should not be handled unnecessarily; neither should it be spun vigorously, because the sphere's alignment is often imperfect and the paper surface may scrape against the meridian ring and be lost. Brass fittings should not be polished, as deposits of metal cleaner on the delicate paper surface can be permanently disfiguring. To facilitate dusting, the globe may need to be turned gently, and a soft, clean duster should be used. If the stand is made of polished wood, it should be treated like a good piece of furniture, and particular care should be taken not to get any polish near the surface of the sphere. Check regularly that the globe is perfectly aligned within the meridian ring and the horizon circle.

Like furniture and other *objets d'art*, globes suffer if the environment in which they are kept is not stable. Both the temperature and relative humidity in a room should be reasonably constant and not too high (see page 181).

REPAIR AND RESTORATION

Globes can incur various types of damage. The surface layer, which is usually varnished, may have discolored badly or become brittle and flaky. Dry conditions may have made the gores split and pull apart, or the metal supports may have become bent or broken. If the sphere or mounts are in need of attention, a specialized globe conservator should be consulted. If a problem arises with a wooden stand – for instance, it may weaken due to loose joints or woodworm infestation – the globe should be referred to a furniture conservator.

A wooden globe may suffer from woodworm, usually indicated by the appearance of little mounds of fine wood dust, and rattles in a metal globe may suggest corrosion. If the internal structure does appear to be failing, and provided the globe is of sufficient importance, then it may be worthwhile to have it X-rayed.

Since each globe-maker had his own methods of globe construction, it is extremely useful for the restorer of a globe to know as much of the history of the various globe designs and their makers as possible.

Conservation

Very often only a small amount of conservation is needed to stabilize the condition of scientific instruments.

Cleaning by a conservator should preserve the original surface finish of the piece. If it is intact, a lacquered surface may be greatly enhanced by light cleaning with a small cotton-tipped swab dipped in a solution of distilled water and 5% non-ionic detergent. The swab should be barely damp, and the conservator should take great care not to scratch the lacquer. It is also important that the piece be well dried. A soft microcrystalline wax can then be applied; this gives a great deal of protection, both from the inevitable handling and from the atmosphere.

Instruments with many intricate parts may need to be taken apart for thorough cleaning. Corrosion may be removed, by a conservator, using manual or mechanical methods, chemical agents and cleaning pastes. Metal cleaners containing ammonia should be avoided.

Restoration

Heavy restoration can, unfortunately, sometimes lead to undesirable effects on scientific instruments, and some thought should be given as to how much restoration is strictly necessary before any treatment is begun.

Bent parts may fracture if an attempt is made to straighten them. It is generally preferable to retain an

Detail of an English globe that belonged to George Washington, c.1789
THIS DETAIL SHOWS HOW THE JOINS OF WILLOW–LEAF–SHAPED GORES RUN VERTICALLY FROM THE POLES. THE VARNISHED PAPER HAS DISCOLORED TO A PALE YELLOW. (LEFT)

Late 17th-century Venetian celestial globe, F. Vincenzo Coronelli
THIS GLOBE'S OCTAGONAL WALNUT STAND HAS EIGHT TURNED BALUSTER LEGS, AND FLAT STRETCHERS. (ABOVE)

original, imperfect part than to ask a conservator to fit a new one. New parts may be necessary, however, to restore an instrument to working order; in this case, the new part should be marked to indicate that it is not original. Retapping of original parts to make new screw holes cannot be recommended in any circumstances.

Original lacquered or patinated surfaces that may be peculiar to certain scientific instruments can be lost through the use of emery cloths or household metal cleaners. Good conservators do not recommend their use on scientific instruments. Neither are buffing machines suitable, since their robust action causes irreversible damage by rounding sharp edges. In addition, scientific instruments were never intended to have a shining, mirror-like finish, and their satin grain can be lost too easily through over-polishing.

LACQUERS AND RELACQUERING

Most old lacquers are resin- and gum-based, containing the insect resin shellac. They were almost always applied by fine brushes (rarely by dipping). Spray-lacquering is a twentieth-century phenomenon.

When the original lacquer has deteriorated or heavy corrosion has been removed during the restoration processes, relacquering is sometimes necessary. Though modern lacquers, which are based on cellulose nitrate or synthetic acrylic resins, are quite acceptable, their appearance can nevertheless be distinguished from that of old lacquers. It is therefore worth asking a conservator to use a lacquer made with gums and resins in the traditional way. Such lacquers can be applied by either spraying or brushing, but both of these methods require a great deal of skill and expertise.

PAINTINGS; MINIATURES

Both paintings and miniatures are sensitive to excesses of heat, light, humidity and dryness. The condition of the surface of the image is often perceived as being of primary importance, but these objects must be considered in their entirety, from the framing or backing to the canvas or panel in the case of oil paintings, or the ivory, card or metal in the case of miniatures, plumbagos or silhouettes.

Canvas becomes increasingly brittle with age and is easily torn or distorted. Oil paint has a tendency to dry, shrink and crack; while mild craquelure is perfectly acceptable in an old painting, more extreme cases can lead to disfiguring flaking and serious paint loss. Paintings on wood are particularly in need of steady environmental control, as all wooden panels will naturally expand and contract. Panels are also sometimes subject to a number of other hazards, including wood-boring insects and, occasionally, dry rot.

The primary requirements of miniatures are a clean atmosphere if colors are to retain their brightness, low lighting levels if pigments are not to fade, and stable heat and humidity levels if the ivory or card on which they are most often painted is not to suffer warping and cracking. The lockets in which miniatures are held should be cleaned only with the utmost care and should never be opened by inexpert hands.

Detail of a Flemish 17th-century painting – after cleaning, before restoration
CANVAS PAINTINGS HAVE OFTEN BEEN TORN OR DAMAGED IN THE PAST AND REMOVAL OF OLD VARNISHES AND REPAINTS WILL REVEAL PREVIOUS REPAIRS. THE PAINTING MUST BE MADE STRUCTURALLY SOUND BEFORE FILLINGS AND RETOUCHINGS ARE APPLIED.

PAINTINGS

Easel paintings are often categorized by the nature of their support, their main structural layer, which is most often canvas or wood panel. "Canvas" supports are usually of linen – although other fibers such as cotton and hemp have been used – and the fabric is usually of a simple plain weave, although more elaborate weaves such as herringbone, twill and damask are found. Canvases are stretched to keep them taut – nowadays over an expandable wooden stretcher, but before the eighteenth century over solid wood panels, or rigid strainers.

Wood types used for panel paintings are usually typical of their country of origin. Thus, early Italian paintings are almost always on poplar, while northern European paintings are very often on oak. Other woods such as fir, beech and fruitwoods were occasionally used – as was pine, despite its inherent instability. Imported woods such as mahogany became popular in the eighteenth and nineteenth centuries.

Both wood and canvas supports were prepared for painting with layers of ground, or priming. For rigid panels, the ground was usually a smooth, rather brittle, creamy-white layer of chalk or gypsum bound with glue. For canvases, a more flexible ground would be used. Light or dark in color, the ground consisted of mixtures of pigments with lead white or chalk, and was bound with a drying oil such as linseed.

Other supports used included copper plates, which were especially suitable for smooth, highly detailed painting styles, and often needed no preparation beyond a slight roughening of the surface to help the paint adhere. Vellum, marble, slate, glass, leather, ivory and zinc have also functioned as painting supports. In the nineteenth century, prepared boards such as millboard became popular for smaller paintings, outdoor sketches, and so on.

Paint layers, composed of colored pigments dispersed in a binding medium such as egg or linseed oil, can vary enormously in appearance: from thin, transparent glazes to thick, opaque impasto. In most paintings, the paint layers are protected and given optical clarity by a layer of clear varnish. Varnishes, composed of natural or synthetic resins, invariably discolor with time, and this is the principal reason why so many pictures are cleaned. Some pictures – Renaissance glue-tempera paintings, and certain Impressionist and Cubist works, for example – were never intended to be varnished and have been irretrievably altered by subsequent varnishing.

The condition of the painted image is clearly of the utmost importance, but the layers below – the support and ground – can have a profound effect on the state of the painting itself. In such a complex structure, the ways in which the various layers interact and sometimes separate from each other have to be understood by those concerned with their preservation. When examining easel paintings and prescribing treatments for them, it is customary to consider the layers one by one, beginning with the support: only if the main structural element is secure will the rest of the painting survive intact.

Display

IDEAL CONDITIONS

Correct environmental conditions are vital if the structure of a painting is to remain stable. The recommended levels for temperature and humidity are 68°F and 55% relative humidity: a range of ± 5% can be tolerated for the relative humidity, but outside those limits, internal stresses can be set up that can lead to deterioration.

Light levels should also be controlled. The materials of easel paintings are not generally as sensitive as those of watercolors or textiles, but some pigments will alter in strong light. A value of 250 lux at the picture surface is the present museum standard and is equivalent to normal diffused daylight in a domestic setting.

Centrally heated houses can become very dry, and humidifiers may be essential in keeping the relative humidity up to the required level. Particularly hot, dry regions are found above radiators or heating vents, so paintings should not be placed there. Wood panels are more affected by extreme dryness than canvases, but neither should be exposed to it.

Obviously, direct sunlight can be harmful. Also to be avoided are cold external walls of houses, where there is a danger of condensation occurring. Hanging paintings over a fireplace can be the worst possible choice: smoke, dust and heat are obvious hazards, and can seriously speed up the deterioration of a panel or canvas.

Although the greatest danger in modern houses is dryness, excess humidity can also be a serious problem. Mold, especially in canvas paintings, is very difficult to eradicate. Exposure to water, from flooding or leakage, can cause shrinkage of canvases, severe flaking of paint, and the blanching (whitening) of paint and varnish layers.

Dutch 17th-century landscape painting
GRAY SURFACE DIRT AND YELLOW VARNISH HAVE BEEN SUCCESSFULLY REMOVED BY CLEANING. (LEFT)

Varnish removal
A COTTON-TIPPED SWAB, DIPPED INTO A SOLVENT, WAS ROLLED ONTO THE PICTURE SURFACE, CAUSING THE VARNISH TO SOFTEN AND DISSOLVE. (BELOW)

Inspection

The most valuable instruction for owners of paintings is to inspect them regularly, front and back. Constant vigilance will detect minor problems before they become major.

The best way of inspecting paintings on the wall is to stoop down and look from below, with the light reflecting off the surface. In this way, blemishes, cracks and raised paint will show more clearly. Photography can also be useful in checking whether a painting is deteriorating. Paintings can occasionally be looked at in direct sunlight; they should not be left there for more than a moment or two, but many minor faults will show up that might not be noticed in a dim domestic setting.

Paintings should be held only by the very edges as greasy finger marks will show on both old varnishes and on fragile paint surfaces. Ideally, they should only be carried around in their frames. These can be vulnerable since moldings might be brittle and the gilding can be damaged by the moisture of one's hand. Wearing white cotton gloves can overcome these problems.

Storage

The storage of paintings usually creates a problem of space. Museums generally have movable racks of heavy mesh on which paintings can be hung. In a private house, they are often placed on the floor leaning against a wall. There are a few simple precautions which should be taken to avoid the damage that can result from this.

Firstly, they should stand on blocks of wood 3–4in deep to keep them away from any possible dampness or standing water. Secondly, paintings should not lean directly against each other, since scratches and dents will inevitably ensue; thin boards should be placed between paintings. Finally, if paintings are stacked in this way, a weight should be placed at the foot of the outermost one to prevent it from sliding forwards.

Transportation

If paintings have to be transported, they should travel in rigid cases with suitable padding inside to cushion against vibration. For short journeys, bubble wrap or soft blankets are acceptable, but they should not touch the surface of the painting. For the transport of valuable pictures, specialized fine-art packers should be consulted, but fragile paintings should generally not be subjected to

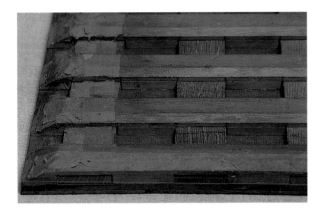

Early 20th-century cradle on a panel painting
THE FIXED BARS (RUNNING LEFT TO RIGHT) HAVE SLOTS CUT INTO THEM FOR FREE-RUNNING CROSS-MEMBERS.

the stresses of travel. Large canvas paintings can, in theory, be taken off the stretchers and rolled. This should be entrusted to an expert, who will know that the painted side should always face outwards on the roller.

Framing

The type of frame chosen for a painting depends on the taste of its owner, but certain structural points should be kept in mind. The frame should be deep enough to contain the entire thickness of the painting, otherwise the back of the panel or stretcher will be exposed and rest directly against the wall. If it is not sufficiently deep, it should be built up with wood strips at the back.

The fixing of the painting into the frame should be with mirror plates screwed to the frame and overlapping the back of the picture. Rubber or some other soft packing material may be needed between the plates and the picture. Holding paintings in their frames with bent nails is a hazardous practice that should be avoided.

The rebate of a frame – the space in which the painting

fits – should be lined with cotton velvet ribbon so that the front edges of the painting are not scuffed by slight movements. If a painting is not flat – a warped panel, for example – the rebate should be modified with shaped slips of rubber or soft balsa wood to accommodate the curvature. The rebate is often slightly too large for the painting; if so, it should be packed with soft spacers (made of a material such as cork or balsa wood) pinned securely to the frame.

Ideally, a backboard should be fixed over the back of the frame to protect the reverse of the painting from impact, dust and sudden fluctuations of temperature and humidity. Glazing is desirable for particularly fragile or vulnerable paint surfaces. In general, however, paintings in sound condition hung in a satisfactory position should not require glass or Plexiglas.

Panel Paintings

Most of the problems that affect panel paintings arise from the sensitivity of wood to atmospheric conditions. As the relative humidity varies, a wood panel moves, swelling across the grain as the relative humidity increases, and shrinking as it decreases. Such natural expansion and contraction should be allowed to happen. If a panel is restrained in any way – even by a tightly fitting frame – it may deform and split as it tries to overcome the restraint.

The constant movement has several consequences. It can set up the regular pattern of cracking (the craquelure) in the paint and ground layers which is quite normal in aged paintings. The craquelure, however, can begin to curl away from the panel and lift at the edges, thus leading to flaking and loss of paint. The movement of wood often results in the gentle convex warp observed in many panel paintings: the layers of paint protect the front of the panel from humidity changes, so shrinkage and swelling only occur at the back. This eventually leads to a permanent compression of the wood cells on the back face, and the consequent warping of the panel with the paint on the convex side. Not all panels do this; some types of wood and cuts of wood are more stable than others.

Nowadays, a slightly curved panel is considered acceptable. It simply needs correct fitting in a frame with slips in the rebate shaped to the correct curvature. However, the attempted correction or elimination of warping by past generations of restorers has done a great deal of harm to panel paintings. Many panels have been thinned and have had heavy wood or metal battens attached to the back across the grain to try and hold them flat. As the panel tries to move with fluctuating humidity,

Stretcher on the back of a canvas painting
WEDGES, WHICH SHOULD BE TIED OR FASTENED TO THE
STRETCHER TO PREVENT THEM FALLING OUT, ARE TAPPED INTO
THE JOINTS TO KEEP THE CANVAS TAUT. (LEFT AND BELOW)

it strains against the battens and generally breaks before they do. Even worse is the practice of cradling. A cradle consists of fixed bars glued to the back of the panel parallel to the wood grain and free-running cross-members passing through slots cut into them. Theoretically, the warp is controlled while natural movement across the grain is permitted, but in practice the cross-members usually become jammed as the panel tries to warp. Moreover, the fixed bars can act as individual restraints and a cradled panel can even become corrugated and split along the line of each fixed bar.

Battens or cradles that are not actively harmful can be left alone. A properly functioning cradle will have cross-members which still move, and there will be no sign of cracking or warping on the front of the panel. Paradoxically, a working cradle was probably not required in the first place. Many cradles which have ceased to work properly are now removed. Where necessary they can be replaced by cushioned backboards; these hold the panel firmly, but also allow it to move.

If a panel consists of more than one member, joins frequently come apart and need regluing. Similarly, splits along the wood grain often require mending. Flaking or blistering paint caused by movement of the support is frequently encountered. Treatment of loose paint with

adhesives and heated spatulas is a routine operation in any conservator's studio.

Finally, wood panels are sometimes attacked by wood-boring insects and, more rarely, by dry rot (see page 33). There are proprietary treatments for domestic use on the market, but some of them can seriously damage paintings. As with all treatments involving valuable works of art, expert advice should be sought.

Canvas Paintings

Stretched canvas is a vulnerable painting support, easily distorted or torn by the lightest impact. Moreover, as it ages, it becomes more brittle and more easily damaged; it loses the small amount of elasticity it once had and will not spring back if dented.

Steady environmental control is important for canvases, although not as vital as for wood panels. If the relative humidity changes, canvases will tighten or sag accordingly. It is tempting to tap out the stretcher of a sagging canvas to take up the slack, but if the humidity changes suddenly, the canvas might become too tight and tear off the stretcher. On the other hand, if a canvas is allowed to sag for too long it can become permanently deformed and impossible to tap out satisfactorily.

A common problem involves lumps of plaster, dust and other, harder, objects falling down between the bottom stretcher bar and the back of the canvas, often causing bulges and flaking paint at the front. Loose stretcher keys are often the culprits, and should be tied to the stretcher to prevent them from falling out. In general, a backboard across the reverse of the frame will protect canvas paintings from these types of accidents.

Inevitably, some canvas paintings will get torn or badly dented. Small holes and minor dents can be treated locally, but for major damages the canvas will require lining. Lining consists of mounting the picture canvas onto a second canvas to give it strength, to correct deformations, and to stick down tears or ragged edges. At the same time, the adhesive used can penetrate through from the back of the original canvas to secure any flaking or loose paint.

Most pre-twentieth-century canvas paintings have been lined, and many have been lined several times. It is a major treatment and, if carried out inexpertly, potentially damaging. Lining tends to be undertaken by specialists because constant practice and alertness to the problems of different canvas types are essential. In the past, lining was carried out indiscriminately, but now it is avoided wherever possible: the integrity and subtle textures of an unlined painting are much valued, and the quite unnecessary lining of many paintings even now is much regretted.

Many canvases can be treated without lining. Flaking paint can be treated locally by standard methods of blister treatment, and dents or distortions can be corrected by gentle pressure with controlled heat and humidity. Weak edges that tear away from the stretcher can be strengthened with almost invisible, gossamer-like fabrics. Sometimes weak canvases can be supported by a loose lining, an unattached canvas placed on the stretcher behind the picture canvas.

Cleaning and Restoration

The cleaning of paintings is the most obvious demonstration of the picture conservator's skill. It not only requires great technical knowledge and experience, but also a sensitive understanding of the aesthetic aims and the intricacies of the painting method of the artist.

Cleaning a painting can proceed through several stages. First, the most recent dirt is removed from the surface; occasionally, this may be all that is required. Usually, however, a conservator has to deal with layers of resin varnish which have discolored, leading to an overall yellowing and darkening of the image. There may also be dirt between successive varnish layers if the painting has

been revarnished more than once. Removal of darkened varnishes with solvents can be a long, painstaking process, but frequently results in a spectacular recovery of the undimmed color of the original paint.

Even then the cleaning may not be finished, as paintings have often been retouched to conceal damages, or repainted in parts to alter the composition. The conservator must be able to distinguish between original and non-original paint and to arrive at a rational judgement about whether to remove all or some of the later paint. This operation is generally more difficult than varnish removal, and may require the use of scalpels and stronger reagents. It is usually worthwhile since old retouchings often cover large amounts of perfectly well-preserved paint around the damages they were put on to conceal.

Cleaning may involve all these stages, but it is important to realize that there may be no absolute level at which a painting is unequivocally "clean." Quite different degrees of dirt, varnish and repaint removal may be appropriate for different paintings. The approach may even be different from area to area within the same painting. Perhaps a painting cannot be safely cleaned

Detail of a Dutch 17th-century landscape
VARNISH HAS BEEN REMOVED DOWN THE LEFT SIDE OF THIS PAINTING. RETOUCHINGS HAVE ALSO BEEN TAKEN OFF TO REVEAL OLD REPAIRS MADE TO SPLITS IN THE PANEL. (OPPOSITE)

Detail of a Flemish 17th-century painting
THE TEARS AND LARGE TRIANGULAR AREA OF DAMAGE HAVE BEEN FILLED WITH A WHITE PUTTY IN PREPARATION FOR RETOUCHING. RETOUCHINGS MUST BE STRICTLY CONFINED WITHIN THE OUTLINES OF THE DAMAGE AND REVERSIBLE IN MILD SOLVENTS. (RIGHT)

Restorer's palette
THIS SECTION OF THE PALETTE SHOWS POTS CONTAINING A VARIETY OF PIGMENTS, A BOTTLE OF CLEAR, SYNTHETIC MEDIUM, AND THE PIGMENTS GROUND WITH THE MEDIUM ON A GROUND-GLASS SLAB. (BELOW)

because the medium is soluble in cleaning solvents, or perhaps a painting is so worn or damaged that to expose its true state would be little more than an archaeological exercise. In such cases, and in other less clear-cut examples, a compromise of partial cleaning may be indicated.

Nevertheless, in many instances it is possible and desirable to proceed through all the stages of cleaning and reveal the unobscured original. Thus, along with the largely unchanged colors of the original paints, some parts may be seen which have altered in tone due to chemical action on the pigments with time, as well as losses of paint caused by past damage.

In the next stage, the conservator decides how much restoration is justifiable – that is, how much old damage should be concealed by new retouching. All restoration is a compromise to disguise disfiguring losses, yet allow the painting to appear gracefully old. For example, normally craquelure is not retouched: an old paint film should be cracked and is not usually disturbing. Only where wide, white shrinkage cracks arise from a technical failure of the paint medium might a small amount of retouching be acceptable.

Paint losses must first be filled with a putty, which should be textured to match the surrounding paint surface. Retouching, or inpainting, is then carried out over the filling, taking care not to encroach onto original paint. There are several aesthetic approaches to inpainting, ranging from the use of plain "neutral" tones to fully deceptive retouching. Fully matched retouching is the usual choice, but for some paintings, visible retouchings may be considered preferable. Whatever the final decision, the paint used should not discolor appreciably and must be reversible – that is to say, easily removed in mild solvents which will not affect the original paint. Either watercolors or synthetic retouching media are generally used nowadays; oil paints are not satisfactory for inpainting, since they discolor and become very hard.

After retouching, it is usually necessary to apply, either by brush or spray, a coat of varnish over the entire paint surface. A picture varnish should be clear, ideally not discolor with time, and remain reversible in mild solvents. However, they will all discolor somewhat as they age, so paintings revarnished now may have to be cleaned again within half a century or even less.

MINIATURES

Portrait miniatures are watercolor paintings on parchment or ivory in specialized, fine techniques. The word "miniature," coined in the seventeenth century, is expressive of technique rather than size, being based on the Latin root *miniare*, to embellish with *minium* (red lead) in book illumination, from which art the separate miniature was descended. Portrait miniatures are not always very small – some are as much as 2ft long – nor, paradoxically, are they invariably portraits – some depict landscape, history, or genre subjects.

Most collections of miniatures attract other small portrait works that are not strictly miniatures: portrait enamels; oil "miniatures" on metal, card, or stone; plumbagos (small monochrome drawings in graphite or Indian ink); silhouettes; and watercolor portraits on card or paper made by miniaturists either as preliminary studies or as independent finished drawings. Because the materials and techniques used in the making of these objects are not the same as those used in miniatures, different conservation treatments will be needed. In the event of their deterioration, these objects should be referred to the relevant specialists – conservators of ceramics, jewelry, oil paintings, or works on paper. Fortunately, however, they normally require no special conditions for display beyond those considered ideal for miniatures.

Climate

The greatest service the owner can do for his miniatures is to provide them with a favorable environment. The miniaturist Nicholas Hilliard (c.1547–1619) pin-pointed the danger of pollution: ". . . the colors themselves may not endure some airs, especially in the sulfurous air of seacoal, and the gilding of goldsmiths."

The optimum condition for the maintenance of miniatures is a climate in which the air has been treated to remove pollutants and is kept as nearly as possible at a constant relative humidity of 55% at 59°F, which is acceptable for miniatures on both parchment and ivory. For permanent display, the lighting level should not exceed 50 lux for watercolor works, although higher levels are permissible for enamels, oil "miniatures," plumbagos, and silhouettes. It is not easy to achieve such conditions in any circumstances, least of all in a domestic setting, but any owner can take sensible precautions to ensure a reasonable, stable environment for his collection.

In a damp atmosphere miniatures will develop injurious mold growths, and sudden decreases in temperature can cause condensation to form on the inside of cover glasses, another potential source of danger to the paint. On the other hand, if miniatures become too dry, ivory supports can warp and split, and the paint may crack and flake away. Continuous fluctuations of humidity can also be damaging, resulting in paint loss or, in extreme cases, ivory fracturing. It follows that miniatures should be housed in a room with a humidity close to the optimum set out above, and which, by its position, is buffered as far as possible from fluctuations of the external climate and, in consequence, from external pollution. Unless accompanied by effective humidification, central heating is harmful to miniatures, as are rooms where fires, including wood, gas, and paraffin types, are used intermittently.

Display and Storage

Many of the pigments used in miniatures fade when exposed to light, an important fact to consider in displaying them. They cannot be seen in the 50 lux illumination recommended for constant exposure unless they are in almost dark surroundings and the eyes are allowed to adapt for several minutes, but displayed permanently in higher light levels they will inevitably fade. It is possible to compromise by viewing the miniatures in a good light, but for very limited periods. One way of achieving this is to arrange them in a frame or glazed table case covered with a thick cloth which is only removed when the miniatures are examined. Miniatures were never designed to be displayed *en masse* in furnished living rooms; to do so is to deny their intended intimacy and to invite deterioration.

Two solutions to the problem were evolved in the seventeenth century by the earliest miniature collectors: the closed cabinet and the cabinet room, both of which are favored by some contemporary collectors, who often use them in combination. The cabinet room can be any small room, normally unlit, which affords the proper climate. Within it the miniatures can be hung on the walls, stored in cabinets with display drawers, or arranged on tables. If miniatures are stored, the conditions should replicate as closely as possible those for display. They should not be wrapped other than temporarily for transportation, when they should be loosely folded in crumpled acid-free tissue.

An Allegory on
Marital Love,
Isaac Oliver, c.1590
$(4\frac{7}{16} \times 6\frac{11}{16}in)$
TOP RIGHT: THIS MINIATURE
ON PARCHMENT, WHICH HAS
BEEN PHOTOGRAPHED IN
RAKING LIGHT BEFORE
CORRECTIVE TREATMENT, IS
INSCRIBED "IO (MONOGRAM)
IN(VENIT)." IT HAS BEEN
DAMAGED BY DAMP, AND A
SUBSEQUENT, ILL-CONCEIVED
ATTEMPT AT RESTORATION
HAS CAUSED THE PARCHMENT
BOTH TO WRINKLE AND
CREASE AND THE PAINT LAYER
TO FLAKE. BOTTOM RIGHT:
THE SAME MINIATURE IS
SHOWN AFTER THE
RELAXATION AND
REMOUNTING OF THE
PARCHMENT AND THE
CONSOLIDATION OF THE
PAINT LAYER.

Home Care

Much damage has been done to miniatures by their owners in well-intentioned attempts to improve their appearance or to search for concealed signatures and inscriptions. Lockets have been ruined by inexpert opening; cover glasses have been broken, causing paint damage; and all too often paint has been wiped off with moisture during misguided attempts at cleaning.

Unlike oil paintings, miniatures are independent of an external environment, their lockets and cases providing each with its own ambient setting. In most instances, these settings were skilfully constructed by jewelers to ensure that they were virtually watertight and could not be opened easily. Thus it requires considerable skill and specialist knowledge to dismantle and reassemble them.

Removed from their settings, watercolor miniatures are vulnerable to all kinds of injury. Unless they are delicately handled, paper-thin sheets of ivory may be cracked, the paint surfaces may be marked or scored, and moisture may bring about damage that will be irreparable.

Owners should limit their conservation treatment of miniatures to superficial cleaning of the lockets, which should be restricted to dusting crevices with a soft brush and light polishing with a soft cloth or leather. The appearance of a miniature is often enhanced by cleaning the *exterior* of its cover glass, using a chamois leather, initially barely moistening it with saliva, subsequently breathing very lightly on the glass and polishing it. It is dangerous to use proprietary metal or glass cleaners since they contain solvents and reagents that can penetrate joints and damage the paint surface of the miniature.

Detail of Mary, Countess of Elgin, *Jean-Baptiste Isabey,* c.1800 (H2in)
RIGHT: THE PAINT SURFACE OF THIS MINIATURE ON IVORY, DAMAGED BY A PROPRIETARY METAL CLEANER USED ON ITS CONTAINING LOCKET, HAS BEEN RESTORED (FAR RIGHT) BY REMOVING THE DEPOSITS ON THE SURFACE AND TREATING THE DAMAGED PAINT.

Examination

Collectors can preserve their miniatures from serious damage by examining them every few months for early signs of deterioration. This involves the closest scrutiny, for the gravest conditions may be heralded by barely perceptible symptoms and, treated by a specialist in the early stages, can be averted. All that is necessary for the examination is a clear, but not brilliant, light and glasses of both × 5 and × 10 magnification. Moving the miniature so that the light approaches it at an acute, raking angle to its surface will often reveal irregularities.

In assessing condition it is important to be certain of the materials involved: whether a miniature is painted on parchment, ivory, card or metal, for example, and whether the medium is watercolor, oil or enamel.

Identifying Materials and Techniques

There are some simple rules of chronology that will help in the initial stage of identifying miniature supports and media. Before 1700, works in watercolor were painted on parchment and, very rarely, on paper; after 1720 they were usually painted on ivory. Paper or card was used by a few artists from the 1770s to the 1830s, and some late nineteenth- and twentieth-century miniatures are on synthetic ivory. Portrait enamels were painted from the second quarter of the seventeenth century and continued to be made into the nineteenth century.

It is most difficult to discriminate between watercolor miniatures on parchment and paper, particularly if the work is painted in opaque color. In this event, recognition depends on the support being visible in an area where the paint is abraded or flaked. Very few early miniatures survive without some paint loss, particularly at the edges, but if this is not the case there is no harm in assuming that the work is on parchment. Under magnification the surface of parchment is composed of unvarying cream or white, densely packed bundles of fibers with a waxy sheen. In comparison, paper surfaces are a matted confusion of fibers, often varied in hue, and in examples earlier than the late eighteenth century are imprinted with the regular parallel laid lines of the paper mold.

In even the most opaquely painted miniature on ivory, the surface is visible in a few transparent areas, chiefly in the flesh and white drapery. It is a visibly hard, compacted material, its long, parallel grain often evident, following the longer axis of the work. The very fine scratches resulting from its preparation with abrasives are usually apparent in raking light.

Because transparent watercolor is not absorbed into the surface of ivory, it has a less "blottesque" appearance than on parchment or paper, and richly gummed, transparently painted nineteenth-century miniatures are frequently mistaken for oil paintings because of their glossy, varnish-like surfaces. Close inspection quickly reveals in pale areas the ivory surface beneath the stippled or hatched brushstrokes with which miniatures are finished.

Conversely, on close inspection oil "miniatures" cannot be mistaken for watercolors, for they are microcosmic easel paintings, with the same dense, broadly brushed paint and a similar impasto in heightened areas. Their supports, of copper, silver, chalk-surfaced card or stone, are frequently revealed by the flaked losses of paint to which they are prone. There is no difficulty identifying portrait enamels, which are painted on domed metal supports with stippled, transparent brushwork over a white ground, and are covered with a smooth glaze.

Signs of Deterioration

Ivory miniatures should be examined with particular care for any distortion of their supports. This usually becomes evident as an even, concave curvature. Many miniatures have a slight warp of this type, but as long as it does not increase or cause the paint to flake and the movement is not constrained by the tightness of a shallow locket, there is no cause for concern. More disturbing is a miniature that is buckling irregularly, a sign of warring stresses between the ivory and an unevenly attached backing card, which will eventually cause the ivory to crack; the very thin ivory sheets were normally stuck to stout paper or card supports. Ivories should also be examined for incipient cracks at the edges, best treated in their early stages.

Invariably prepared with great care, the parchment tablets used for early miniatures rarely give cause for concern. They are frequently curved, often because they were squeezed originally into over-tight lockets, but such long-standing distortion is of little consequence. If there is flaking of the paint associated with curvature, it is probably due to more recent ill-use. Occasionally the parchment may separate from its card backing at the edge; this, too, is unimportant unless it is progressive and threatening to cause paint loss.

Portraits on paper should be examined for the visible signs of the degradations that are incident to all works on paper – discoloration and foxing – and if an object of this type happens to develop a strained appearance, like a badly stretched drum skin, it should be professionally treated before the stress results in tearing (see page 117).

It is important to be alert for signs of paint loss through flaking, usually caused by fluctuations in humidity; lifting paint needs to be secured even if the conditions have been stabilized. Molds damage watercolor paint and can be infectious, but are not active in less than 65% relative humidity. Miniatures showing signs of mold growth, seen as yellowish or white matte spotting on the paint surface, should be isolated and treated by a conservator. Inspec-tions should include the hair compartments on the backs of lockets, where mold growths are often initiated.

Advice should also be sought if the paint discolors or blanches. The development of gray or black patches in areas of white or pale opaque paint is due to the action of atmospheric hydrogen sulfide on white lead. Its treatment is desirable only on account of its displeasing visual effect; it does no permanent damage to the paint. In many early miniatures touches of black in jewels and armor may be due to the tarnishing of silver paint, and for this there is at present no remedy.

Occasionally the cover glass of a miniature may develop a misting of moisture, both inside and out. If no other glasses in a collection are affected, this is probably "glass disease," or devitrification, rather than condensation (see page 46); in either case the miniature should be dismantled as soon as possible, and if the glass is devitrifying it should be replaced with a new one.

The paint of most oil "miniatures" has a network of fine age cracks (craquelure), and these occasionally become the focus of losses, apparent in the early stages as slight cupping of the minute islands of paint. Often the varnish layer is a contributory factor, and it may be sensible to have it removed by a professional.

Portrait enamels are the most durable of objects, but the majority are painted on copper, which can corrode and slough off the paint layer. Advice should be sought if verdigris forms at the edge of a work.

Restoration

There are few conditions affecting portrait miniatures which a skilled conservator cannot improve beyond recognition, but there are limitations both to what can and what should be done in the way of restoration. Central to these limitations is the fact that close scrutiny of a restored miniature, aided by magnification, will highlight the slightest flaws and reveal any restoration work.

The retouching of miniatures is unusually complicated because paint matching must take into account the texture, comparative gloss and brushwork, as well as the hue of the original material. Many miniatures include passages where the paint has been floated to a perfectly even layer without any brush marks. It is impossible to float in a missing patch in such an area without causing obtrusive joins at the edges, and the alternative is to hatch or stipple color to cover the patch in the least visible brushwork possible; such a restoration should not be obvious on a close synoptic scan, but it will become visible under a degree of magnification.

DRAWINGS; WATERCOLORS; WORKS ON PAPER

 Most works of art on paper are susceptible to two main problems: the deterioration of paper and the fading or discoloration of pigments. Exposed to strong light, paper darkens and becomes brittle. Being made of cellulose fibers, it may be attacked by silver-fish and other insects, and under humid conditions foxing and mold can develop. Impurities in the paper itself, as well as those absorbed from the atmosphere, may also cause deterioration.

The inks used in drawings, prints and maps vary in permanence; while some are stable, others fade or become discolored if exposed to strong light. The pigments in watercolors are particularly vulnerable, and tempera and gouache have a tendency to flake and crack.

Photographs, unique in consisting of chemically coated paper, are particularly unstable. They require special storage in cool, dry and dark conditions, and should be kept free of surface dust and protected from damage caused by handling, such as fingerprints.

Wallpapers are also complex to maintain; not only sensitive to strong light and excess humidity, they can also suffer from an impure domestic atmosphere and from day-to-day rubbing and scuffing.

Jedburgh Abbey from the South-East, Thomas Girtin, c.1800 MOVED BY THE BEAUTY OF THIS LOCATION, GIRTIN PAINTED SEVERAL VIEWS OF THIS SUBJECT FROM SKETCHES HE MADE IN 1796. THIS VERSION IS UNFADED BY LIGHT AND TRUE TO THE ARTIST'S ORIGINAL COLORS. THE MAJORITY OF HIS WORKS, MOUNTED AND FRAMED FOR MANY YEARS, ARE NOW PALE SHADOWS OF THEIR ORIGINAL STATE.

PAPER CONSERVATION

Paper

Since paper is made from biodegradable vegetable fiber – commonly linen, cotton, wood, mulberry or esparto – natural agents such as damp, mold and fungi, as well as atmospheric gases and damage caused by insects and animals (including humans), are liable to destroy it. Therefore, all works on paper – books, manuscripts, prints, drawings, watercolors, photographs and objects of ephemera – require the closest attention in terms of the conditions in which they are kept.

To make paper, fibers are suspended in water by turbulence and lifted out onto a screen or mold. The water is drained away, and the web of fibers is turned out onto a felt. Pressure is put on a group of wet paper and felts to remove the surplus water, and the sheets are then allowed to dry. Sizing or waterproofing of paper is done either at the pulp stage or after the sheets are made. The structure of the mold determines the form of the paper: either laid, with distinct chain and laid lines; or wove, giving an even transparency when held up to the light. These processes can be done either by hand or machine.

Paper was first made by the Chinese between the first and second centuries AD. It came via the Silk Route to Persia and Turkey, and in the twelfth century the Arabs brought the technique from North Africa to Spain. Paper-making in Europe and the invention of movable type in the fifteenth century are inextricably linked: thereafter there was a tremendous expansion and refinement of paper-making, to fill the huge demand for paper brought about by an increasing number of printers. New manufacturing methods were sought and, finally, after years of making paper by hand, the Industrial Revolution brought about fully automated machine paper-making. Apart from the machinery, new fibers to satisfy the demand were found to replace costly linen rags; hence, wood pulp was introduced. These developments did not have the effect of improving paper quality: new machinery introduced metal particles into the papers, and new fibers were not as pure (not as acid-free) as the old ones.

CHEMICAL INSTABILITY
The introduction of wood pulp created paper with built-in self-destructive elements, as the impurities found in wood pulp – particularly lignin (an acidic substance) – worked to break down the paper fibers.

All paper fibers have to be purified during manufacture, but some types are innately more pure than others. Early in the history of European paper-making, linen – a long, strong and reasonably pure fiber – was most commonly used, and even today papers from the fifteenth century (if they have been properly stored) are still robust. It is difficult and expensive, however, to make wood pulp completely pure, but if its impurities are left in the paper, they will destroy the fibers. In some processes, damaging chemicals left in paper will eventually break it down and cause it to disintegrate, while certain sizing materials can damage the cellulose; as with atmospheric pollution, this damage will be indicated by yellowing of the paper.

When drawings are executed on paper made from impure fibers, they should be preserved in as stable an environment as possible. They should be stored away from polluted environments, dust and dirt; light should be kept to a minimum; and storage areas must not be damp. Professional de-acidification may also be possible.

ATMOSPHERIC POLLUTION
The causes of the modern phenomenon of acid rain damage paper. Emissions from industry, automobiles, and heating and air-conditioning systems contain gases which in time completely break down paper. Most damaging is sulfur dioxide, which is readily converted to sulfuric acid on the surface of paper, helped by the absorption of atmospheric moisture into the hollow centers of the paper fibers. In poor-quality paper the process is speeded up. Items stored in environments with filtered air will not be attacked in this way. Old mounting boards of wood-pulp paper (usually showing tan bevels) emit acidic gases which will damage paper lying against them.

Dust and dirt act physically and chemically on the surface of prints and drawings. In cities such grime is often oily and can adhere permanently to paper; likewise, microscopic particles can get trapped between paper fibers. These particles are generally disfiguring and will also cause chemical damage to the paper.

Hence, the environment must be kept as free as possible from pollutants, dust and dirt – an extremely difficult task in urban areas. Books should be protected by keeping them in cabinets behind glass doors or certainly dusted regularly. Works of art on paper should be properly mounted, and either stored in boxes or contained within secure conservation framing (see page 118).

LIGHT

All light is dangerous to paper. Within the light spectrum both visible and ultraviolet rays can destroy the delicate web of vegetable fibers. Visible radiation takes up a larger part of the spectrum than does ultraviolet, but the latter causes greater damage to paper.

Standard practice for museum display specify 50 lux as the highest level of light for paper objects. Ultraviolet barriers (in clear film form) on windows, and in frames, light filters and blinds provide some protection against light damage. Nevertheless, collections of prints and drawings are best displayed in rotation.

HEAT

Heat can dehydrate and embrittle paper fibers. It will also speed up chemical reaction, either from within the paper or from the environment. Heat combined with moisture will accelerate mold growth and rot. Temperatures should not be allowed to rise above 59°–64°F, and objects should be stored away from direct heat coming from light or other heating sources.

HUMIDITY

Paper contains moisture and hence is sensitive to changes in relative humidity. Paper expands with an increase in humidity and contracts when this decreases, so works of art should be allowed to move freely in their mounts with no constriction put upon them. The ideal relative humidity for paper artifacts is 50–60%.

A relative humidity of above 65% provides a perfect environment for the culture of mold – and also encourages the micro-organisms which cause the discoloration known as "foxing" to develop. These small brown marks, which are commonly found on paper, thrive in high humidity and are probably encouraged by small metal particles in machine-made paper.

Sizing agents, gums and pigments on paper, especially pastels, also attract atmospheric moisture. A constantly high relative humidity, such as that in tropical climates, will eventually rot paper. Properly calibrated monitoring equipment (thermohygrographs) are inexpensive and readily available, as are monitoring strips that change color with changes in relative humidity.

Britannia watermark in handmade English laid paper, c.1760
FROM THE BEGINNINGS OF PAPER-MAKING IN EUROPE IN THE TWELFTH CENTURY, MAKERS HAVE SEWN WATERMARKS INTO THEIR MOLDS TO IDENTIFY THEIR PAPERS. THESE MARKS CAN ALSO BE USEFUL TO ART HISTORIANS IN THE DATING OF PRINTS AND DRAWINGS.

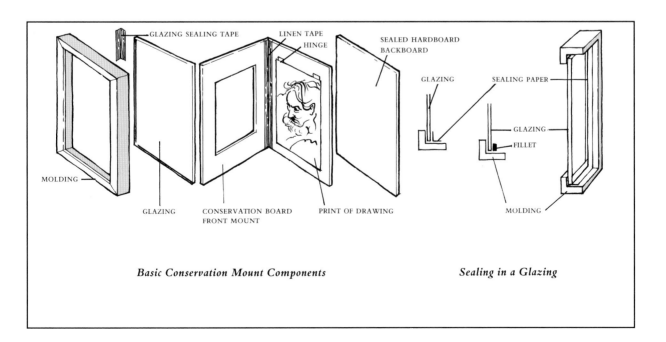

GLAZING SEALING TAPE — LINEN TAPE HINGE — SEALED HARDBOARD BACKBOARD — GLAZING — SEALING PAPER — GLAZING — FILLET — MOLDING — GLAZING — CONSERVATION BOARD FRONT MOUNT — PRINT OF DRAWING — MOLDING

Basic Conservation Mount Components   **Sealing in a Glazing**

To maintain the correct relative humidity, full air-conditioning may be necessary in tropical climates, but in more temperate zones dehumidifiers can be used. Areas must be properly aired so that damp cannot linger. Bookcases should have ventilation at the back, or books should at least be placed on the shelf with a gap between them and the wall (see page 144).

INSECTS AND OTHER PESTS

Various insects and animals, including book lice, silverfish, wood-boring beetles, mice and rats, eat paper. The nibbles of silverfish are common on prints, drawings and book spines, as is the damage caused by wood-boring beetles. Rodents use paper to make warm, comfortable nests. Regular inspection and close scrutiny will spot these invaders, which should be dealt with by an exterminator.

MANHANDLING

Human beings have practised numerous bad habits over the centuries which have taken their toll on paper objects. Books are badly handled, often with dirty fingers; drawings have been stored in attics that are too hot, too cold, or have leaking roofs; and treatments to conserve the objects may have had contrary effects. General carelessness, such as tearing, staining and abrading book pages and other paper artifacts, is all too common.

Often proper storage conditions have not been fully understood by owners or custodians, and the wrong materials may have been used. Particularly prevalent are instances of poor-quality mounting and framing, the use of acidic boards, self-adhesive tapes and inadequate protection from ultraviolet rays.

Mounting and Framing

A wide range of pure materials and components is available for proper conservation mounting and framing of works of art on paper. The following information should be helpful both for those collectors wishing to do their own mounting and framing, and those enlisting the services of a professional framer.

MOLDING AND GLAZING

Apart from choosing a molding for aesthetic reasons, it is also important that it is both strong (particularly at the corners) and deep enough to house the other components.

Different types of transparent materials may be used for the glazing: glass, Plexiglas and other acrylics (some have built-in ultraviolet protection), or polycarbonate. Acrylics and polycarbonate have a static charge and are unsuitable for pastels, charcoals or other media which might be pulled off. Glass can easily break and is inappropriate for works that have to be transported.

PROPER MOUNTING

Mounts or mats made of so-called "museum board" or "conservation board" are suitable for paper artifacts; both are readily available in different thicknesses and colors. Museum board is purer than conservation board, although both are alkaline in content and will protect objects from acidic attack and therefore deterioration. Storage folders, too, need to be made up of these boards. Any other boards should be avoided.

A proper mount should be made up of two parts joined by strong linen tape, one having a window in which to display the work. The mount with the window must be deep enough to hold the surface of the work away from the glass: therefore, the larger the work, the thicker the mount should be. A pastel's mount should hold it at least $\frac{1}{4}$in away from the glazing.

If a work is to be close-mounted to the molding, fillets should be put in place to hold it away from the glazing. All these materials should be acid-free.

SECURING WORKS INTO A MOUNT

This should be done with hinges at the top edge only, using strong Japanese paper and pure starch paste – not tape. These hinges may be arranged to suit the particular object, taking into account whether it is to be displayed fully or overmounted. Adhesives used in mounting and framing must be pure and alkaline in content.

FRAMING AND BACKING

A picture's glazing may be sealed onto the molding or, along with the mount and object, it may be sealed as a package, using tape with a water-soluble glue or gum. Self-adhesive tapes with water-soluble gums may be used with Plexiglas and other acrylic glazing.

A good, strong backing board will stabilize the molding and protect the work from damage. Good-quality hardboard, $\frac{1}{8}$in thick, is best, but it may need a coat of varnish to seal off impurities. It should be secured into the frame with strong, non-rusting pins. The air gap should be sealed with gummed brown paper.

STORAGE BOXES

The Solander box is the most suitable and sturdy for storage. However, it is expensive, and it is possible to find an alternative in cheaper conservation-card boxes, that are available in different designs and sizes.

DRAWINGS AND WATERCOLORS

Until the Industrial Revolution glass was very expensive, so it was uncommon to hang drawings and watercolors on walls. Before the early nineteenth century these works were usually mounted and stored out of the light – in folders, boxes or bound albums. Only afterwards, when glass became cheaper, were drawings more often hung, thereby exposing them to damaging elements, particularly light and atmospheric pollutants.

Drawings on paper are likely to suffer from all the problems related to their supports, as well as to specific problems brought about by the different pigments, dyes and binding agents used in the drawings themselves. They may have incurred damage from pollution in the atmosphere, too much light or damp, or insects and from uncaring or mistaken treatments by past owners.

Often paper supports are laid onto old mountings that are causing them harm; these should be removed. However, if works are attached to original wash-lined mounts, these should be preserved; this matter should be discussed with an art historian or conservator. Watercolors were frequently executed on laminated paper; this lamination should also be preserved, if possible, unless there is a danger of its harming the watercolor.

All works of art on paper must be regarded as three-dimensional objects. Paper has its own characteristic surface, on which a layer of pigment often lies, held by light gum. The application of wet washes of color can put tensions on paper, making it wrinkle and pucker; these should not be tampered with as they must be considered an aspect of the artist's intention. On the other hand, if an artist has constricted the paper's movement with the use of a sketching frame or tapes, in order to drum out the paper, the watercolor will appear very flat.

People who are owners of drawings and watercolors should be sensitive to the various techniques the artists have used, and not seek to alter them in any way. They should therefore be vigilant in looking for signs of deterioration and, if these are found, advice should be sought from a paper conservator.

Transportation

All drawings on paper are delicate, but some media are more friable than others, particularly pastel, gouache and some modern media. The paper or animal skin on which the drawing is made expands and contracts with changes

The Lighthouse, Naples, *James Müller, 1839*
THIS DRAWING IS EXECUTED IN WATERCOLOR, GOUACHE AND PENCIL ON PAPER. OVER A PERIOD OF YEARS THE WHITE LEAD OXIDE PAINT USED IN THE SKY HAS TURNED TO BLACK LEAD SULFIDE THROUGH THE CHEMICAL ACTION OF SULFUR DIOXIDE PRESENT IN THE ATMOSPHERE. DELICATE CONSERVATION WORK HAS ENABLED THE BLACK LEAD SULFIDE TO BE TRANSFORMED INTO STABLE WHITE LEAD SULFATE, THUS RESTORING THE IMAGE AS CLOSELY AS POSSIBLE TO ITS ORIGINAL APPEARANCE.

in relative humidity and can cause loss and cracking of the pigment. If an individual work is in a particularly perilous state or of an especially delicate construction, it should not be allowed to travel at all. If there is any doubt about this, a conservator should be consulted.

All works should be carefully packed when they are being transported (see page 183). For regular travel, strong plastic cases are available.

Metal Points

The use of a stylus made of different metals (gold, silver, copper, lead, tin and various alloys) has its roots in the art of Medieval manuscripts. When the area to be used for text was measured and drawn up, a stylus was employed to define the areas for writing and illustration. The metal of the stylus is deposited on the writing material to produce a mark like that of a graphite pencil.

Styli have been used by artists from the fifteenth century to produce fine-lined drawings which, except in the case of the lead stylus, were executed on paper with a layer of specially prepared ground made of pulverized substances, including white lead, bone and shell, bound with various agents (linseed oil, glues or gums). Artists sometimes also tinted these grounds with powdered pigments. The use of metal point, however, had become less common by the seventeenth century.

CONSERVATION

When metal point drawings were first executed, they were a pale gray tone overall. Oxidation occurred shortly afterwards, producing a color that was anticipated by the artist. We may not be sure of the intended color since pollution caused by industry in the last hundred years may have further changed the color of these works.

If the tinted ground is of a light-sensitive nature, ultraviolet protection will be needed. Above all, abrasion must be avoided, as grounds are often very soft and delicate. Moisture is also damaging to the grounds, because violent changes in relative humidity will cause the paper to expand more than the ground, which is likely to become loose and fall off. Because the grounds are highly absorbent, they pick up grease from fingers; likewise, any other substance which falls on them will readily penetrate them. Removing these stains is rarely possible, so handling should be done with white cotton gloves and kept to a minimum.

Black Inks

This method has its roots in the Oriental use of black carbon inks, which were introduced into Europe perhaps as early as the eleventh century. Inks similar in content, commonly known as Indian or Chinese inks, were made in Europe in the twelfth century; they comprised soot from a variety of woods and resins, and were bound with gum or glue. Chinese and Japanese ink sticks are still available today and used by artists; liquid carbon inks are manufactured in Europe and the East.

CONSERVATION

Since they are made of pure carbon, these inks are very stable and will not fade; nor will the paper supports be damaged by these inks. However, some contemporary artists use over-thick applications of ink, which may flake off.

The introduction of chemical aniline dyes in the late nineteenth century led to the production of a blue-black ink, which can look deceptively like a carbon ink. This ink fades to a bluish-gray or pale brown in light and is extremely difficult to identify.

Brown Inks

In all ink-making, manufacturers have endeavored to produce a fine suspension in a liquid which would freely flow from the pen. When an artist wanted a warmer line to a drawing, he preferred a brown-toned ink, which also gave a greater depth of tone in washes. There are three different types of brown ink: iron-gall, bister and sepia.

Iron-gall ink, generally made from ferrous sulfate and oak galls containing tannic and gallic acids, was used for writing from very early on in Europe. Artists from the fifteenth century created this cheap, easy-to-make ink in their studios; it was often mixed with soot and gums to give a darker tone. By the seventeenth century iron-gall ink, then known as "common ink," was made commercially; at that point it was used mostly for writing, but many European artists continued to use it up to the early nineteenth century. Iron-gall ink varies in color from very light yellow-brown to darker orange-brown to blackish-brown, depending on the recipe. Many contemporary artists have used it for sketches.

CONSERVATION

This medium is the most delicate used in drawing, from a conservation point of view. As its content is derived from acids, the paper upon which the drawings are executed is liable to be eaten through by the inks and, very often, to be in a totally fragmented state, the heavier areas of ink having dropped out completely. Another possibility is that the moisture in the atmosphere will draw the inks away from the original lines, giving a fuzzy appearance. When drawings are fragmenting, it will be necessary to ask a paper conservator to restore the damage with a fine tissue. Any wetting of these drawings will be likely to result in bleeding of the ink, and will make the acid move into and damage the paper.

All drawings executed in iron-gall ink will fade in light, so they should either be kept in the dark or have ultraviolet protection and be lit by not more than 50 lux.

Bister Ink

Made from the tarry, sooty deposits accumulated in chimney stacks, bister ink is easily confused with iron-gall. It was not used as a writing ink; rather, artists made it up themselves, first filtering out the larger particles of soot, then reducing it over a flame to the desired liquidity. These inks were often bound and thickened with gums, which made a layer of the ink lie on the paper surface. Bister ink has a darker look than iron-gall and, sometimes, when artists have not filtered out all the larger soot particles, it is more readily distinguishable.

CONSERVATION
Bister is easily damaged by light and should either have ultraviolet protection, be shown at a light level not exceeding 50 lux, or be stored away from light.

Sepia Ink

This rich, brown ink, introduced in the nineteenth century, is made from the liquid that cuttlefish and squid eject to cloud the water and thereby protect themselves. Although its name is often used in descriptions of its color, it is not a common form of drawing ink.

CONSERVATION
This ink is moderately stable in light, but nevertheless ultraviolet protection should be used on such drawings.

Colored Inks

From the fifteenth century artists have used a great variety of colored inks. Drawings in colored inks vary in their ability to withstand light and in their tendency to harm the paper on which they are drawn.

The twentieth century has seen the invention of many different colored inks, adopted by many artists who are either unaware of or disregard the inks' instability. Ballpoint and felt-tip pens have been used in modern works, but in most cases these will not last long. Artists often use such inks to sign their works, but the signature will fade in time. Ball-point inks are easily recognizable, while felt-tips may pass as watercolors. Since they are dyes, not pigments, these inks fade dramatically, with some colors fading more than others.

CONSERVATION
Drawings that are executed in colored inks should be properly protected from light and, in the case of felt-tip

A paper conservator repairing wormholes in an 18th-century Japanese wood-block print
GOOD NATURAL LIGHT AND CLEAN, WELL-EQUIPPED WORKSHOPS ARE NECESSARY FOR THE RESTORATION OF PAPER ARTIFACTS. JAPANESE PRINTS SUCH AS THE ONE BEING WORKED ON HERE PRESENT PARTICULAR PROBLEMS, AS THE ARTISTS USED RICE PASTE-BASED INKS WHICH ATTRACT INSECTS AND MOLD.

pens and markers, with their mostly light-sensitive dyes, they should always be kept away from light (however, some of the dyes are also unstable in the dark). These inks need ultraviolet protection and should be shown in a light level of 50 lux, but this will not be of major help since the modern dyes may have built-in self-destructive elements. If they have to be displayed, drawings in colored inks should be rotated in quick succession.

Charcoal

This modest material has long been used to produce cartoon drawings as well as small, delicate renderings. It is made from sticks of willow, plum, linden and other woods, as well as from vines. These are carbonized in heated chambers from which air is excluded (so that the sticks are not reduced to ash).

Charcoal is distinguishable from black chalk in that it is softer and more matte in appearance. Nearly all drawings from earlier centuries have been rubbed and smudged, so if a drawing is found in a completely fresh state, with its surface richness of black soft carbon intact, every effort should be made to preserve this.

Study of a Kneeling Woman, with Detail of Drapery and Foot, Simon Vouet, *1640*
THIS DRAWING, EXECUTED IN BLACK AND WHITE CHALKS ON BUFF PAPER, IS LAID ONTO A MOUNT FROM THE COLLECTION OF PIERRE-JEAN MARLETTE (1694–1774). IT IS IMPORTANT TO PRESERVE THIS TYPE OF EVIDENCE OF PROVENANCE.

CONSERVATION
The delicate nature of a charcoal drawing's surface should be of paramount concern. Deep mounts should be made so there is no contact with the glazing, which should be glass. Acrylic glazing becomes static and will pull off the particles of carbon. Keeping charcoal drawings in folders or boxes will rub and destroy their surfaces. Since they are made of pure carbon, there is no danger of light damage.

Chalks

Artists from the fifteenth century employed this medium, most commonly in the natural colors of black, white and red ocher. Some combined moisture with it to make washes and to blur lines. After the end of the eighteenth century, fabricated chalks became common, popular for their greater consistency and variety of colors.

CONSERVATION
As chalk lies on the surface of paper, it is vulnerable to rubbing and smudging. Chalk drawings should be mounted as charcoal, in a deep mount behind glass. These chalks are stable in light.

Graphite or Pencil

Graphite is the natural successor to metal points. The best-quality graphite, or plumbago, was found in the 1560s in Cumberland, a former county in northwest England. It was fashioned into a stylus and fixed into a port-crayon (holder) or used as a lump. The embargo on the shipment of graphite from England to France in the late eighteenth century led Nicolas-Jacques Conté to the successful transformation of inferior Continental graphite into a paste-like mixture; pressing it into rods and producing, in 1795, the prototype of the first modern pencil.

Like charcoal, graphite is made from pure carbon. The drawings have a metallic surface and they can range from a very light gray to almost black.

CONSERVATION
Graphite or pencil drawings are absolutely stable in light and will not harm the paper support they are on, although paper itself is prone to yellow in light. However, some fixatives used to secure their surfaces will darken.

When the surface is a rich, thick layer of graphite, care should be taken not to rub this or press anything against it, and it should ideally be mounted.

Pastel Drawings

Fabricated chalks, or pastels, have been used by artists since the sixteenth century. They are made from dry pigments and binding agents, such as gums, honey water and, more recently, methylcellulose. Mixtures of pigments result in an enormous range of shades of color, and the pigments and binding agents are blended to achieve fine differentials in hardness and softness of line.

Pastels can be executed on paper or animal skins. The papers chosen in the eighteenth century were often rough in texture to provide a "tooth" to hold the pastel; their colors, including brown and green-gray, provided a muted background for the works, largely portraits.

The skins varied from vellum to chamois and, as with paper, were prepared with a "toothed" surface. These supports were usually secured to stretchers, sometimes with linen or cotton canvas behind them. Pastels remain a popular medium to the present day.

Portrait of a Woman, *Anon., 1848, shown before and after conservation*
THIS PASTEL PORTRAIT HAS BEEN BADLY AFFECTED BY MOISTURE, CAUSING MOLD GROWTH AND SEVERE COCKLING AND DISTORTION OF THE VELLUM SUPPORT. THE BINDING AGENT (USUALLY GUM TRAGACANTH) USED IN THE MANUFACTURE OF PASTEL MAKES THIS MEDIUM SUSCEPTIBLE TO MOLD ATTACK.

CONSERVATION

Because of the soft, delicate surfaces of pastel drawings, the nutrients in their binding agents, and the common method of mounting them on stretchers, these works demand the utmost care in terms of conservation.

If the atmosphere is too moist mold will grow, and if too dry their papers and skins will become too taut on their stretchers and cause them to tear and wrinkle. In fact, being mounted in this way can be harmful if their backs are not well protected. Pollution will move through the canvas, paper or both, and the paper will suffer and deteriorate; the drummed nature of the arrangement makes them vulnerable to accidental puncturing from the front or rear. Another problem is static electricity: if a glazing has this property, it may draw the pastel off the surface onto its own surface. Some pastel pigments are particularly light-sensitive – for instance madder,

Vandyke brown and alizarin – and will fade. As with all fugitive pigments or dyes, this reaction begins as soon as they are exposed to light.

Pastels should be left on their original stretchers, if possible, especially in the case of skins, since these keep them in position. However, if these supports are causing physical problems of any kind to the paper or skin, a conservator should be consulted.

Many artists used certain fixative agents to consolidate their pastels while they worked on them. In the eighteenth century this was not usual, but the Impressionists often built up their works with layers of pastel, using fixatives of gum and other natural materials. In this century artists have used modern fixatives made from various polymers which can distort the colors and will slowly darken them over time. They should never be applied to pastels during conservation, or at any other time.

Jedburgh Abbey from
the South-East,
Thomas Girtin, c.1800
THIS WATERCOLOR HAS ONLY
VERY RARELY BEEN EXPOSED
TO THE LIGHT, AND DISPLAYS
ITS ORIGINAL BRIGHT
FRESHNESS. THE DEEP INDIGO
USED IN THE SKY HAS A
TENDENCY TO FADE RAPIDLY
IN LIGHT, AND IT IS UNUSUAL
TO FIND IT SURVIVING IN
WATERCOLORS BY THE SAME
ARTIST THAT HAVE BEEN
MOUNTED AND FRAMED AND
THEREFORE EXPOSED TO LIGHT
FOR SOME YEARS.

Watercolors

The term "watercolor" has come to mean the application of thin washes of pigment on paper, with commonly added "body color" and gums to highlight certain areas. It has its roots in Medieval manuscript illumination, but the technique flourished in the late eighteenth and early nineteenth centuries, when it was elevated from a sketching medium and began to rival oil painting as a medium of artistic expression. By the Victorian era, the enthusiasm for watercolors was so great there was a continual search for new and more permanent colors to expand the palette; it continues to be a popular medium.

CONSERVATION

Some pigments in watercolors fade badly, and the chemical effect which some pigments have on others will also cause fading. The pigment layer is thin and therefore more prone to suffering in this way from fading than are oil-bound or more thickly spread pigments. All light is dangerous to watercolors, but ultraviolet is the most hazardous, although the heat generated by infrared rays is damaging to both paper and watercolor. The process is often a slow one, with subtle changes of tone occurring and imbalances developing, thus shifting the emphases –

so much so that some works become virtually unrecognizable from their original appearance.

Papers also discolor in light, and this darkening will distort the color balance. Such damage is irreversible, but may be minimized if watercolors are displayed only for short spells; rotation of a collection is recommended. A glazing with an ultraviolet barrier must always be used while watercolors are on display. Ideally, they should be kept in the dark but, when display is necessary, the 50 lux level for lighting should be adhered to.

Atmospheric pollutants, which tend to be acidic, can destroy some pigments in watercolors as well as the paper they are on. Conservation mount boards will provide the drawing with an acid-free environment. Proper sealing arrangements to secure the backing boards will also minimize the movement of pollution into the framed package. Foxing is a common phenomenon on water-colors, and problems of this nature should be discussed with a conservator (see page 128).

The darker areas of a watercolor were often made richer with a layer or two of gum arabic or tragacanth; some artists covered large areas to give them an almost varnished appearance. These have often cracked as the gums have shrunk and the paper expanded and con-tracted; this matter should be discussed with a conservator.

A 19th-century foxed watercolor

FOXING IS AN INDICATION OF THE NATURAL BIODEGRADABILITY OF PAPER. IT CAN SOMETIMES BE REMOVED BY SKILLED PAPER CONSERVATORS. (ABOVE)

A Master Wrestler, Ottoman, c.1610

MINIATURES EXECUTED IN PIGMENT BOUND WITH ANIMAL GLUE AND OTHER GUMS HAVE A THICK SURFACE, FREQUENTLY PRONE TO CRACKING.

Tempera and Gouache

Tempera is a method of binding fairly coarsely ground pigments with egg yolk. Gouache, or "body color," is a type of watercolor that is less finely ground and therefore can be applied more thickly to form an opaque layer, although it can be diluted to create a wash. Binding agents for gouache include gums, honey and animal glue.

CONSERVATION
Tempera and gouache on paper are prone to flake and crack, due to the differential in expansion and contraction between the pigment layer, which is rigid, and the paper, which moves with changes in moisture levels. Flexing of paper supports for these media will also cause cracking and further damage. Moreover, if these works are painted on skins, gouache in particular will flake badly with any expansion or contraction of the support. A conservator may be able to consolidate this damage.

Although tempera is a medium which is fairly resilient to fungal attack, the binding agents which are used in gouache are attractive to microorganisms. These can produce ugly, almost black, spots, which are often impossible to rectify without resorting to restoration. Another fairly common problem in gouache paintings is

that the white lead carbonate becomes blackened. This can usually be altered to another white lead compound, but this is something that must be done by a conservator.

Oil Paints and Acrylics

Pigments bound with oil and acrylic are more often used on canvas, but even in the seventeenth century artists were painting with oil on paper with a gesso base and, in the twentieth century, they often painted directly onto paper. Acrylic, a twentieth-century invention, may be thinned down with water or acrylic medium to produce thin washes, when it closely resembles watercolors.

CONSERVATION
Oil can and will spread out into paper, causing a halo effect at the edges of the drawing, particularly visible on white paper. If the paper is totally covered, the oil will oxidize and make the paper brown and brittle. A conservator can help perhaps by reducing the staining, and certainly by arranging a lining and support for fragile drawings.

There are not many problems with acrylic, although fading may occur in strong light and intense heat can actually change the colors. Again, the recommended light level is 50 lux.

PRINTS AND MAPS

A print is essentially an image produced by a process that allows it to be multiplied. To be able to print the image, it must first be cut, carved or drawn. This is done into or onto the printing surface, made of materials such as wood, metal or stone. The idea of printing multiple images as they are conceived of today originated around AD 100 in China.

The vast majority of printed images are on paper, but some are on silk, vellum and other supports. Prints can be produced with black ink (some of these are hand-colored afterwards, often with watercolors) or with colored inks. The stability of inks is directly linked to the stability of the pigments they contain, and some colored pigments are particularly light-sensitive. If the ink is black it is likely to contain carbon, which is extremely stable.

Fine-Art Prints

The "fine-art" print developed from what started out as primarily a utilitarian and educational facility. As printing technology and communications became more mechanized, hand-printing processes became exclusive, thus giving artists more reason to explore the rich, creative scope within the various printing techniques. To maintain the rarity value, many artists print limited editions. In the past, though several images could be printed from the same plate, with some techniques it was only possible to print a limited number of impressions before the plate wore out. Today, it is possible to harden the copper surface, enabling a relatively large number of good impressions to be produced.

There are four broad categories of printing – relief, intaglio, planography and stencil printing.

RELIEF PRINTING
Wood-cutting was the first technique used for relief printing on paper in Europe; the earliest examples may date from the mid-fourteenth century. The technique is called relief printing because the printing surface is raised above the background "in relief." Wood is the most common printing surface, but materials such as card, metal, linoleum or vegetables are also used.

Because woodcuts proved particularly suitable for book illustrations, they were closely linked with the first printed books in the fifteenth century. Many early woodcuts were colored by hand, but by the beginning of

Christ Returning from the Temple with His Parents, *Rembrandt, etching and dry-point, 1654*
SUCH PRINTS USE STABLE INKS AND HIGH-QUALITY PAPER. (TOP)

Mondschein, *Edvard Munch, woodcut, 1896*
THIN PAPER CAN MAKE CONSERVATION DIFFICULT. (ABOVE)

the early sixteenth century printed color woodcuts had developed, only to be eclipsed by engraving and etching by the end of the century. But for a few exceptions, such as Thomas Bewick (1753–1828), it was not until the late nineteenth century that the technique of wood-cutting was revived.

Also within the category of relief processes are metal-cutting, wood-engraving and lino-cutting.

INTAGLIO PRINTING

In intaglio processes, the printing surface is sunk beneath the areas that are to remain blank. The ink is rubbed into the grooves or pits made on the plate, which is usually highly polished copper, although steel, brass, bronze and zinc are also used. Intaglio prints can be engravings, in which the grooves and the pits are cut with a burin, and etchings, in which they are bitten out by acid. As a technique for printing on paper, engraving developed from the goldsmith's long-established practice of decorating metal with engraved patterns, and was first used in the second half of the fifteenth century.

Etching, originally developed by armorers to decorate weapons and first used for printing in the early sixteenth century, uses the corrosive action of acid to "bite" a furrow into the metal plate. The plate is first coated in a thin layer of "ground," a mixture of wax and pitch which is unaffected by the acid. Once the ground is set all over the plate, the design is drawn into the ground with a fine needle. When the entire design has been cut into the ground, the plate is immersed in acid, a process that etches grooves into the metal plate where it is not protected by the ground.

The large category of intaglio processes also includes dry-point, mezzotint, soft-ground etching, aquatint and stipple engraving. The most recognizable feature of an intaglio print is the much-valued plate mark, the imprint of the edge of the plate into the paper, which is produced by the heavy pressure needed for printing. It should be noted that plate marks can be damaged easily by careless pressing and poor storage.

PLANOGRAPHIC PRINTING

Lithography relies on the chemical treatment of the lithographic stone or plate to accept ink and repel water, and is called a planographic ("flat writing") technique. Developed by Alois Senefelder in 1798, lithography gave printing the potential of total mass production of images. As a means of reproducing paintings, full-color lithography came into use in around 1820.

Apart from lithography, there are other planographic processes such as transfer lithography, photolithography, offset lithography and collotype.

STENCIL PRINTING

The stencil method, in use since ancient times, relies on covering the areas that are to be left blank, and printing the design through the holes of a cut-out stencil. The technique of attaching stencils to a mesh of fabric, such as silk, and then printing the design onto paper, is known as silk-screen printing. This process is widely used in twentieth-century commercial printing, and was particularly popular in the 1960s, when leading artists became attracted to the "fine-art" possibilities of this technique.

"IMITATIONS"

Some printing techniques set out to emulate other art forms. Engraving in the crayon manner, for example, attempts to replicate the appearance of a chalk drawing, and a nineteenth-century oleograph, which is an ordinary color lithograph impressed with a canvas grain and then varnished, imitates oil painting. An awareness of such imitations can avoid confusion when choosing correct conservation treatments.

Conservation

The various processes outlined above have in common conservation problems that relate to their paper support. Different problems may arise, however, in regard to the nature of their inks and textures.

DUST AND SURFACE DIRT

Prints on display should always be enclosed in tight-fitting, acid-free mounts and frames, but some may come into an owner's possession in less than perfect condition. If the print has only a light covering of fine dust, it may suffice to dust it down with a fine, soft-haired brush, taking great care not to ingrain the dust or produce a streaky effect. It is extremely easy to spoil a print by trying to clean it with inappropriate erasers, so more heavily soiled items should be referred to a conservator.

DISCOLORATION

Overall discoloration of a print can be the result of a poor-quality wood-pulp paper support, containing either raw lignin or chemicals such as bleaching residues and unstable sizings (or both). Such poor paper has an innate tendency to degrade, and discoloration can only be slowed down by ensuring that the print is displayed in an acid-free mount and stored in the correct conditions (see page 116). In some cases it is possible for a conservator to deacidify such paper, although this process can be fraught with complications. If the print contains colored inks, these may change color or fade during deacidification. Sometimes the combination of chemicals in the paper pulp may be such that, though it is possible to neutralize the acid in the paper, the deacidification process may darken the paper further. This may be acceptable for preserving an important document, but is usually unacceptable for a decorative print.

LOCALIZED DISCOLORATION

If a print becomes discolored in a particular area, it is most likely because that section has been in contact with something else containing acid, such as a mount board, wooden backboard, tape, label or glue. Like other works of art on paper, prints have often been glued down onto wood-pulp mount boards. If this is the case, the discoloration can come from both glue and wood-pulp boards – a state often compounded by slats of wood placed behind the mounted print. With age the slats shrink and move, thus allowing atmospheric pollution to penetrate from the back; this causes discoloration in stripes directly corresponding to the gaps in the wood on the back.

Prints are often mounted in window mounts, which is generally acceptable – as long as museum-quality, acid-free mount card is used. However, as was often the case in the past (and sometimes still is), the mount boards are made from lignin-containing wood pulp sandwiched between thin layers of better paper. The bevel, or angled edge, of the window mount exposes the wood pulp, and the acid from the decomposing pulp will migrate to the print, often producing a dark brown line around the edge of the aperture. It is easy to spot an acid mount by looking closely at the bevel: if orange-brown in color, it can be assumed that the mount is made from wood pulp.

DAMAGING TAPE

Pressure-sensitive, self-adhesive tapes are responsible for a great deal of often irreversible damage and discoloration. The adhesives in these tapes alter their chemical nature very quickly when reacting with oxygen in the atmosphere. An old piece of transparent self-adhesive tape can become yellow, dry and crisp, completely lose its ability to stick, and leave a dark, yellowish-brown stain on paper. Such tapes and stains are extremely difficult to remove from paper, and only an expert should attempt the task. The solvents needed are very strong and often toxic, and can damage printing inks – and the conservator.

MOLD DAMAGE

The small brown marks that disfigure many works of art on paper are called "foxing." There is much debate about the reasons why the spots occur in different quantities on similar paper stored in the same conditions, but the general consensus of opinion is that foxing is a type of mold infestation that flourishes in an acid and damp environment. Any paper stored in a damp setting surrounded by papers or boards made from lignin-containing wood pulp may develop foxing, as well as risk general discoloration and a breakdown in the paper fibers.

If a print has developed such marks, seek the advice of a conservator, who will first consider how acid the paper is. A conservation laboratory can determine this using sophisticated equipment, but usually an experienced conservator, by simply looking at and lifting the paper, can tell whether it is dangerously acidic, and whether the foxing can be removed. It is necessary to consider the stability of the inks used in the printing before embarking on any treatment. In some cases, foxing is best left alone because removing it may involve bleaching, which can be very damaging. In fact, the foxing may not be so disturbing once the print is in a fresh acid-free mount. An expert may also decide that it is safe to deacidify but not to bleach a print. Whatever the choice, to prevent the foxing from getting worse or recurring, the print should be safely preserved and displayed in acid-free mounts (see page 118), and stored in a stable environment with a relative humidity of less than 55%.

Other types of mold may appear on prints as marks and stains of various sizes and colors: pink, purple, brown, gray or black. Such stains occur when an object has been left wet or damp for some time, and, because they are extremely difficult – sometimes even impossible – to remove, require the attention of a conservator.

It is an altogether different matter to arrest mold growths entirely, since spores are always present in the air and will only remain dormant in drier environments. It is therefore imperative that the environment does not fluctuate and hence encourage molds.

WATER DAMAGE

A damp or wet environment is a breeding ground for mold, but water and damp can also make the paper support distort and cockle. Paper is hygroscopic, having the ability to absorb moisture and also to lose moisture in a dry environment. The paper support of a print will always move a little as small environmental changes take place; this is natural and should not be interfered with. The slightly undulating surface of a good piece of paper is part of its aesthetic value, so prints should not be glued down to cardboard or dry-mounted with synthetic resin onto rigid supports. The former is sometimes reversible, but the latter is rarely rectifiable and may destroy the intrinsic and financial value of a print.

If a print is exposed to greatly varying humidity levels, the paper will cockle. If the print, due to some accident, has become completely wet, it should be dried on clean blotting paper in a well-ventilated room. If then, upon drying, it has cockled to such an extent that its aesthetic appearance is lost, it should be taken to a conservator.

An Alchemist, *William Pether, mezzotint, 1775*
WITH THEIR RICH, VELVETY SURFACES, MEZZOTINTS ARE MORE
VULNERABLE THAN PRINTS WITH HARD, SIZED SURFACES, AND
FREQUENTLY SUFFER SCRATCHES AND ABRASIONS IF NOT WELL
CARED FOR. (ABOVE).

MEZZOTINTS

The main feature of mezzotints is their rich, velvety surface, often accentuated by the use of soft, unsized paper. Because of the lack of size, however, the surface of mezzotints is vulnerable to scratches and abrasions. A framed mezzotint should have a double window mount cut to give extra depth to the aperture, creating a greater distance between the glass and the surface. If they are unframed, such prints should be protected by layers of acid-free paper when stored.

JAPANESE PRINTS

Japanese woodcuts present specific conservation problems. All are printed on handmade paper, and the printing inks differ from European inks in that their pigments are not held in oil, but in a smooth rice paste; this is much more sensitive to moisture, and can also attract insects and molds. Since the ink is so water-sensitive, there are greater limitations to the conservation treatment.

The pigments used in Japanese prints are dyes, earth colors and metallic pigments, some of which are especially light-sensitive. Therefore, the prints should ideally be displayed in rotation under low light levels so as to cut down the overall exposure. These prints often include special features, such as delicate embossed lines and finely ground mica or metals sprinkled on areas stenciled with glue, which can be rubbed and flattened easily. These embellishments produce additional storage and conservation problems.

Fuji in the Clear
Weather, *Hokusai,*
print from the series The
Thirty-Six Views of
Fuji (1831–1833)
THIS QUINTESSENTIAL
JAPANESE PRINT
DEMONSTRATES THE WOOD-
BLOCK TECHNIQUE. ITS
VIBRANT PIGMENTS ARE HELD
IN A RICESTARCH MEDIUM,
WHICH IS PARTICULARLY
SENSITIVE TO MOISTURE AND
ALSO TENDS TO ATTRACT
INSECTS AND THE GROWTH OF
MOLDS. (RIGHT)

Le Chapeau Epingle,
*Pierre Auguste Renoir,
lithograph, c.1898*
FIN-DE-SIÈCLE
EXPERIMENTATION WITH
PIGMENTS – THIS PRINT
FEATURES ELEVEN COLORS –
AND DECLINING PAPER
QUALITY HAVE LED TO LATER
CONSERVATION PROBLEMS.
(RIGHT)

The Melody Haunts
My Reverie, *Roy
Lichtenstein, silk-screen
print, 1965*
THE SMOOTH SURFACES, FLAT
COLORS, AND OFTEN HEAVILY
LOADED ART PAPERS OF SUCH
PRINTS MAKE THEM
VIRTUALLY IMPOSSIBLE TO
RESTORE. (ABOVE)

19TH-CENTURY LITHOGRAPHS

In the mid-nineteenth century synthetic aniline dyes were discovered, making it possible to produce myriad new colors. Also, the production of paper dramatically increased – its quality tended to decrease – and many lithographs (including posters) and screen prints were printed on an extremely inferior wood-pulp paper. Many of these new dyes were particularly light-sensitive and it was found that, within weeks, they could fade away completely. Because of this sensitivity, such prints should, if they are to be displayed at all, only be exposed to very low light levels, below 50 lux.

MODERN COLORED PRINTS

Twentieth-century colored prints present specific conservation problems due to the many commercial combinations of dyes, oils and solvents mixed to produce their printing inks. When restoring a print, conservators often do not know how the inks will react – mainly because the manufacturers keep their formulas to themselves and are rarely specific in their trade descriptions. The papers of contemporary prints are also often complicated. Modern paper production uses a variety of chemicals and fillers to manufacture papers of the right color and texture at the right price.

Storage

If prints are stored in boxes, these should be made from acid-free boards and papers. Solander boxes, which seal out dust and moisture when closed and lie flat when opened, are specially made for this purpose. Each print should be mounted individually and the mounts then stacked in Solander boxes, with acid-free tissue inside each window mount. Each mounted print should be separated by a piece of acid-free card. If prints are stored unmounted, they should be separated by acid-free papers.

Wooden or metal plan chests are suitable for bigger collections. The drawers should be lined with acid-free card, and the prints stored within should be interleaved with acid-free tissue. Prints should not be kept in plastic sleeves as condensation may form, or the plastic may deteriorate and give off harmful chemical vapors. Prints stored in portfolios should be carefully interleaved with acid-free paper and the inside of the portfolio lined with the same paper or card. The environmental conditions apply for storage equally to prints and maps.

Handling and Display

A print should be picked up carefully, between clean thumb and fingers, using a piece of clean paper folded to form protection between the fingers and the print. Ideally, white cotton gloves should be worn unless they make the handler feel clumsy, in which case well-washed hands may be safer. The print should be held at opposite edges or corners so as not to cause the paper to buckle.

The value of a print is directly related to its condition. If the print is mounted and framed correctly, hung on an inside wall, and only exposed to light levels below 50 lux in a constant atmosphere of 55% relative humidity, then there should be little risk of diminishing its value. The environmental conditions recommended for the display of prints and maps are the same as for other works on paper (see page 117).

Transportation

If prints are to be transported, they should be packed carefully with acid-free paper. Ideally, they should be carried in a sturdy portfolio or in a hard traveling case specifically manufactured for transporting pictures. If it is necessary to transport prints in a tube, the cylinder should have as large a diameter as possible and should be made of very strong card. The recto (front) of the print should be protected with a sheet of acid-free tissue.

The Comte de Vaudreuil, *F.-H. Drouais, 1758*
IN THIS PAINTING THE COUNT EXAMINES TWO MAPS, WHICH, NO DOUBT, WERE LINED ONTO LINEN FOR SUPPORT.

Maps

Most maps are prints, printed in color or colored by hand. Maps are sometimes laid onto a secondary support of fabric to strengthen them when folded for portability. These folds often wear out, however, causing both paper and fabric to weaken and break. When handling a large map, it is best for two people to lift it. Make sure the surface it is placed on will accommodate its size fully, with no overhang at the sides.

In general conservation terms, maps are treated much like other printed works of art on paper. However, if a map is hand-colored, it should be dealt with as a watercolor (see page 124), and a conservator should be consulted. Large maps should be referred to a conservator accustomed to treating oversized objects.

The storage and transportation of maps are the same as for prints. If a map collection is extensive, it would be worth building a plan chest to store the maps flat.

PHOTOGRAPHS

Since the birth of photography in 1839, both photographers and manufacturers of photographic materials have been attempting to increase the longevity of photo images, which are inherently unstable objects.

A photograph's components are the primary support, or base on which the image is printed – which can be paper, metal, glass, or flexible film – and a transparent binder layer of either gelatin, albumen, or collodion. Light-sensitive salts in the binder layer form the final image, and can comprise metallic silver, platinum, iron compounds, pigments, or organic dyes.

Each part of a photograph can deteriorate at a different rate. Not only can its constituents react with one another, but the deterioration of one constituent may act as the catalyst for the breakdown of another. Therefore, it is advisable for photographs to be stored by type and chemical composition.

Non-Paper-Based Cased Objects

DAGUERREOTYPES
Invented by Louis J.M. Daguerre (1789–1851) in France, this expensive process flourished from c.1839 to 1865. It produced, on silver-plated copper, negative images which seem positive when viewed at the correct angle.

Most daguerreotypes were set within cases made of materials such as leather, wood, papier-mâché, and inlaid mother-of-pearl. Some European examples were not cased but instead sealed with passe-partout, strips of strong, gummed paper. Most prevalent was the American-made Union case, produced by mixing shellac, wood fibers, and gum, adding dye, heating the mixture, and then pressing it into a mold. Cases were usually velvet lined and sometimes had the maker's name stamped in gold leaf on the outside. The packaged object contains the plate, with its highly polished surface, a brass mount, and a cover glass, all of which were sealed together at the edges before being placed inside the protective case.

Most damage to daguerreotypes is the result of curiosity. For many years the sealed images were safe in their pollutant-free microclimate. Unfortunately, people often dismantle the packages, breaking the seals in order to examine plate marks (which establish the silver's thickness and sometimes the maker). Once air and outside environmental factors attack these vulnerable objects, interference rings – the coloring of which resembles oil on water –

appear from the edges inward. Plates may even go black.

A common problem with sealed cased-glass objects is crizzling, or weeping glass (see page 46). If there is high humidity in the case, tiny water droplets will appear on the image side of the glass; if the humidity drops appreciably, the droplets turn to crystals. Both states affect the silver and the copper of the image base: the former will tarnish, the image-bearing layer becoming pierced, leading to greenish copper corrosion of the secondary support. Moisture in the enclosure will also cause corrosion of bronze or other metal mounts.

The silver image-bearing layer is extremely sensitive. In the past it has even been subjected to silver-cleaning solutions. These not only obliterate the image but also scratch the plate surface.

AMBROTYPES, COLLODION POSITIVES
Because of the prohibitive expense of daguerreotypes, means to mass-produce photographs were constantly being sought. Two results were the American ambrotype, popular from c.1854 to 1890, and its European equivalent, the collodion positive. Formed by silver held in the collodion layer attached to glass, the images are positive and often hand-colored. The image becomes visible by placing black paper, velvet backing, or black varnish on the glass's non-emulsion side. The cases are similar to those of daguerreotypes.

Components of cased photographic images
FOREGROUND, FROM LEFT TO RIGHT: "PINCHBECK" MOLDING WITH GLASS COVER; IMAGE PLATE; BRONZE MOUNT. BACKGROUND: PADDED LEATHER CASE. (OPPOSITE)

Collection of 19th-century cased images
CLOCKWISE FROM TOP LEFT: AMBROTYPE; OPALTYPE; AMBROTYPE; AMBROTYPE; LEATHER CASE; DAGUERREOTYPE. (RIGHT)

The most common problem with these objects, apart from broken seals, is the flaking of varnish or, if uncased, the breakage of the glass layer; such breakages should be stored in strong enclosures to await expert advice.

TINTYPES, FERROTYPES

American tintypes (or English ferrotypes) are collodion positives on japanned-tin bases. If cased, they are difficult to distinguish from ambrotypes. Uncased examples are easy to identify: they attract a magnet. These are also prone to bending metal supports and flaking emulsion. The paper casing may show rust stains.

Paper-Based Photographs

The earliest paper prints, salt prints, flourished from 1839 to the 1860s, with a brief revival at the turn of the century. They differ from other images in that the light-sensitive silver salts lie entirely within the fibers of the paper. The other silver image-bearing processes are albumen (1850–1900) and gelatin (late 1800s–present); prints can be matte or glossy. Early papers were hand-coated.

The non-silver paper processes include platinum (1873–*c.*1920) and cyanotype (1842–*c.*1950); the latter images are commonly known as blueprints. Color photography (*c.*1935–present) is usually a non-silver process, and prints consist of organic dyes in a gelatin binder.

The most common form of deterioration to all but platinum prints is fading, caused by strong light or residual chemicals from processing. Dyes in some color prints can fade in both light and darkness. Residual iron salts in platinum prints and cyanotypes can cause ferrotyping, whereby a second image forms on an adjacent sheet; such objects should be interleaved with acid-free paper.

Generally, the paper bases of photographs are of good quality. Early salt and albumen prints were often on writing paper containing watermarks and laid lines. In the late 1960s, resin-coated papers for black-and-white and color prints were introduced. These have a plastic coating on both sides, enabling them to be processed rapidly and preventing prints from curling. They are not as stable as conventional paper, however, so if deterioration is noticed, a new copy print should be made.

Glass Images

The earliest glass-plate negatives had a collodion binder layer, soon to be followed by albumen and then gelatin. Collodion negatives were often varnished to protect them. Positive processes on glass include lantern slides (often hand-colored) and autochromes (dyed starch granules with gelatin-silver emulsion); although heavy, these are fragile and can break easily. The main problems with emulsions are cracking and lifting.

Flexible Film

The main types of flexible film – cellulose nitrate, cellulose acetate, and polyester – exist in roll and sheet forms. Introduced in the 1890s and in continual use until the 1950s, cellulose nitrate was employed mainly in the film industry in roll form and as X-rays in sheet form. It is highly unstable, can self-combust and, when kept in bulk in inappropriate conditions, constitutes a fire hazard and serious health risk. Extreme brittleness indicates an advanced state of deterioration, when toxic gases will be given off. Most film archives therefore copy their valuable material onto more stable bases and keep the originals in cold storage.

The instability of cellulose nitrate led to the production of "safety-base" film in the early twentieth century. This exists in several forms, including diacetate and triacetate. If kept in high temperatures and too dry an atmosphere, the plasticizers in the base are gradually lost, compounds added as fire retardants become reactive, the base shrinks, and the emulsion layer comes under great tension, pulling, distorting, and making the image illegible. High humidity can lead to mold.

Although possessing high dimensional stability and a greater ability to withstand temperature extremes, polyester has not totally replaced acetate. Research continues to find a suitable adhesive to bind the emulsion to the base.

Color transparencies and slides suffer from fading. When overexposed to light sources, such as constant printing and projection, the organic dyes within these images can lose their brightness and clarity.

Photomechanical and Carbon Processes

These include photogravure, collotype, and photolithography. Usually paper-based, these techniques are widely used for posters and illustrations. The images tend to be stable, but the supports are subject to the normal degradation of prints and drawings (see page 116).

Albumen photograph of the Forum, Rome, Anon., c.1860
THIS PRINT HAD BEEN FOLDED CAUSING PARTS OF THE IMAGE TO BECOME PARTIALLY DETACHED FROM ITS SECONDARY AND TERTIARY SUPPORTS (RIGHT). THESE WERE REMOVED, AND IT HAS BEEN RESUPPORTED ON FRESH CARTRIDGE.

Carbon prints, which date from *c.*1860 to the 1930s, were produced in a range of colors and on various supports. These prints, which are sometimes indistinguishable from photographs, are generally stable. Their most vulnerable aspect is the delicate gelatin binder which is prone to abrasion if not handled carefully.

Causes and Prevention of Deterioration

The main sources of deterioration of photographic materials are inherent instability (as outlined above), improper processing, and poor environmental control.

TEMPERATURE AND HUMIDITY

Ideally, photographic materials should be kept in cool, dark, dry conditions. Fluctuating temperatures and humidity cause the most damage to the binder layers. Silver content becomes reactive in the presence of moisture (including high relative humidity), leading to oxidation (silver corrosion). Silver ions in the image layer become mobile and migrate to alternative sites, usually to the edge of the print or glass base, a phenomenon known as a "bloom." In such conditions, staining, fading, and image loss can also occur, the binder layers can become brittle, and emulsions can break and lift up.

Optimum conditions are a temperature range of 59°–77°F, with relative humidity at 30–35%. Relative humidity should never rise above 60% as this can promote mold and insect attack. Many archives, however, use cold and/or lower temperature storage. Cold storage implies a temperature below the freezing point of water (32°F), with relative humidity of 25% (±5%); lower temperature storage implies a temperature of 59°F, with a relative humidity of 30% (±5%).

POLLUTANTS AND LIGHT

Airborne pollutants such as abrasive dust can be extracted mechanically or prevented from damaging the materials by the use of suitable enclosures (see below). Harmful noxious fumes and gases include those from oil-based paints, varnishes, ozone (from photocopiers), ammonia, and peroxide (from cleaning fluids), and car exhausts, as well as sulfurous and nitrous gases in the atmosphere.

The effects, on photographs, of ultraviolet and heat damage from light are the same as for other paper artifacts (see page 117); in addition, oxidation can occur. Most susceptible to light damage are salt and albumen prints, photographs on resin-coated paper, and those with applied color. These should be displayed at no more than 50 lux, preferably below.

IMPROPER PROCESSING

If "fixing" solutions have not been completely washed out or exhausted solutions have been used, the residual sulfur compounds will tarnish the image silver.

Storage Materials

All enclosures, boxes, hinges, adhesives, and cabinets should be chemically inert. Material in direct contact with photographs should be unbuffered 100% rag for color negatives, cyanotypes, and salt, albumen, and color prints. Slightly alkaline material, specifically produced for pho-tographic storage, is preferable for collodion negatives, tintypes, cellulose nitrate, and cellulose acetate.

Storage materials should be free from reducible sulfur, which can attack the silver in the image and cause it to tarnish. Wood, medium-density fiberboard, and chipboard should be avoided. The last two contain formaldehyde, which cross-links with gelatin and causes its breakdown. Cabinets should be made of nonflammable baked enamel or powder-coated metal produced without solvents. While rooms are being decorated, photographs should be moved to another part of the house for at least two weeks while the paint dries.

Pressure-sensitive tapes and petroleum- or rubber cement-based glue should not be used as they can cause disfiguring and irreversible staining. Rubber bands should not be used as they contain sulfur. Fading and staining can also occur if envelopes with adhesive central seams, such as glassine, are employed.

Polyester sleeves are recommended, and can be bought in a variety of sizes. The material is transparent, chemically inert, and will protect against fingerprints. But it is not suitable for all images, such as those with flaking pigments or ballpoint pen "crop" marks, and fragile prints should be supported in the sleeve with an appropriate board. Avoid frosted polyester (which often contains harmful plasticizers) and polyvinyl chloride (PVC).

Photographs should not be stored in "self-seal" albums, as the adhesive degrades and stains, and the plastic sheet can damage a print's emulsion. Archival-quality albums are ideal, and products made of polypropylene can be used safely for both prints and color slides. Prints can be stored either horizontally or vertically, whichever is safer and more convenient. Glass plates should be stored vertically, as the weight of horizontal piles can cause breakage.

Handling and Transportation

Photographs should be handled by the edges only, because fingerprints cause irreversible damage; preferably, wear clean cotton gloves. If information needs to be documented on a photograph, use a soft pencil on the back, preferably in the margin (if there is one).

Many prints, especially modern ones, have highly static surfaces which attract dust. A soft-bristled brush or photographer's air brush should be used to remove dust, but avoid brushes that shed their hairs.

Framed, mounted, and otherwise well-supported photographs should be transported in the same manner as paper objects (see page 119). Cased objects, however, should be treated as miniatures (see page 110).

WALLPAPERS

Once dismissed as a lesser decorative art, wallpapers are today much more appreciated and studied as significant cultural relics. They are also more understood in scientific terms, and even the tiniest paper fragment discovered under a baseboard can often be accurately identified using modern techniques.

Although the history, development, and production of wallpapers differ a great deal from those of drawings, watercolors, prints, and other paper artifacts, they have many of their inherent properties in common – albeit on a much larger scale – and therefore also procedures of handling and care. However, the early, often idiosyncratic, methods of producing wallpaper – in both the East and West – can lead to unexpected difficult problems, which only a conservator should address.

The Development of Western Papers

The use of paper as a wall covering was a gradual process, which followed on directly from earlier uses of paintings, tapestries, gilded-leather hangings, brocades, damasks, and ornate plasterwork as wall decoration, and from advances in paper-making technology during the sixteenth and seventeenth century. In the main, wallpaper evolved as a more economical, practical and adaptable alternative to these other types of decoration, many of which they were made to resemble, from the small-scale designs imitating Tudor stitchwork to the imitation-leather hangings of the nineteenth century.

EARLY PAPERS

Since the development of wallpapers was a gradual process, it is extremely difficult to establish an entirely accurate date for their introduction in the West, but the earliest surviving examples in England date back to the sixteenth century. Initially, these papers were produced on a very small scale. It is not known whether they were made primarily to line deed boxes, instruments cases and the interiors of case furniture, or to be hung on the walls of houses.

The paper employed was handmade in molds from recycled rags, and then printed from hand-carved wooden blocks or stencils using black carbon and colored inks. It seems that some inks contained an additive making it resistant to insect attack, so many early papers have survived in remarkably good condition.

MOLD-MADE PAPERS

The size of early handmade wallpaper was limited to that of the mold used in its manufacture. Molds were built with a wooden frame and a woven mesh of brass wires to support the paper pulp, and were both heavy and unwieldy. Analysis of existing examples suggests that until the late eighteenth century, linen was widely used as a paper-making fiber; later it was mixed with, then replaced by, cotton. Jute, hemp, and horsehair would also be added to strengthen the paper, giving it a rough texture. In about 1750, a wire gauze mesh replaced the woven brass wires. This produced smooth wove papers that became renowned throughout Europe for their fine textures.

These factors enable early Western papers to be dated, as do pigment and fiber analysis. Also useful are the duty stamps which can be found on the reverse of papers made between 1712 and 1836.

COLORS

Until the end of the eighteenth century, only a limited range of pigments was available. These included vermilion and blue verditer, and earth pigments such as terre verte and yellow ocher. Natural organic dyes such as indigo and rose pink were also used, often mixed with whiting to create delicately colored grounds. Unfortunately, organic dyes have little permanence to light, and many of the papers produced in these early days have faded considerably. Alternatively, these sensitive colors were applied and then covered with varnish, both to deepen the colors and to make them more durable. Evidence of this technique can be found in the grounds of flock wallpapers of the eighteenth century.

FLOCK WALLPAPERS

These luxurious papers, which were used in the grander rooms of aristocratic houses, were made by sprinkling chopped cloth, usually wool, but sometimes silk, onto a stylized design block-printed or stencilled with a slow-drying adhesive. The result was a rich, velvety, three-dimensional pattern. Because of the high quality of the materials making up these papers, many have survived in reasonably good condition. Often however, the varnish has oxidized, altering the original color considerably. Because of the friable nature of the flocked surface, and also health and safety considerations, flocked paper should be cleaned or dusted only by an expert.

OTHER EARLY PAPERS

Wallpapers imitating stucco or decorative plaster were usually printed in shades of white, gray, brown, and black, and were recommended for use in "well-lit halls" and stairways in the mid- to late eighteenth century. Because the pigments they tend to contain are generally unaffected by light, they can generally remain (or be rehung by an expert) in their original position. However, even with such hardy pigments, windows and other light sources should be filtered against harmful ultraviolet rays.

LATER EUROPEAN PAPERS

By the 1830s, mold-made papers were superseded by the continuous roll of paper produced on a paper-making machine, a process that was quicker and more economical for manufacturers and resulted in a lower-priced product. The demand had so increased by the middle of the

The Golden Age *wallpaper, designed by Walter Crane, 1887* THIS HEAVILY EMBOSSED PAPER WAS PROBABLY INTENDED TO IMITATE LEATHER HANGINGS. THE RICHNESS OF EFFECT WAS ACHIEVED BY DECORATION WITH METAL, FOILS, AND APPLIED COLOR, MAKING IT PARTICULARLY VULNERABLE TO SOME CLEANING TECHNIQUES. AS WITH MANY HISTORIC WALLPAPERS, THIS EXAMPLE WAS REMOVED INTACT (ABOVE) FROM ITS ORIGINAL LOCATION, THEN CLEANED, CONSERVED, AND REHUNG WITHIN A MUSEUM ENVIRONMENT, WHERE CONTROLLED TEMPERATURE, HUMIDITY, AND LIGHT LEVELS ARE MAINTAINED (LEFT).

century, that wood pulp (which was more plentiful) was introduced widely as a rag substitute, reducing both the quality and longevity of available papers.

Despite this general deterioration in quality, some outstanding papers were being produced in Europe in the later nineteenth century. In France, magnificent *panoramique*, or "scenic," papers were made, with rich, painterly surfaces that were likened to frescoes. In England, William Morris created over sixty wallpaper designs in distinctive floral and other patterns, often using traditional hand-blocking techniques. In addition, complex relief effects were achieved on some English papers, such as Walter Crane's heavily embossed "Golden Age" design, which glittered with stamped foil and brilliant color in imitation of expensive leather hangings.

Chinese Papers

Even the finest European flock wallpapers of the eighteenth century could not compare to the splendid, hand-painted papers from China. Shipped to the West as early as the seventeenth century, these papers were often confusingly termed "India papers" or "Japan papers."

Chinese wallpapers were hand painted with richly colored pigments, such as malachite and azurite. Eighteenth-century examples depicted scenes from life – people planting in paddy fields, selling oranges, catching fish, and making fireworks – while the later papers were more flamboyant, with fantastic scenes such as birds and butterflies amid peonies and bamboo.

Rolls were made up of joined sheets of paper, which were formed in lightweight bamboo molds. Paper materials included fibers from the paper mulberry, rice, white straw, and bamboo. Mica was sometimes sprinkled onto the surface, imparting a lustrous, silky quality, but occasionally when silk itself was employed, it could become very brittle and prone to fragmentation.

SPECIAL PROBLEMS

Chinese wallpapers in the West were both expensive and fashionable, and were carefully hung by specialized firms. Walls were often prepared and lined using tacked canvas and sheets of lining paper to which the wallpaper would be applied with a mixture of flour paste or animal glue. These composite structures have proved highly vulnerable to deterioration, a problem exacerbated by the hygroscopic nature of Chinese paper, which makes it especially prone to damage from dirt, dust, and smoke.

A specialized conservator should be engaged to remove such paper from the walls and to restore it, if sufficiently

stable, often with special aqueous treatments. Repairs and relinings should be done using Oriental materials, and retouching should be kept to a minimum.

Conditions, Care, and Handling

Like other works of art on or comprising paper, wallpapers are vulnerable to a variety of external elements and internal damage (see page 116).

LIGHT AND HEAT

Many sensitive pigments will fade if exposed to light. Most damage is irreversible, but correct precautions will prevent further harm. Ideally, paper artifacts should be kept below a maximum light level of 50 lux. Direct radiant heat from sunlight should be excluded by the judicious use of blinds (see page 117).

TEMPERATURE AND HUMIDITY

Wallpaper will respond to changes in temperature and humidity, causing stress, distortion, and often severe physical damage. The temperature of rooms containing antique wallpapers should not exceed 59°F. The recommended relative humidity is 55–65%, but the paper may have become used to far from ideal conditions over the years. Since uncontrolled or fluctuating temperatures and humidity levels can cause significant damage, it is advisable that regular readings be taken.

Hand-painted Chinese
"bird and flower"
wallpaper,
late 18th century
A CONSERVATOR
CONSOLIDATES THE ORIGINAL
FLAKING PIGMENT AND TRIES
TO REMOVE HARMFUL LAYERS
OF HOUSE PAINT USED IN
PREVIOUS "RESTORATIONS."
(OPPOSITE)

Hand-painted Chinese
"garden party" wallpaper,
early 18th century
ALTHOUGH THE COLORS IN
THIS SCENE HAVE REMAINED
REMARKABLY FRESH, THERE
ARE OBVIOUS SIGNS OF WATER
DAMAGE. (RIGHT)

SMOKE AND POLLUTANTS

Wallpaper is sensitive to smoke from fires, candles, and gasoliers, and to general atmospheric pollution. All of these have contributed to physical and chemical deterioration, resulting in high acid levels with attendant staining, discoloration, embrittlement, and weakening. While this acidity can be treated effectively by a professional, once the paper has been rehung precautions should be taken to prevent it from deteriorating further. Methods to be considered could include lining the walls with a protective barrier of acid-free paper, introducing air-filtering systems, and the controlled use of ambient heating.

DAMP AND OTHER DAMAGE

The extensive use of glues and adhesives, both to hang papers and bind their pigments, makes them particularly vulnerable to damp. Mold and insect attacks are common causes of damage, as are delamination and discoloration of certain pigments, particularly the copper-containing colors that imitate gold.

French *panoramique* papers are especially susceptible to damage, as their heavy pigment layer requires considerable amounts of adhesive binder and is, therefore, prone to mold attack. Also, if the adhesive fails, cracking, flaking, and losses may occur. Consolidation of these and other similar pigment surfaces is complex, and should be attempted only by an expert. Surface dirt on such papers can be easily cleaned by a professional if the pigment surface is sound, but in high humidity dirt can easily be absorbed into paper and become virtually impossible to remove.

Some of the worst damage caused to historic wallpapers is physical, and includes scratching and rubbing from humans and animals. While such damage can be repaired, it can be prevented only by introducing a protective layer of rigid polycarbonate sheeting. To many this may be offensively intrusive, so simpler preventive measures of caution and traffic control should be followed.

Professional Treatment

While some papers attached to sound walls can be treated *in situ* by experts, others must be removed and dealt with in purpose-designed studios and laboratories. If the latter is the case, papers can be taken off either by the controlled use of steam, moisture, or complex facing techniques adapted from fresco conservation. Further treatment will usually include removing old canvas, paper linings, and glues, followed by washing, deacidification, and repair. As regards Chinese papers especially, methods and materials as close to the original as possible should be used. Retouching or inpainting should be minimal and restricted to areas of patching or repair. All treatment should be fully reversible, and any techniques and materials used should be thoroughly tested over a long period of time. Once conserved, wallpapers should be rehung only when environmental conditions have reached optimum levels.

BOOKS AND MANUSCRIPTS

 Bound volumes suffer principally from two different problems: one concerns the materials from which they are made, the other is connected to the peculiar flaws inherent in conventional Western binding. The materials of which books consist — paper and board (vegetable fiber), parchment and leather (animal skin), wood and adhesives — can each be damaged to varying degrees by excessive heat, light and humidity. They all must be protected against attack by insects or by mold growth, and all can be severely affected by heat and water damage.

The standard Western bookbinding, in which the leaves are held between rigid covers, is subject to strain as books are opened, closed and handled. Where a book's spine and joint materials have become less flexible, opening it will cause structural damage. Text-block drag, the tendency for leaves to pull away from covers, has affected most books since the custom of standing books vertically on shelves was established in the sixteenth century.

Beyond keeping books free of dust and providing them with a favorable environment, the simplest way of protecting them is to support them adequately when they are shelved or used. This reduces structural strain and wear to fine bindings. The closed book protects illuminations and illustrations, as well as textual matter and the leaves themselves.

The corner of a traditional library, showing 18th- to early 20th-century calf and Morocco bindings SOME OF THESE BOOKS APPEAR IN DECEPTIVELY GOOD CONDITION, BUT THEIR MATERIALS ARE NOT ALWAYS DURABLE. FOLD-OUTS, FOR EXAMPLE, MAY HAVE BECOME BRITTLE AND MUST THEREFORE BE HANDLED WITH EXTREME CARE. THE PAPER SHOWN HERE IS DISCOLORED, BUT STILL FLEXIBLE, AND IN REASONABLE CONDITION.

Over the centuries texts have been inscribed, written or impressed on a wide variety of materials, which include stone, clay, palm leaf, bark and planks of wood. When the text continues from one leaf or plank to another, and these are grouped together and joined along one side, the result is a codex. Since classical times the support material used for writing in the West has been dominated by papyrus (vegetable fiber), parchment or vellum (animal skin). In Europe from around the twelfth century AD, the support has increasingly been paper, written onto with a quill or reed and ink. The two major book forms have been the roll (sheets joined to form a continuous surface), which prevailed in the classical world and died out around the third or fourth century AD, and the codex.

Book Construction

Fundamental to the codex or Western book form is a text-block built up from folded sheets of parchment or paper. The sizes of available animal skins determined the various format dimensions, which probably influenced paper mold sizes when they were introduced.

The broadsheet (mold size), folded once across its shorter dimension, produced a folio – two leaves or four pages (a page being the surface of the leaf). Folding the sheet again, but at right angles to the previous fold, created a quarto, that is, four leaves or eight pages; further folding produced an octavo (or 8vo), 16mo, 32mo, and so on. Other types of fold created 6mo, 12mo, etc. Any given sequence of folds was usually at right angles to the previous one. The last fold creates the spine fold, through which the sewing-thread passes to hold the leaves together. This folded sheet forms a "quire" (in manuscripts), or a "section" or "signature" (in printed books).

BOOKBINDINGS

During the Middle Ages, a wide variety of bookbindings were produced. Whatever the sewing structure, whether chain-stitch, long-stitch, tacking or sewing onto bands, the thread or thong always went through the spine fold. Sewing the text-block to bands – the most common form of Medieval binding structure extant today, as well as the most prevalent form of later European binding – is a technique thought to have developed in the Carolingian Empire (AD 751–987). In this method, the band slips are usually laced into wooden boards and the covering is of alum-tawed (mineral tannage) skin. From the twelfth to the fifteenth century, the majority of these well-constructed bindings were protected by a "chemise," a skin or textile overcover, the skirt of which could be extended in any direction. After the bookshelf came into vogue, book owners often removed the chemise.

Soon after the invention of printing in the fifteenth century, the quality of binding construction deteriorated and abbreviated techniques began to be used. By the nineteenth century there was also a decline in the quality of materials. With few exceptions, alum-tawed skins, often colored with stains, were used until the fourteenth

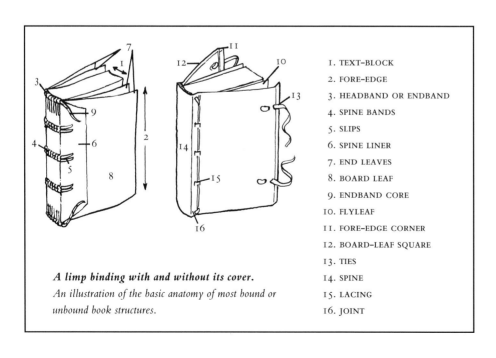

1.	TEXT-BLOCK
2.	FORE-EDGE
3.	HEADBAND OR ENDBAND
4.	SPINE BANDS
5.	SLIPS
6.	SPINE LINER
7.	END LEAVES
8.	BOARD LEAF
9.	ENDBAND CORE
10.	FLYLEAF
11.	FORE-EDGE CORNER
12.	BOARD-LEAF SQUARE
13.	TIES
14.	SPINE
15.	LACING
16.	JOINT

A limp binding with and without its cover.
An illustration of the basic anatomy of most bound or unbound book structures.

century, after which oak-tanned calf gradually came into use. In late fifteenth-century Italy, boldly colored goatskin leathers – referred to in the West as "Turkey" leathers – were imported from Islamic countries; generally, these are still in good condition. During the first decades of the eighteenth century, "Morocco" (goat) leather started to be imported into Europe. Appreciation of these leathers was such that European imitations were produced, which may explain the varying quality of Morocco leather – some are in splendid condition, whereas others have fared poorly and need professional treatment.

Other leathers that have been used in the last three hundred years are tanned pigskin and sheepskin. The latter is often stamped in a variety of different grain patterns, thus making it difficult for the layperson to identify.

THE HOLLOW BACK

When the leather covering is stuck directly to the spine of the text-block it is described as a "tight back" binding. Bindings whose coverings are not stuck to the spine of the text-block are referred to as "hollow backs." There are two essential types: "casing hollows" (as in early vellum-covered bindings and the case bindings of modern publishers), and "tube hollows." In this latter binding, in use from the 1820s, a flattened paper tube was glued to the spine of the text-block to prevent the leather cover from creasing when the book was opened (as happens with "tightbacks"). Often false bands were added to the tube hollow, which gave the appearance of a tight back over

raised cords. The boards being set tight against the backing shoulders cause the leather to crease sharply at the joints when a board is swung back and the hollow opens.

It is characteristic of the hollow back for the cover of the spine to become more convex – and the spine of the text-block to become more concave – as the book opening increases. This convexity must never be flattened – for example, by opening the book on a table – because strains will occur at the joints, down the center of the spine covering, or text-block, or in the paste-downs at the joint. Whichever is the weakest point will be endangered. A book constructed with a hollow back should only be opened on a book rest constructed with a space into which the hollow spine can expand freely.

Grain patterns of three commonly used leathers
THE FOLLICLE PATTERN OF TANNED SHEEPSKIN (CENTRE) AND GOATSKIN (BOTTOM) IS EXTREMELY SIMILAR, BUT THE GRAIN SURFACE OF SHEEPSKIN HAS A TENDENCY TO PEEL, AS IS OBVIOUS HERE. TANNED CALFSKIN (TOP) HAS A MUCH FINER GRAIN PATTERN. (RIGHT)

Detail from the Ghent Altarpiece, *Jan van Eyck*
THE VIRGIN HOLDS A MANUSCRIPT THAT HAS ITS BINDING COVERED WITH A GREEN TEXTILE CHEMISE. THE BALLS AT THE CORNERS SERVE AS WEIGHTS TO HOLD THE BOOK OPEN. (LEFT)

18th- and 19th-century bindings
THE TWO MATCHING 19TH-CENTURY VOLUMES RESTING ON THE 18TH-CENTURY MOROCCO LEATHER VOLUME HAVE RECESSED CORDS AND FAKE DOUBLE BANDS. (RIGHT)

THE PROBLEM OF THE BOOKSHELF

In the Middle Ages, books were stored closed and on their side; thus they were under no structural strain. But at the end of the sixteenth century the bookshelf reached England, and for the first time books were being stood vertically on shelves. Standing a binding vertically causes the text-block to "drag" downwards within its boards.

Gradually, to compensate for text-block drag, book spines were over-rounded and over-lined until, by the second half of the nineteenth century (and often in the present-day trade), clamshell-like bindings were the result. The thicker the lining and covering material added to the spine, the more the opening becomes restricted. The boards hinge from the very crown of the backing shoulders and have no influence on a usually solid text-block. Thus the strain is directly at the joints, and although a binding may seem in excellent order, its boards often have become detached. If this is the case, gather the separate pieces together and tie them gently with soft cotton tape, then wrap in crepe bandage and take to a good binder or conservator.

The Housing of Books

During the last fifty years our bibliographical heritage has suffered greatly from a general loss of knowledge of the environmental and handling requirements of natural materials, and lack of awareness of books as functioning physical objects; rather, if considered at all, the bindings have been thought of as adjuncts to decoration. As a result, central heating, adverse environmental conditions, and poor handling and storage have led to deterioration of materials, mold growth and broken bindings. In many cases, particularly with nineteenth- and twentieth-century bindings, substances within the materials used or techniques employed to make the books can in themselves cause damage.

IDEAL CONDITIONS

In rooms containing books the curtains or shutters should, whenever possible, be closed against light. The temperature should be as cool as possible, not exceeding 68°F, and the relative humidity should be regulated. A constant humidity of 53–58% is recommended for skin materials, and is suitable for all but modern papers (see page 181).

A bookbinding is formed of several materials in close juxtaposition and, as the environment changes, all move at different rates. The ideal environmental conditions, therefore, relate to those prevailing at the time of original construction (particularly to relative humidity, probably

Early 20th-century Morocco leather bindings
THE OLIVE-GREEN SPINES HAVE DISCOLORED OWING TO LIGHT DAMAGE, BUT THIS IS LESS GRAVE THAN THE UNSEEN PROBLEM OF DRYING OUT AND EMBRITTLEMENT.

60% and above in an unheated bindery or scriptorium). But more important is not to allow the relative humidity to fluctuate. This is particularly apposite to Medieval manuscripts with heavy layers of paint and gilding, because the parchment support is extremely hygroscopic and must not be allowed to expand and contract. Stiff-board parchment bindings are an excellent gauge for noting the moisture content of a collection, the problem is that if it dries out, the parchment contracts, distorting the boards and even breaking the joints.

PREVENTING MOLD

Brick- or stone-walled buildings with no rising damp and a reasonable exchange of air show a remarkably stable temperature and humidity throughout the year. It is only recently, with the advent of central heating and insulation, that the situation has dramatically altered, thus facilitating the growth of mold. Good ventilation and movement of air in every corner of a room and bookshelf, including behind the books (and backing panel), will keep mold spores from germinating, but it is difficult to eradicate mold entirely since most varieties thrive in hot, moist conditions. Not allowing the humidity to climb above 65% and having the temperature below 64°F will help to hinder regrowth, as will basic good housekeeping. If a condition is particularly extreme, advice should be taken from a conservator. However, many fumigation remedies that were in use in the past have been proven harmful to the environment and are no longer available – so that even the most painstaking professional treatment may not produce satisfying results.

WATER DAMAGE

If books have become extremely wet, much can be done if remedial action is swift and correct. A wet text-block should not be opened, and the possibility of mold growth must be dealt with immediately. The affected area must be kept as cold as possible; open windows and create a fast exchange of air by using fans.

Sort out and treat all parchment-bound books, as these must not even begin to air-dry. Because inks and pigments are often water-soluble, manuscripts also have special problems that should be dealt with by a conservator. If text-blocks comprise printed paper (as long as it is not clay-coated "art" paper), then place each book between polished millboard, wrap it up in a stretch bandage (trying to retain the original shape), and deep-freeze it until it can be dealt with by a conservator at a later date. Single sheets of parchment need to be deep-frozen and then treated by a conservator, whereas loose sheets of paper should be laid out to dry on clean blotting paper prior to treatment by a conservator, who will use the same method as for cockled prints (see page 128).

Each book must be considered for treatment on an individual basis, but generally speaking, where adhesives have not been softened, books can be air-dried by standing them on end and fanned open, supporting them as necessary. Books whose adhesives have been affected will have to be supported until the adhesives have reset. Never dry wet leather or parchment with heat.

SHELVING

Book shelving, or any surface with which the sides of a binding may come into contact, must be smooth. The vertical members may have holes or grooves for adjusting shelf height; these are best covered by a smooth archival-quality, acid-free card, and the shelves, if new or newly painted, should also be covered with this material. The bookshelf must be stout and unbending, and bookends must relate to the format size of the books on a particular shelf and stand exactly vertical. The bookends should be sturdy, at least as large as the books they are to support, and preferably made of either old wood or metal lined with an archival-quality board.

As indicated earlier, Western binders have never mastered the stress factors present in the vertically housed book. The drag of the text-block within the boards causes flattening at the head of the spine, increased rounding at the tail and breaking of joints, starting at the head of the spine. Such stresses are exacerbated when the book is free to open partially at the fore-edge, or to fall diagonally when a neighboring book is extracted. To allay such

problems there is a tendency to pack shelves tightly – not a good idea as any difficulty in extracting a book encourages damage to headcaps and spines, and also abrasion to the sides. It is therefore advisable not to pack books tightly on shelves, and, when extracting a book, to fill the vacated space with an acid-free block.

Laying a book horizontally on a firm, flat surface is ideal, but is usually feasible only for the most valued bindings and those in extremely fragile condition. It is not always possible (because of space limitations), nor is it even desirable, for example when bookshelves or cases are part of the decor. Alternative solutions would be to provide some supporting book-box or wrapper.

BOOK-BOXING

Good book-boxing is extremely beneficial to the preservation of books or loose sheets. Such enclosures should not only supply physical support and protection, but will also reduce damage from light, pollutants, water, fire, rodents and insects.

There are a wide variety of box designs, but careful choice must be made to solve a particular problem as the use of an inappropriate design or material can do harm. Archival-quality materials should be used wherever possible. A good book-box should meet the following requirements: the way in which to open the box must be obvious and, upon opening, the box must allow the book to be grasped firmly before removing (if the book is large and heavy, then the box design should allow two hands to be used). The box should also permit the book to be removed without scuffing or rubbing – and should exert gentle overall pressure on the book when it is closed.

The most satisfactory design is a drop-spine box with a pressure flap, and if the book has deep squares or is particularly thick, the tail wall of the base (which carries the text-block support) must hinge away. Slipcases, pull-off boxes, ribbon pulls, or any other enclosures or elements that may cause abrasion are unsuitable.

Priority items for boxing include any binding with projections such as bosses or chains; textiles, including book cloths and bindings with very light-sensitive colors; silk ribbon ties (if fragile, press gently and fold flat inside bookcovers with Japanese paper "retaining bridges"); stiff-board vellum bindings; and any other especially vulnerable binding. The only books unsuitable for boxing are those for which slowing the rate of air exchange would exacerbate a problem, such as volumes containing highly acidic paper or inks, and ones whose spines should be able to be viewed. In the latter example, a compromise is to use a "book shoe." This is like a slipcase, only with an open

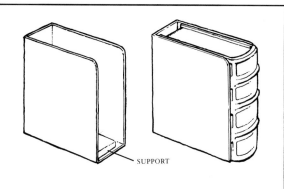

A protective slipcase or "book shoe"
Book shoes are extremely useful for storing books when
their spines need to be open to view. Made of acid-free
millboard creased and cut to fit the individual volume, it is
important that they also contain a text-block support
tailored to the book's tail-square.

top, flexible walls and a text-block support. The book is
slid in at an angle, thus limiting abrasion to the sides. Book
shoes should be made of acid-free millboard that has been
creased and cut to fit the individual item exactly.

Handling and Transportation

To extract a book from a packed bookshelf, never pull on
its headcap. Instead, reach over the head to the fore-edge
and then ease it out, making sure that neighboring books
are not dragged with it; if this is not possible, push in the
books on either side until you can grasp the sides of the
one you wish to remove. Extra-heavy books must be
supported along the tail-edge when halfway out, then as
soon as possible turned horizontally. Never carry more
books than you can firmly hold.

The more frequently books are moved for routine care
or consultation, the more abrasion and risk of damage
they face. Trolleys or carrying boxes should be used when
books are to be moved any distance – whether from room
to room, through doors, or from floor to floor. When
moving books on a trolley, always place them horizontally. When it is necessary to transport books any distance
it is best to wrap each book in tissue and polystyrene sheet,
and place them in a stout case surrounded by inert foam
blocks so that no book can move in any direction.

Books with fragile parts or surfaces must be handled
extremely carefully. Never place a book onto either an
open book or a binding with projections or fragile sides. It
is also inadvisable to stack books in piles of more than a
few, since this puts great stress on the spines. Loose boards
or spine pieces can be kept in place by tying the book with
a soft cotton tape (never string or elastic bands), tied in a
bow. A better solution still is to use acid-free card
wrappers or simple boxes that are made from archival-
quality board.

General Maintenance

Before starting a cleaning or housing project on whatever
scale, it is always best to carry out a condition check at the
same time. Look on shelving for book fragments that have
fallen off; you have a better chance of finding where they
belong before you displace any books. Always keep a
lookout for signs of rodents, insects or mold bloom.
Obviously, depending upon the pest, the remedies will
differ substantially. It is really a matter of identifying the
cause, for which purpose a conservator may need to be
consulted (see page 118).

Working with books can be time-consuming and
repetitive, and it is often difficult to retain concentration
over a long period. However, careful handling is required
at all times, since a moment's carelessness can harm a book.
Always treat books as though they were fragile objects –
as, indeed, most of them are – and keep them closed as
much as possible. Never thrust a book down on a
bookshelf, because even a slight shock increases text-block
drag on the sewing structure and joints. Remember, too,
that a gilt-leather cover is no indication of the value of the
binding or its contents: many times a scruffy, seemingly
utilitarian item is of more interest and value.

CLEANING
Zealous overcleaning has ruined many books. When
cleaning, always err on the side of caution; "institutional"
dirt may be removed, but not "evidential" dirt.

The amount of dusting and cleaning necessary depends
on the environment. A layer of dust retains a higher
moisture level on a surface than the surrounding atmosphere, and becomes a fertile ground for mold growth.
Cleaning should be done in an area away from where the
books are kept, preferably outside (in a shaded area);
otherwise the dust is simply spread to other items. Keep
your hands clean at all times, to avoid transferring dust or
oil from one book to another. For most dusting, and
particularly for heavy dust deposits, use a low-suction
vacuum cleaner with a piece of gauze across the nozzle; the
amount of bibliographically interesting fragments lost
due to careless cleaning must be staggering.

Removing the dust from a solid headedge with a hogshair brush
USE A SOFT BRUSH AND, WHEN DUSTING IN THE VICINITY OF OTHER BOOKS, WORK BY AN OPEN WINDOW OR DOOR SO THAT THE DUST IS CARRIED OUTSIDE.
(FAR LEFT)

Collection of side-stitched 17th-century pamphlets
ALTHOUGH STAINED AND RUBBED, THE CONDITION OF THE PAMPHLETS IS STABLE. DO NOT CLEAN OR BIND, BUT IDEALLY HOUSE IN A TAILOR-MADE 'DROP-SPINE BOX.
(LEFT)

Books with solid headedges – gilt or waxed – may be dusted with a hogshair brush. Grip the fore-edge of the book firmly closed and brush from spine to fore-edge. This avoids brushing dust into the headband. Where dust has penetrated down into the leaves, rest the book on inert foam supports and, using a soft-haired brush, move the dust out towards the page edges.

If the headedge of a text-block is not solid, then the book or album must have enclosed housing. An enclosed bookcase can save a tremendous amount of work and damage, as can a well-designed and tailored book-box.

Unless there is mold present, do not clean the central folds of the text block of any book. Leave any loose items (such as leaves, fragments and straw) where they are; all such evidence has a bearing on the history of the book or collection. If unsure, leave the item in place and make a note of what you have seen. If a loose fragment must be removed from a book, it should be placed in an envelope on which should be noted its position in the book and the position of the book on the shelf.

OTHER IMPORTANT POINTS

Several other points should be kept in mind regarding the care and preservation of books and manuscripts. First, do not erase or lose any previous shelf marks, as these form an important record of the book's provenance. Likewise, keep intact any paper or parchment bookseller's wrapper or publisher's cover; such covers may once have been purely utilitarian and even meant to be discarded, but they are now extremely rare and vital to bibliographical history. Fold-outs are best left undisturbed, except when removing dust along the edges and from neighboring leaves. Never allow any manuscripts or books – even scrapbooks and albums – to be broken up. Before lending a book for display, record the book's condition very carefully and, once it has been deemed fit for travel, make sure it will be well cared for in a suitable environment. Exposure to light will irreparably alter a book's original condition; therefore it is very important for exposure times and light values to be guaranteed by the borrower. Finally, remember that the closed book has proved to be the finest protector of manuscript illuminations, paper quality, and prints and watercolors.

Professional Treatment

Dry-cleaning and the removal of deposits should be left to a conservator. So should leather dressing (oiling) and minor repairs, since such tasks undertaken by untrained amateurs can lead to much damage. Likewise, seek advice from a professional if the paper or parchment of a book has torn or otherwise been damaged, if the spine is breaking, or if the binding has become detached or degraded. Sensitivity to differences in the qualities of materials and a great deal of experience are needed for all the specialized tasks mentioned above.

CARPETS
AND RUGS

Oriental carpets and kelims, Chinese silk carpets, rag rugs and woven tapestries serve a dual purpose, being suitable both as floor coverings and as wall decoration. The way in which they are displayed depends largely on their size and condition. Although carpets and rugs that are to be used on the floor should be in reasonably robust condition, they can be preserved by thoughtful positioning and regular cleaning. Those that are to be hung on the wall may need to be protected and strengthened by attaching a suitable lining.

All carpets should be protected from sunlight if their characteristically warm and mellow colors, mostly obtained from vegetable dyes, are to be preserved. Spotlights which focus on wall-hung carpets should also be checked for levels of heat and brightness. Since the wools, silks and cottons from which they are made are often attractive to insects, carpets should be examined from time to time for clothes moths, carpet beetles and other pests.

Structural damage to carpets, particularly those that have been used on the floor, is most likely to occur at the edges, where the weave may have come unravelled. Tears may also appear in worn or fragile pieces. Carpets which have suffered in this way can be restored effectively with materials sympathetic to those of the originals. All such restoration is best left to those with professional expertise.

Section of a West Caucasian Akstafa long rug, wool, late 19th century
THE COLORS OF THIS LARGE RUG HAVE BEEN PRODUCED BY ORGANIC DYES. THESE ARE USUALLY PRONE TO DETERIORATION FROM MOISTURE AND EXCESSIVE SUNLIGHT, ALTHOUGH THIS EXAMPLE IS IN AN EXCELLENT STATE OF PRESERVATION, WITH ITS COLORS STILL BRIGHT AND WELL DEFINED: A FITTING TESTIMONY TO A SENSIBLE PROGRAMME OF CONSERVATION.

In addition to the popular Oriental knotted carpet, many other types of knotted or woven floor covering exist. The same basic principles regarding care and conservation apply to knotted rugs and carpets and to most other forms of covering, be they hooked or rag rugs, Aubusson needlework carpets, woven tapestries, or Middle Eastern woven kilims, collectively known as textiles.

Carpets and woven textiles are warp- and weft-based. The vertical foundation is the warp, usually of wool, though sometimes of cotton or hemp. The carpet has woven horizontal rows of wefts, alternating with a row of knots over pairs of warps. Wefts, which are made of a material similar to that of the warps, generally are in pairs, though occasionally they occur in threes or more.

A carpet is made from bottom to top, one row at a time. The design or pattern of a carpet is created by the change in color of the wool that makes the knots. In contrast, the design of flat-woven textiles is created by the wefts; like carpets, these are generally of wool, though highlights may be in cotton or silk.

Use and Display

Unlike many other works of art, carpets can serve a practical as well as an aesthetic purpose. Using them as they were originally intended, as floor, wall and furniture coverings, can only add to an owner's enjoyment of them. The manner of displaying a carpet largely depends on its condition and how often it needs to be handled or cleaned. Two of the best qualities of wool (some 75% of carpets and other weavings consist of pure wool) are its translucence and its tactile nature, both of which may influence how a piece will be displayed.

FLOOR USE

Use common sense when positioning a carpet on the floor. The carpet may look wonderful on parquet, but the constant tread of high heels or heavy shoes on its surface without any cushioning between it and the hard floor may cause serious, irreversible problems.

Underlay is a good protection against a carpet wearing out. A double-sided underlay is suitable on both hard (wood or stone) surfaces and wall-to-wall carpeted floors. Such an underlay has a slightly "tacky" surface for use against a hard floor; when on top, it will stop the carpet "walking around." For soft, carpeted floors, turn the underlay over so it will hold onto the flooring. Never glue underlay – or anything else – to carpets.

A popular place to display a floor piece is under the dining-room table. Moving chairs over it, however, can

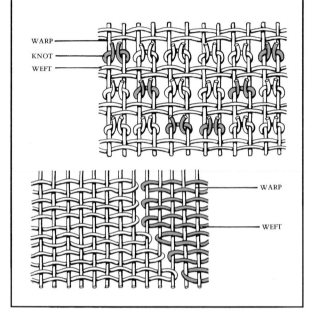

Carpet and weaving structures

THE UPPER DESIGN SHOWS A STRUCTURE OF VERTICAL WARPS AND HORIZONTAL WEFTS, WITH SYMMETRICAL "TURKISH" KNOTS, AS USED IN THE MAKING OF CARPETS AND RUGS. THE DESIGN OR PATTERN IS CREATED BY USING DIFFERENT-COLORED KNOTS. BELOW IS A SLIT-WEAVE WEFT DESIGN, THE BASIC CONSTRUCTION FOR TAPESTRIES AND KILIMS; HERE THE DESIGN AND COLOR CHANGES ARE IN THE WEFTING.

WARP
KNOT
WEFT

WARP

WEFT

cause damaging – and unsightly – wear, and the proximity of food and drink can lead to staining and cleaning problems. Furniture legs that come into contact with the carpet should be covered with rubber and, if possible, repositioned regularly so as not to cause permanent indentations on the surface of the carpet.

WALL DISPLAY

Carpets and textiles of all sizes can be hung relatively safely, either vertically or horizontally. Such a display, especially if artfully illuminated, can greatly enhance an object. Preparation for hanging a carpet or textile can be done in one of three ways, all of which are best undertaken by a conservator.

The first method, known as tapestry-style lining (after the traditional method for hanging tapestries), entails attaching a lining onto the back and a strip of Velcro along the top of the textile, and then stapling the other half of the Velcro to a wooden batten, which is hung on or screwed to the wall. This technique, which is used for larger carpets and kilims, leaves the lining loose at the bottom, enabling the piece to "breathe," with the weight spread evenly and the back protected. Whether displayed horizontally or vertically, a heavy carpet will also need wide support tapes (attached vertically on the back) to help spread the weight.

The second technique, suitable for displaying smaller fragments, consists of the textile being stabilized, conserved onto a lining (which may be dyed), mounted taut onto a wooden stretcher and again attached to the wall using Velcro. A molded Plexiglas cover can be added to protect the mount and the textile from dirt, and a shield can be incorporated into the Plexiglas to stop ultraviolet damage and fading.

The third method, applied to lighter textiles, also involves hanging them with Velcro, a band of which is sewn to a cotton tape stitched to the back of the textile. The other half of the Velcro is stapled to a wooden batten, which is hung on or screwed to the wall. This method is far superior to the one that employs hooks or rings, as the weight is spread more evenly, and it is easier both to hang the textile straight and to take it down.

A piece should neither be hung in direct and/or strong light, nor in a place where it may be easily pulled and torn.

Handling

Never move a heavy carpet by pulling one handful near the edge. Get hold of two or more substantial folded handfuls and then gently pull the carpet into position. Always lift, never drag, furniture, and carry it over a carpet. If a piece is already hanging on the wall, it is preferable that two or more people move it.

Cleaning

The removal of loose dirt and dust from carpets is of extreme importance, and must be attended to regularly.

VACUUMING

An upright vacuum cleaner with rotating brushes and a cylinder vacuum cleaner (without rotating brushes) are the two best tools for cleaning carpets. Average domestic vacuuming will not harm a carpet, but beware of loose threads being drawn into the machine. When using rotating brushes, it is best to work from the bottom to the top of the carpet, so that they revolve with the pile. A kilim should be vacuumed horizontally with the weave.

The back of a carpet should be vacuumed at least twice a year with either machine, depending upon the delicacy of

the object. Sweep up the loose dust on the hard floor and then vacuum the front of the piece, carrying on this process until no more loose dust collects on the floor. Test a piece by turning over one of its corners and gently beating it onto a piece of white paper, which should be inspected for more dust. Dust can be very harmful as it gets lower into the knots, where it acts as sandpaper, slowly grinding away at the base of the knot.

Hanging textiles may be dusted and vacuumed on the wall. Once or twice a year they should be taken down and treated more thoroughly on both the back and front with a vacuum cleaner. If the piece in question is a silk or other delicate textile, it should not come into direct contact with the vacuum cleaner, so place a sheet of filtration fabric or a nylon mesh on top of the textile and then vacuum over it, using a cylindrical cleaner without rotating brushes.

WASHING

Washing a carpet or textile should never be undertaken without the advice of a professional. Washing changes the physical structure of a carpet and must be done carefully, since the process is a balancing act between improving the carpet's aesthetic (surface) qualities and weakening its (internal) structure. Leave the problems of dealing with pH factors, de-ionized water, and drying to an expert, who may decide to use one of a variety of cleaning techniques depending upon the problems encountered. Do not attempt to use an "off the shelf" carpet shampoo as any wet-cleaning process carries significant risks.

DEALING WITH STAINS

Instant first aid must be applied to stains. First, soak up any surplus liquid with an absorbent material – do not rub, just dab at it gently. The remaining liquid can then be absorbed by a large heap of salt, which should be left to dry until it is vacuumed off. Any stain that remains after this must be dealt with by a professional cleaner.

The professional will be limited in his methods of stain removal, however, if the carpet contains synthetic dyes, thought to have first been used in 1870. These dyes are seldom fast, and will bleed if the textile is washed. The back of a carpet is the best place to look for the presence of synthetic dyes, the clue often being a large difference in the strength of colors compared to the front. For instance, a sharp, bright orange on the back and a mellow, faded orange on the front signal the presence of synthetic dyes, and should be considered a warning in regard to future cleaning. Shades of purple and green may also indicate the use of such dyes. A specialist will carry out specific tests before determining the method of cleaning.

Domestic pets may cause damage to a carpet by soiling or scratching it. Commercial products are available to spray on a carpet in order to prevent an animal from returning to a favorite spot. Test the product first on a small section, leaving it on for a day or so and then inspecting it for fading or staining.

Avoiding Damage and Deterioration

Always be on the look-out for signs of wear. Move the carpet around regularly, if possible, to spread and even the wear. After a while the wear may be deemed unacceptable, in which case a different location should be found for the carpet. Since heavy shoes are not usually worn in a bedroom, that room (or even a wall) may be preferable for a softer-wearing carpet.

DAMP

When a carpet is up for cleaning, examine it for damp patches. Water from central heating is especially damaging in terms of both staining and fast rot, since the pipes contain antifreeze. Where the temperature is not kept constant, central heating can also cause other problems. A higher temperature than the 63°F recommended for storage is generally acceptable, as long as it does not exceed 70°F, but if a carpet gets too hot and dry the loss of the wool's natural oils can do damage.

LIGHT

Spotlights can cause damage if bulbs are too close to a hanging, so inspect the object closely for the amount of direct heat affecting it (the heat may not only dry it out, but may also burn it). Lighting that is too strong may also lead to fading, so it might be wise to seek advice from a lighting engineer to make sure the level of artificial lighting is satisfactory. Museums recommend 50 lux.

As direct sunlight is very harmful and should not fall on antique carpets, windows should be properly filtered against harmful ultraviolet rays or covered with a fine muslin screen. Blues and indigo-based colors are not affected as quickly as reds and madder-based colors.

MOTHS

When packing a piece for storage, take every precaution against moths; if possible, check the storage area regularly for moths in their larval state. Hanging pieces are also susceptible to moths and should be inspected, especially if a tapestry-style lining has been used (insects may get behind the lining). Regular vacuuming can help to alleviate this problem.

Corner of an early 19th-century Shirvan Caucasian rug
ONCE SERIOUS DAMAGE (TOP) HAS BEEN RESTORED (BELOW), THIS TYPE OF RUG IS SUITABLE FOR FLOOR USE. A SKILLED RESTORER IS ABLE TO REPRODUCE THE ORIGINAL COLORS VERY CLOSELY. THE RESTORED CARPET SHOULD BE POSITIONED TO AVOID HEAVY WEAR AND STAINS, AND ANY FURNITURE STANDING ON IT SHOULD BE REPOSITIONED REGULARLY.

TAPING THE ENDS

Taping and securing the ends of a newly acquired carpet is a good preventive measure that should be undertaken by a professional. The edges, and possibly even the sides, of the carpet are sewn and secured to the back with cotton tape that is $1\frac{1}{4}$–2in wide. Doing this before there is a chance for any damage to be caused by cleaning or general floor use is a small price to pay compared to rebuilding and restoring a piece.

Storage and Transport

ROLLING

The rolling and transporting of any sizeable carpet must be done in the correct manner, preferably by two people. First, locate the top of the carpet by stroking a palm up and down the length of it; one direction is smooth, and where this smoothness begins is the top of the carpet. Then roll the carpet down the pile from the top, flattening and positioning the lie of the wool as you proceed, preferably over a stiff tube. The rolled carpet can then be moved or stored for a short period of time.

For long storage, open the piece and turn it over so that it is face down on the floor. Cover it with acid-free tissue paper and roll from the top onto a tube – the best type is plastic plumber's tubing – that is slightly longer than the carpet and has been covered in tissue paper. Cover the rolled carpet with more tissue and afterwards tie it lightly with wide ribbons, preferably inserting it finally in a clean linen sheet or a purpose-made cotton sleeve. Store it off the floor on bracket supports touching only the tube ends, not the carpet. The room temperature should be a constant 55°F and the relative humidity 45–55%.

FOLDING

A carpet should be folded only for temporary storage since, after a period, creases will begin to show and need to be ironed out on the back (with a cloth between the iron and textile). Some textiles are liable to crack, so before folding, test a small part for pliability by listening for any cracking and simply feeling if it is too stiff to fold.

Once it has been established that the carpet can be folded without causing it undue harm, lay it face down on the floor and cover it with acid-free tissue, then fold down the length in three and fold up the strip into a block. This way the foundation is protected when bent and has no sharp creases in it, thus avoiding cracking or splitting. Store the carpet off the floor, making sure it is touching neither heaters nor walls. The room temperature for folded carpets or textiles should be a constant 55°F and the relative humidity 45–55%. It is vital to check the carpet regularly for infestation by moths (see above).

TRANSPORT

Whether the carpet is rolled or folded, it should be wrapped in bubble wrap, taped tightly to keep it airtight and waterproof, and preferably crated for long-distance transport. This protective covering should be removed after transport, as the textile should not be left in an airtight package.

Conservation and Restoration

The care of carpets extends to treatment by a professional. Detailed and unambiguous discussion of the work that is to be undertaken is of the utmost importance, as many textiles have been changed irreversibly for the worse owing to misunderstandings between the owner and the conservator or restorer.

Discuss carefully the materials or products to be used for cleaning, repair, or whatever else is being done. If a piece is to be lined, discuss the color of the lining, especially if dyeing is necessary in order to match existing colors. Close cooperation is needed for this sort of work; the owner should be able to envisage how he wants the piece to look – and to communicate this to the expert.

Restoration of a 19th-century northwest Persian carpet
THE RESTORER HAS BUILT A NEW FOUNDATION DOWN THE SIDE OF THE CARPET, AND HERE IS USING A NEEDLE AND KNIFE TO REPLACE THE KNOTTING. REPAIRS OF THIS TYPE, AND ANY CLEANING BEYOND DUSTING, VACUUM CLEANING, AND INSTANT FIRST AID, SHOULD ALWAYS BE UNDERTAKEN BY PROFESSIONALS. OWNERS SHOULD TAKE CARE TO DISCUSS THE MATERIALS, PRODUCTS, AND COLORS TO BE USED WITH THE CONSERVATOR OR RESTORER BEFORE WORK IS BEGUN.

TEXTILES

Antique textiles are potentially vulnerable to almost every aspect of the domestic environment. Exposure to light, heat, humidity and atmospheric pollution, the work of insects, and the effects of bad handling, poor storage and incorrect methods of display can all have serious consequences. Certain procedures, however, will minimise the risks of damage, and in cases where the condition of a textile has already seriously deteriorated, there is much that can be done in the way of restoration. Textiles comprise tapestries, curtains, silks, velvets, brocades and lace, and also include embroidered boxes, stumpwork and beadwork, samplers, silk and woolwork pictures, and fans, hats, shoes and costume. In many instances, the combination of fabrics with ivory, leather, wood, metal and other sensitive materials complicates the methods of care and conservation of this sensitive group of objects.

All textiles have a propensity to degrade in the presence of strong light, and this is the root cause of many of their problems. In silk and woolwork pictures, for instance, colors are devalued and structure weakened, and beadwork is spoiled when its threads begin to rot. The natural ability of textiles to absorb moisture brings other problems; for instance staining is caused by the growth of molds and the oxidation of metal threads and buttons. Moisture also draws atmospheric pollution into the fibers of fabrics. While cleaning can improve appearance and conservation strengthen textiles and go some way towards repair, faded colors can never be renewed, and are lost forever.

English embroidered portrait panel, c.1670
THIS PANEL, FROM A CABINET IN GROOMBRIDGE PLACE, KENT, ENGLAND, IS EMBROIDERED IN SILK ON A SILK GROUND FABRIC. THE PORTRAIT IS EDGED WITH SILK-WRAPPED PARCHMENT LOOPS, AND SILK-WRAPPED WIRES. FREQUENTLY WITH THIS FORM OF DECORATION, THE LOOPS AND WIRES BECOME LOOSE AND THE SILK UNRAVELS. A CONSERVATOR WILL BE ABLE TO REATTACH LOOSE DECORATIVE ELEMENTS, AND REWRAP AND SECURE UNRAVELLED SILK.

Textile objects come in all shapes and sizes, ranging from delicate pincushions and purses, to enormous, heavy tapestries. They can be made from natural or synthetic fibers, or they can be composite, incorporating organic materials such as bone, shell, feathers or hair and inorganic materials such as glass and metals. Textiles can be woven fabrics or felted and pressed; they can be dyed, printed, painted, embroidered or decorated with applied work or with stamped or embossed designs.

The nature and complexity of textiles make them fragile and difficult to deal with, particularly when old and damaged or degraded. Damage may not immediately be apparent, but a textile left undisturbed for a number of years may have become brittle and thus be more liable to tear when moved. Careful examination is essential at regular intervals to determine the condition of a textile object, and to check that its condition is stable and not deteriorating. It should be thoroughly examined before any cleaning or remounting work is undertaken, particularly if this involves removing flat textiles or embroideries from frames or taking down tapestries, large hangings, or curtains from walls. The conservation of these objects is complex, demanding work, and should usually only be undertaken by trained professional conservators.

Causes of Damage

Textiles are vulnerable to damage by light, heat, moisture, atmospheric dirt and pollution, insects and pests, bad handling, poor storage and incorrect methods of display.

LIGHT
Bright light, both natural and artificial, will cause colors to fade and fibers to become brittle, tender and discolored. Light also makes fibers go brown, particularly cellulosics (cotton and linen) and some protein fibers (silk). Textiles should be displayed in a low light no higher than 50 lux, and spotlights should not be used. Display should be for short periods only if the light level is higher than that recommended. Textiles that are not intended for display should be carefully stored and kept in the dark.

HEAT
Heat may cause shrinkage of sensitive organic materials, particularly composite objects in which leather, parchment, ivory and wood have been incorporated. Heat can cause drying out and embrittlement of fibers, and can help accelerate chemical degradation processes, particularly in unstable materials such as modern synthetic polymerics, referred to here as "plastics." The ideal recommended temperature for most textiles is no higher than 66°–68°F. When coupled with changes in atmospheric humidity, violent fluctuations in temperature can cause rapid shrinkage, warping, distortions and splitting of degraded fabrics as they tighten on their mounting stretchers. For these reasons textile objects should never be hung above central heating radiators. Also, as hot air rises, the moving air currents help attract atmospheric dirt and dust, which can be deposited on the textile or sucked into ill-fitting frames. Heat is most damaging to textiles when it is coupled with high humidity.

HUMIDITY AND MOISTURE
The ideal relative humidity for the safekeeping of textiles is a stable 55%. Some textile objects need to be kept in drier conditions at no more than 40%, but this is directly linked to particular types of damage and is not the norm.

Textiles should not be kept in damp conditions. There is a risk of mold growth, which can lead to unsightly marks that are often impossible to remove, even by professional conservators. In the case of pieces embellished by metal threads, decorations, buttons or fastenings which contain copper, there is a greater risk of verdigris being formed in a damp environment. Similarly, oxidation of silver and silver-gilt metal threads on embroideries may be accelerated in damp conditions.

In extreme dampness colors that are not fast may migrate from the embroidery into the ground fabric, causing disfigurement of the textile. Likewise, if a fabric is stored folded or with other textiles, color may transfer from the embroidery to the fabric it is folded against.

POLLUTION, DIRT AND DUST
Dirt and dust quickly build up on the surface of an unprotected textile. Likewise, sulfur dioxide, a component of atmospheric pollution, can cause metal threads to tarnish and fabric degradation to accelerate. Because of their material, nature and construction, some textiles cannot be cleaned so it is essential that they be protected from dirt and dust. Textiles should never be displayed in the open. The simplest method is to seal the textile in a glazed frame or protect it in a Plexiglas box or permanent glass display case. Large furnishing textiles cannot be protected in this way so they should be regularly vacuum-cleaned to stop a build-up of dirt and dust.

INSECTS AND PESTS
Insects may often feed and lay eggs on textiles. Indeed, moths, carpet beetles and other fiber-eating pests can cause untold damage to textiles. They frequently penetrate into

Embroidered motif on 19th-century Turkish towel
TEXTILES SHOULD NEVER BE STORED IN DAMP CONDITIONS AS
THESE CAN CAUSE MOLD OR, IN EXTREME CASES LIKE THE ONE
SHOWN HERE, MIGRATION OF COLORS INTO THE SURROUNDING
FABRIC. SUCH DAMAGE IS USUALLY IRREVERSIBLE.

the dark corners and edges of ill-fitting picture frames
where they may live and feed, unnoticed, until they
eventually emerge by eating their way into the main body
of the textile. It is usually at the larval stage of its
development that the insect does the most damage.

Health and safety regulations do not permit the general
public to use strong insecticides, so a clean environment,
regular inspection, and good housekeeping are essential to
combat damage. When pests are found, advice should be
sought from a trained conservator to determine the best
method of dealing with the problem.

If rodents get into a place where textiles are stored, they
will chew anything available from which to make their
nests. They are highly destructive and must be eliminated.

Handling and Storage

Careful handling of textile objects is all-important. They
should never be dragged or picked up by the corners; the
weight should be supported evenly throughout, or the
textile may split or tear when moved. Care should be
taken not to scuff the surface of a textile; when degraded
the surface can easily be rubbed away.

Textiles should be stored in the dark, either flat or
rolled. They should never be folded as hard creases may
form, which will eventually crack and split along fold

lines. Interleave the textiles with acid-free tissue in
preparation for storage. If rolled they may be wrapped in
cotton lawn, calico or another fine, closely woven fabric.
Polyethylene should never be used as a dustsheet or when
preparing a textile for storage as it attracts dust. Three-
dimensional textiles or heavy pieces should never be
stacked one on top of another. Enough space should be
allowed around each object to facilitate handling and
access. Mixed-media objects should be assessed on the
merits of the object as a whole, particularly taking into
account the most vulnerable element when preparing
them for storage or removal.

"Plastics" should not be stored with other textile
objects because they give off degradation products as they
age and break down, which could damage nearby textiles
and may cause tarnishing of metal threads either incorporated into the weave structures or used for embroidered
decoration. "Plastic" textiles and costume accessories
should not be stored in enclosed spaces.

Display

Textiles should not be on permanent display, but changed
and rested at intervals. The time of display depends on the
nature and condition of an object, and a conservator or
other expert should be able to advise on the period for
which it may be on view.

Time, care and money spent in providing the appropriate, dust-proof environment – with the correct light level,
relative humidity and temperature – will greatly help slow
down degradation and maintain the object in good
condition while on display. Ideally, a textile should be
displayed in a dark hallway or on a shaded wall – not in
front of a window or in a bright room.

Embroidered Boxes and Caskets

Antique raised-work, stumpwork, beadwork and other
embroidered boxes are particularly fine textile objects.
They were used for jewelry as well as writing and sewing
tools. Some are simply constructed with a single compartment and a padded and embroidered top, but the larger
(and more common) ones may have three levels, a high
hinged top, a lift-out tray, numerous drawers and at least
one secret compartment.

The casket lid is usually prevented from opening wide
by a silk ribbon fixed to one side. If the ribbon is damaged
or missing, the open lid may fall back, strain the hinge and
risk splitting the back section of the casket. Provision must
be made for a restraining mechanism for the lid.

Charles II beadwork picture, c.1660
THE COLORS OF BEADWORK DO NOT USUALLY FADE, ALTHOUGH THE GROUND FABRIC MAY SOMETIMES DEGRADE AND BECOME DISCOLORED. HEAVY DISCOLORATION MAY ALSO INDICATE THAT THE THREADS HOLDING THE BEADS ARE WORN AND LIABLE TO BREAK IF NOT TREATED WITH GREAT CARE. THE APPEARANCE OF THE BEADWORK MAY ALSO SIMPLY BE DULLED BY SURFACE SOILING WHICH, HOWEVER, IS MUCH LESS SERIOUS AND CAN GENERALLY BE REMOVED SUCCESSFULLY BY A SKILLED CONSERVATOR.

STORAGE AND DISPLAY

Embroidered caskets should be stored closed and in the dark in a dust-free place. Those embroidered with stumpwork should not be wrapped in tissue or fine fabric because the free-standing motifs and raised work may be crushed. Any loose or detached motifs should be collected for reattachment by a conservator.

If displayed, it is essential that these caskets be protected to prevent dirt and dust settling on the surface. Ideally they should be placed in glass display cases or protected by a Plexiglas box cover. Repeated cleaning is undesirable, expensive, and not to be recommended.

CONSERVATION

Embroidered boxes should only be treated by a professional conservator. Surface dirt and dust can be removed. Curled up or torn free-standing motifs can be supported, repaired and reattached if they have fallen off or been wrongfully placed during previous repairs. Loose floating silk threads coming away from the laid work can be secured back in position. If the silk embroidery is faded the color cannot be restored, but often general cleaning will serve to brighten the appearance overall.

Beadwork

Care must be taken when seventeenth-century beaded boxes, mirror frames and pictures are cleaned because often the silk or fine linen threads holding the beads are degraded and will break when touched. Usually a few beads will come away during the cleaning, and these must be accurately and expertly refixed.

A guide may be given to the strength of the securing threads holding the beads – and therefore the overall condition and fragility of the object – by looking at the ground fabric. Much early beadwork was worked on a creamy-white, fine silk-satin ground. If this is heavily discolored, yellowed or even brown, then the threads holding the beadwork are also likely to be degraded and the beads may fall off if treated without due care.

Beadwork responds well to cleaning. Usually the color of the beads has hardly faded, and removal of surface grime will reveal their original bright hues. If patches of beadwork are missing, it is not aesthetically or ethically acceptable to rebead the area. It is impossible to match antique beads with products made today, so anything other than original beads will be inappropriate.

BEADED BAGS

Beadwork bags and purses may have beads woven or knitted into the structure, not embroidered onto the surface, to form the design. The most common damage found in these is the degradation of the threads holding the beads. Careless handling can cause the threads to break, beads to fall out, and the design to unravel and be lost.

To save the object it may prove necessary to support the beadwork fully with an interlining, onto which the fragile beadwork and detached beads can be stitched. If the bag already has a silk lining stitched inside, it will be necessary to release this in places to allow the support lining to be inserted and the repair carried out. The original silk lining should then be restitched back in place. These objects should not be conserved directly onto their original silk linings. This work can prove difficult, and should only be undertaken by an experienced conservator.

17th-Century Embroidered Pictures

The silk ground fabric on which these embroideries were worked has frequently discolored, degraded and split. Although unable to reverse the discoloration, a conservator will be able to support the ground fabric to give it cohesion of structure and make the object sound enough to be remounted and framed.

Stumpwork and other embroideries of this date, particularly portrait pictures, were frequently finished with broad free-standing edgings composed of bands of silk-wrapped parchment loops and silk-wrapped wires. With time the silk frays or becomes unraveled, and the loops sometimes fall off. It is a simple matter for a conservator to rectify this damage, providing all the detached pieces have been kept.

Silk Pictures

Painted and embroidered silk and woolwork pictures were made towards the end of the eighteenth century and early in the nineteenth century. They were mostly naïve in style, and depicted pastoral scenes, religious subjects, and literary or architectural themes. Some were mourning pictures, whereas others comprised floral designs or exotic-bird motifs. Painted parts – usually the faces, hands and feet of the figures and the sky areas – are sometimes incorporated on these pictures.

The embroidery was worked through two fabrics: a fine silk was laid upon a linen backing to help take the weight of the heavy, closely worked woollen and knotted parts of the embroidery. Sometimes the linen was omitted if the embroidery was not too heavy in weight and was made only from silk. The completed embroideries were stretched taut and usually nailed onto wooden stretchers, then framed. Many of them have painted and gilded glass mounts.

The most common signs of damage to silk pictures are the fading of the embroidery, yellowing of the ground silk, and a brittle, dried-out appearance. Those pictures in poor condition suffer from split ground silk which, at worst, has shattered and dropped out in places. In some instances, a fine film of dry silk dust that has broken away from the embroidery may adhere to the inside of the glass, where it is clearly visible.

All silk pictures must be treated as extremely fragile objects. Most can be assumed to be in a far worse condition than is immediately apparent. When the pictures were first mounted, tension lines were set up between the nail points on opposite sides of the stretchers, and vibration or shock will cause silk, when it has degraded and become brittle, to split along those lines. The interface between the solid areas of embroidery and the background fabric is a particularly weak point, and the ground silk may break away and peel back from this point.

CONSERVATION

In some instances it is possible to clean, conserve and remount silk pictures, but for most treatments it is necessary to remove them from the stretchers – a hazardous practice, as it means the highly tensioned strain lines are released and the brittle silk may spring and shatter at the moment of relaxation.

Occasionally it may be possible to clean silk pictures with solvents, but care must be taken to ensure that the surface is not scuffed or rubbed. Stain removal or spot treatment for localized soiling should never be done. If the pictures are not embroidered onto a linen backing or support, the ground silk can usually be supported using a thermoplastic adhesive technique, which is similar in concept to relining a painting; thus, effective conservation can be achieved.

On the other hand, if there is already a linen backing present, the adhesive method of treatment is extremely difficult to apply. Conventional stitching techniques of repair are also rarely suitable for these objects because of their extreme brittleness.

Painted and embroidered silk pictures should not be removed from their frames – even for inspection – without seeking the advice of a conservator. Of course, no attempts should be made at treatment, except by an experienced conservator.

Samplers

Embroidered samplers were originally made to show samples of stitches and motifs used in domestic embroidery, and are possibly one of the most commonly found textile objects. Traditionally made by children, samplers generally have wool or linen ground fabrics worked in colored silk, wool or linen embroidery threads. Some were made in monochrome, usually in black or red on a white background. Any combination of floral and animal motifs may be found, together with initials, verses, alphabets and family details incorporated around houses, trees, figures and occasionally ships. Many are worked with religious subjects, such as a prayer or a psalm, and most have decorative borders completed with stylized leaves, fruit or flowers.

Usually samplers are framed but the glass is frequently ill-fitting, allowing dust and insects to collect on the object. Sometimes the mount is acidic and brittle, and the frame is often found open, allowing dirt and pests to enter.

If the frame is dirty and the glass loose, the sampler may be removed and the glass and frame cleaned, both inside and out. The frame should be checked for woodworm, which should be treated, if necessary, before the piece is replaced in the frame. However, current practice and up-to-date advice should be sought from a furniture conservator before attempting to deal with the woodworm (see page 18). The glass should be sealed into the frame with brown gum strip. Any tape with a sticky and unstable adhesive should *not* be used as it will quickly break down and may cause problems.

Samplers are usually found nailed onto wooden stretchers. Sometimes tapes are stitched around the sides of the textile; these are used to nail into, thus preventing the nails from penetrating the edges of the piece. When the nails have rusted in, the rust marks may have migrated into the fabric surrounding the nailheads, causing large brown stains. If left untreated, the stains will worsen and continue to creep into the sampler edges. Ideally, the nails should be removed, the sampler generally cleaned and the rust marks treated separately.

It is seldom possible to wash a sampler as the colors may run, causing irreversible disfigurement. In the right circumstances solvent cleaning is possible, but testing of all the colors present is essential before treatment. The textile may then be remounted by stitching it onto a fabric-covered, acid-free mounting board (for method, see facing page). It should then be replaced in its original frame, prepared as described, and the back sealed using brown paper and gum strip, the simplest method.

English embroidered picture, c.1720
NAIL HOLES CAN BE SEEN AROUND THE EDGES OF THIS PICTURE, INDICATING THAT AT SOME TIME IT HAS BEEN NAILED TO A WOODEN STRETCHER. WHERE POSSIBLE, RUST MARKS OF THIS TYPE SHOULD BE REMOVED BY A SKILLED CONSERVATOR.

Flat Textiles

Flat textiles – including woven fabric lengths, silks, printed cottons, velvets, brocades, damasks and lace – are not straightforward to clean. Apart from possible fragility due to age, many have finishes or dressings that may be dissolved during cleaning, thus radically damaging the fabric. Metal threads, which may be incorporated into the weave of some of these fabrics, increase cleaning problems because of their individual and complex structures and tendency to snag the cloth.

Velvets can be particularly deceptive. They may seem sound, robust fabrics, but in reality their pile is fragile and deteriorates easily. Careless scuffing of the surface or even stroking the hand over the pile can result in silk loss and the appearance of bruising. Once the pile has been lost the damage is irreparable. Conversely, the pile of a velvet may be crushed but the fiber structure may still be intact. In this case, treatment by light steaming will cause the fibers to relax and lift up, giving an immediate visual improvement.

Velvet should only be lightly steamed and should not be allowed to get too damp – and certainly not wet. During steaming the pile should not be touched or brushed. Ideally, a small hand steamer (available from some electrical shops) should be used, which emits light steam for a few minutes. If, alternatively, a tea kettle is used to steam the velvet, take care not to get the textile too wet or to hold the kettle too close to the surface of the textile, since the heat of the steam will damage the fabric.

Flat textiles should never be ironed. The direct application of heat by ironing can lead to accelerated degradation of an already deteriorating fabric. Steaming a fabric and then allowing it to dry while hanging is a useful method of removing creases from textiles.

PREPARING TEXTILES FOR FRAMING

If a flat textile is to be displayed, it should be mounted by stitching it onto a fabric-covered, acid-free, board that is cut slightly larger than the textile to be mounted. This allows for some stretch in the textile when it is laid out, and creates space for the rebate of the frame into which the board will be fitted.

The board must be covered with a suitable fabric. A heavy cotton or linen that is strong and closely woven is ideal, but if a silk or velvet is chosen an undercover of cotton must be applied to the board first.

Cover the board with the fabric, making sure that the grain is straight and that the fabric is smooth and will stretch evenly in both directions. Cut the fabric about 3–4in larger all around than the board. Use a water-soluble woodworking adhesive to stick the surplus fabric to the back of the board, leaving the front free but the fabric firmly stretched across it. The corners of the fabric should be mitered to ensure that they fit tightly around the edges of the board.

When the fabric at the back of the board is dry, it may be trimmed back to 2in, if necessary, and the edges masked off with a single strip of acid-free brown gum strip in order to give a good finish.

Place the textile object squarely on the front of the prepared fabric-covered board and, if it is strong, put it under slight tension to prevent the possibility of sagging. Pin the textile out. If possible, the pins should be placed between the weave structure, so as not to pierce fragile threads. Stitch the textile to the fabric with a curved needle, keeping the direction of each stitch at right-angles to the object's edge. Remove pins as the stitching progresses. If mounted in this way, the object will be suitably prepared for framing. It is important to make sure that any textile on display is kept out of direct sunlight.

Lace

Lace can make up wedding veils, dress flounces, fichus, small lappets, handkerchiefs and costume trimmings. It may be made from linen thread, silk or cotton and be cut work with needle-woven insertions, bobbin lace (worked with a variable number of threads), or needle lace (worked with a single thread in a series of detached looped stitches). Decorative lace motifs may have been applied onto a net ground or worked directly into a ground, or the motifs and ground may have been made together as one. Sometimes separate motifs were joined together with linkages that form the structural basis of the piece.

It is important to identify the fiber from which the lace is made before considering any treatment. It is also important to identify the method of manufacture as different tensions are created within the lace by different methods of construction.

The most familiar type of lace is cream, but it can also be black (as in Chantilly lace) or colored. Some lace is made

Detail of an 18th-century Brussels lace wedding veil
LARGE PIECES OF LACE SUCH AS WEDDING VEILS SHOULD BE HANDLED WITH GREAT CARE, AND ARE PARTICULARLY FRAGILE WHEN WET. WHILE IT IS FREQUENTLY POSSIBLE TO REMOVE STAINS, IT IS NOT ADVISABLE TO WASH FINE LACE AT HOME WITHOUT SEEKING THE ADVICE OF A CONSERVATOR.

from gold (silver-gilt) or silver metal thread and, occasionally, silk-wrapped parchment bands. White lace was rarely, if ever, a bright white; rather, it was a creamy-white shade. Much antique lace has been damaged by ill-advised chemical treatments that have rendered it unnaturally white.

When lace is found gray or yellowed with age, it can be brought back to creamy white. Stains may be removed or reduced to a cream color, and even dark brown stains may be reduced to pale yellow by skilled treatment. Once lace has been harshly bleached to a bright white little can be done to bring it back to a more appropriate soft shade. Dyeing it back to a more natural color would not be acceptable, as to follow one harsh treatment with a chemical dyeing process would only cause more problems and increase the risk of long-term damage.

Professional conservators are usually able to remove iron stains from lace. Mold, damp marks and other stains can be removed or lessened providing the lace is made from a cellulose fiber (linen or cotton). If, however, the lace is made from a protein fiber (silk) or constructed on a silk net ground, fewer treatments are possible. Some types of lace, such as eighteenth-century silk "blond," were a pale straw color by design and should be kept that color.

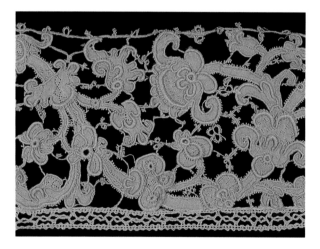

Italian gros-point needle lace, c.1660
IN THIS TYPE OF LACE, SEPARATE MOTIFS MADE FROM FINE LINEN THREADS ARE JOINED TOGETHER BY FANCY LINKAGES THAT FORM THE STRUCTURAL BASIS OF THE PIECE. THIS TYPE OF CONSTRUCTION CAUSES UNEVEN AND DIFFERING TENSIONS WITHIN THE LACE, WHICH MUST BE TAKEN INTO ACCOUNT IN ANY CLEANING OR CONSERVATION WORK. PARTICULAR CARE MUST BE TAKEN WHEN WASHING THIS TYPE OF LACE AS IT IS LIABLE TO CURL UP AND BECOME DISTORTED IF NOT TREATED PROPERLY.

Lace should be handled with consideration because of its open texture and fragility. Fingernails should be filed smooth to make sure they have no jagged edges, and rings should be removed to prevent claws or stones catching in the mesh. When examining lace it is often helpful to lay it upon a dark background fabric to make the pattern, broken linkages, old cobbled repairs and areas where motifs are missing easier to see. Crude repairs should be removed. Unpicking old repairs and constructing new ones is highly skilled, exacting work, which often requires the conservator to work with magnifying lenses.

The beauty of fine lace may be better appreciated when it is set against a contrasting silk or velvet background fabric. When sewn to the fabric-covered board the stitching must not pierce the structure of the lace in case lace threads are broken, but be laid across them.

Large pieces of lace are difficult to handle because of their size. They should not be washed at home as they are likely to be particularly fragile when wet.

Fans

Fans are among the most difficult of textile objects to conserve as they are highly delicate in construction. Fans may have a fixed leaf, they may be folding, sometimes opening out to form a complete circle, or they may comprise sticks strung together, as in *brisé* fans.

Fan leaves can be made from plain silk, silk gauze, lace, paper, leather or parchment; they may be painted, stamped or embellished with embroidery, sequins and other applied decorations. The sticks of a folding fan could be made from wood, bone, ivory, lacquer, mother-of-pearl, tortoiseshell, metals (base and precious), jade or plastic. They may be heavily carved and ornamented, gilded and mounted with jewels, or left plain or polished.

DAMAGE AND CONSERVATION
Most fans comprise mixed media, and all parts – leaves, sticks, and the ribbons used for stringing the sticks together – are subject to damage. Fans were made to be used and because of this it is common to find that they have previously suffered damage and have been repaired. These old repairs can cause problems for the conservator.

Sticks, particularly heavily carved guards, are often dirty, and have dark deposits of dust ingrained into the carving which may be sticky with a film of skin grease. It is normally possible to clean sticks without having to remove the fan leaf. However, if the leaf itself needs repair or cleaning, it may be necessary to remove it from the fan and treat it separately.

Italian fan with straw-work appliqué, c.1620
FANS ARE USUALLY MADE OF MIXED MEDIA (HERE STRAW AND
SILK) AND ARE HIGHLY VULNERABLE. THEY SHOULD IDEALLY BE
STORED IN A STABLE ENVIRONMENT. (TOP)

French embroidered fan, c.1760
EMBROIDERED ON SILK, WITH IVORY, SEQUINS AND PAINTED
CHINOISERIE FACES, THIS FAN POSES COMPLEX PROBLEMS FOR THE
CONSERVATOR. (ABOVE)

Folding fans should only be worked on with the
support of a tailored and specially shaped sloping fan
board, precisely graded and designed to give full support
along the length of each stick. This is important when
cleaning sticks as they break easily with light pressure.
Because sticks are brittle and break easily, cleaning is
usually better left to a professional conservator.

STORAGE AND DISPLAY

Fans should be stored closed, either in their original boxes
(if possible) or individually wrapped in acid-free tissue.
When displayed open, fans should be sealed in glazed
frames, fan cases or a dust-proof display cabinet. Fan-
shaped cases are available from specialized picture framers.
If mounted on a rectangular board, this should be sealed in
a deep frame, ensuring the fan does not touch the glass.

Hats

Like other mixed-media objects, hats pose complex
problems as far as care and conservation are concerned.
Where severe damage is found – such as trimmings and
ribbons torn and crushed, and the basic structure altered –
then the advice of a professional must be sought.

If a hat is not badly damaged but only a little crushed and "tired-looking," a light steaming may prove beneficial. The hat must be thoroughly examined beforehand to make sure the trimmings are not heat- and water-sensitive. Steam may damage wax flowers and cause curled feather decoration to loose its curl. After steaming the hat should be left on a stand to dry out thoroughly.

An expert will often be able to repair broken construction wires and support damaged fabrics. Feathers can be cleaned and broken ones mended if all the parts are present. Wires supporting flower and leaf sprays can be replaced, and the sprays made to stand up again. Straw can be repaired, and lace and veiling cleaned.

STORAGE

Hats should never be stacked one on top of another. Large, heavy hats should not be stored resting on their brims, which in time will sink down under the weight of the crown and trimmings, causing damage.

Ideally, each hat should be cushioned on a support stand and stored in an acid-free box or clean, spacious cupboard. Strong but simple-to-make stands may be constructed using acid-free tissue. Tissue rings and sausages are first made, then joined together and fashioned to fit each hat exactly. For a conservator, to make a stand for even the most complicated shape, such as a bonnet, should take only ten to fifteen minutes. Ribbons, bows and loops may be cushioned with small sausages of tissue to prevent a hard crease forming in the fold line.

For permanent display, tailored stands can be constructed using acid-free card, polyester wadding and a fabric cover. If a hat is professionally conserved, it would be advisable to ask for a stand to be provided for permanent safekeeping and display of the hat.

Many hats are soiled on the band inside the crown with hair grease, sweat or make-up. A hat should not be stored in this condition as insects may be attracted by these types of soiling. A conservator should advise on the most appropriate methods of cleaning.

Shoes

Shoes also fall into the category of mixed-media, three-dimensional objects. When stored they should be padded with acid-free tissue or have a purpose-made polyethylene terephthalate insert so they hold their shape. Shoe trees can be used, but only in strong leather shoes – providing they do not overstress the fabric of the shoe and are not made of a plastic, possibly unstable, material. Tissue padding is much safer for fragile fabric shoes.

If a single shoe from a pair is displayed, a light level of no higher than 50 lux must be ensured and display should be for only a short time, the exact period depending on the condition of the object in question. Both shoes will fade, but the shoe on display will probably fade more quickly than the one in storage, thus spoiling the pair's integrity.

Plastics

Many twentieth-century shoes and bags, especially couture pieces, are made from or incorporate "plastics." "Plastics" can harden rapidly when the polymers break down and set in whatever shape they happen to be in. If a plastic object is crushed or misshapen due to bad storage, then it will harden into that malformed shape. Other "plastics" go granular or sticky as they break down.

Without scientific analysis it is impossible to determine the composition of the plastic and therefore what degradation products to expect, but it is wise not to store plastics with other textiles and to give them plenty of space in an airy, cool, dark environment.

Historic Costume

Historic costume should never be worn. Fabrics and stitching may be weak, and the risk of splitting should not be minimized. If soiling with perspiration, food or drink occurs, it may not be possible to remove it.

Costume should not be stored in a dirty condition. Historic costume – men's as well as women's – is usually not strong enough to withstand commercial dry-cleaning in a tumble-action machine, however, so advice and treatment by a conservator are advisable.

Alterations may have been made to a costume, and it may be desirable to return the item to its original style. This is specialized conservation work, since stitch marks, pleat lines, wear lines and other evidence of the original style may be overlooked by an untrained eye.

BEADED COSTUME

Beaded costume can cause particular problems as beads and sequins may be made of many different substances and have further applied coatings or finishes. Beads can be made of glass, metal, natural stones, coral, pearls (natural and artificial) and plastic. Glass beads may be solid or thin-walled and hollow, sometimes filled with wax; they may have an iridescent pearlized coating or be painted. All these materials may be water- or solvent-sensitive. Also, beads may be stitched onto a fine net which is possibly at risk because of the weight of the beads.

*French late 18th-century
silk-satin open robe*
HISTORIC COSTUME SHOULD
BE STORED AND DISPLAYED
WITH CARE TO ENSURE THAT
IT IS ADEQUATELY
SUPPORTED, WITH NO POINTS
OF STRAIN. IT SHOULD NOT
UNDER ANY CIRCUMSTANCES
BE WORN, AS THE STITCHING
IS FREQUENTLY NOT STRONG
ENOUGH TO WITHSTAND
WEAR, AND IRREVERSIBLE
DAMAGE CAN BE DONE BY
PERSPIRATION OR FOOD
STAINS. (RIGHT)

*Detail of open robe
showing front lacing*
IT IS IMPORTANT TO EXAMINE
THE DETAILS OF
CONSTRUCTION CAREFULLY,
AS THEY OFTEN REVEAL
ALTERATIONS THAT MAY
PROVIDE EVIDENCE OF
RESTYLING AND OF CHANGING
FASHIONS. (ABOVE)

Some glass beads, usually found on costumes of the late nineteenth and early twentieth centuries, suffer from a phenomenon known as glass disease. The beads were usually manufactured using soda glass or potash glass, and, in the presence of atmospheric humidity above 42% alkali, mineral salts leach out from the beads, causing cracking and crumbling of their structure. It may also cause spots of color to be bleached out of the dress fabric where the beads touch it. Costume with glass disease must be kept at or below 40% relative humidity.

STORAGE AND DISPLAY

Most costume should be stored hanging on padded hangers and covered with cotton-lawn dust covers or dust bags, not plastic dry-cleaning bags. Costumes should not be packed too tightly together when hanging.

Fragile costume, including 1920s beaded net dresses, should be stored flat, the folds padded out with acid-free tissue sausages. If parts of the garment are folded over, tissue should be interleaved between the layers.

If costume is displayed, it should be in a dust-proof case. The costume should be prepared on a purpose-made stand that is the correct size to support adequately. Underpinnings such as petticoats are essential to support a heavy skirt and prevent sagging.

Costume should not be on permanent display. Despite the measures taken to protect them, they still suffer some damage from light, pests and pollution, which is why most museums prefer to rotate the exhibition of their collections of historic garments and accessories.

Large Textiles

Large textiles come in many forms, including tapestries, bed hangings, curtains, copes, altar frontals and tent hangings. Their most common conservation problems are due to a combination of size, weight, and the fragility caused by degradation of the fabrics.

ENVIRONMENTAL CONDITIONS

All textiles are hygroscopic in that they react physically to moisture and dryness and are therefore vulnerable to changes in environmental conditions. An increase in humidity will cause the textile to take in moisture, relax and drop if it is hanging. As the temperature rises and the textile dries out, it will tighten and may return to its previous dimensions. Large textiles have an equally large capacity for reaction to environmental changes and will gain weight if they take in moisture. Stability of the environment is thus important in preserving textiles.

Detail of Belgian 18th-century tapestry showing damage
THIS SORT OF DAMAGE, WHERE AREAS OF THE SILK WEFT HAVE DEGRADED AND FALLEN OUT, LEAVING WARPS BARE AND WEAK AREAS GAPING, IS TYPICAL OF THE WEAR AND TEAR SUFFERED BY TAPESTRIES. A TAPESTRY IN THIS CONDITION SHOULD NOT BE HUNG, AS THE FORCE OF ITS OWN WEIGHT IS LIKELY TO INCREASE DAMAGE FURTHER. THE SIZE, WEIGHT, AND FRAGILITY OF SUCH HANGINGS MAKE THEM DIFFICULT TO REPAIR.

HANGING

A large textile that is intended to be hung for display should be lined in order to stop dust from penetrating its fabric from behind. However, the lining should not be stitched and linked in too tightly or the textile will pull against the lining as it moves.

The most commonly practised method of hanging large textiles today makes use of Velcro. Sometimes it is stitched directly onto the back of the lined textile, and sometimes with heavier objects, such as large tapestries and rugs, it is first sewn onto a band of heavy fabric, which is in turn stitched onto the object.

When a tapestry or large textile is hanging, the weight must be evenly distributed along the top edge; first stitching the Velcro to a band which is then sewn along the top edge of the hanging will help spread the load and save having to sew through all the layers of fabric and Velcro at once. When applying Velcro directly to a hanging, large enough stitches should be made so that they pass over two or three warps of the fabric.

Conservators repairing a 16th-century tapestry
THE REPAIR OF TAPESTRIES IS PARTICULARLY TIME-CONSUMING AND REQUIRES A GREAT DEAL OF SPACE, AS THE TAPESTRIES MUST BE LAID OUT FLAT BOTH FOR EXAMINATION AND FOR TREATMENT. IT IS ALSO A VERY COMPLEX PROCEDURE, AS IT MAY INVOLVE RESEWING SLITS, SUPPORTING DAMAGED AREAS WITH PATCHES AND REPAIRING THEM BY COUCHING, AND REWARPING AREAS THAT ARE MISSING. IF THE TAPESTRY IS VERY WEAK, IT MAY ALSO NEED A FULL SUPPORT OR INTERLINING IF IT IS TO BE HUNG. THE PROCESS OF REPAIR IS OFTEN A LENGTHY ONE, AND CAN TAKE MANY YEARS.

CLEANING AND STORAGE

It is not a viable proposition to wash or solvent clean large textiles constantly, but surface dust should be vacuumed off on a regular basis, perhaps once a year. The nozzle of the vacuum cleaner should be covered with fine net to prevent any loose threads from the object being pulled and sucked into the cleaner, thus causing the textile to tear. If the textile can be taken down and laid flat, a piece of fine nylon net may be stretched across it to form a protective screen before vacuuming is carried out (see also page 151).

Large textiles should be stored wrapped around rollers with a diameter of at least 4in, which are strong enough to support the weight of the textile. They should be interleaved with a heavyweight acid-free tissue or with cotton sheeting, and be wrapped in a cover of strong, dust-proof cloth. The rolls should be stored lying down on shelves or racks, or, better still, suspended by their ends so that no part of the textile is resting on a hard shelf. They should not be stored on the floor, where they will pick up dust, or upright.

REPAIR AND RESTORATION

The repair of large textiles is particularly time-consuming due to their size, and several factors have to be considered before embarking on it. The condition of the textile will dictate if repair by patching will be sufficient, or whether a full support of interlining will be needed. If this is the case, it will be necessary to carry out the work on a frame.

Old repairs may be causing distortions and have to be removed before any new work is carried out. Many weeks may be needed for the preparation work before actual repair is started. A space where the whole object can be laid out flat for examination and treatment, possibly for some time, is essential. Large textiles are therefore not the sort of objects to repair in a domestic situation where space is a problem and time to concentrate on the work is limited. The conservation of tapestries is a particular skill and should not be undertaken by inexperienced people. It can involve cleaning, slit sewing, rewarping and couched repairs, all of which can cause further damage to the object if not carried out correctly.

SCULPTURE AND STATUARY

Despite the apparent stability and resistance of stone and metal, from which sculpture and statuary are frequently made, they run a gamut of risks in the garden, the conservatory and the home.

The visual pleasure which these works of art give depends on their surface finish, their sculptural detail and their structural integrity. Since surface degradation and loss of patina, as well as scratches, bruises, fractures and structural damage are especially difficult to repair or disguise, preventing misadventure assumes primary importance.

Outdoors, pollution and rain combine to attack the surface of stone and marble. Frost, moisture and soluble salts, and the action of lichen, moss and ivy also degrade their surface, and plants in close proximity cause staining. Bronze and lead statues are at risk from severe cracking and distortion when moisture corrodes their internal armatures. Conservatories are also unsuitable for statuary, with their high levels of humidity and profusion of plants.

Indoors, staining, discoloration and overzealous cleaning, as well as accidental knocks, are the greatest hazards facing bronze statues, marble tabletops, stone fire surrounds and alabaster reliefs. Sculptures in wood, ivory and bone are likely to suffer from a dry as well as humid atmosphere, and from the effects of strong light.

A Priestess of Isis, attributed to John Cheere, 1740s
THIS PIECE, NOW AT SALTRAM HOUSE IN DEVON, ENGLAND, HIGHLIGHTS THE NEED FOR REGULAR CARE OF GARDEN SCULPTURE. WHILE OWNERS WILL READILY ACCEPT THAT HOUSES SHOULD BE KEPT IN SOUND STRUCTURAL CONDITION, SCULPTURE IS OFTEN NEGLECTED AND IS RARELY SUBJECT TO THE SORT OF MAINTENANCE THAT FORMS THE BASIS OF ALL GOOD CONSERVATION.

Sculpture embraces an enormous range of natural and synthetic materials. Very often several materials are combined together in one object (for instance marble, bronze and ivory), which can create problems for their conservation because the different materials may need to be treated or stored in ways that are mutually deleterious.

Frequently sculpture is placed in extremely hostile environments, which will guarantee its eventual decay. Marble, stone and bronze statues are often sited in gardens or conservatories and around swimming pools, where it is difficult to control variations of temperature and humidity. Museums try to stabilize the atmosphere in which objects are displayed by sealing them in glass cases or in air-conditioned rooms, but for the private collector these measures are often too expensive or inappropriate for normal living conditions. Therefore, it is necessary to take some simple precautions – with the advice of a professional sculpture conservator – in order to reduce the effects of environmental damage.

Art Deco chryselephantine figure

THIS FIGURE COMBINES IVORY, BRONZE, MARBLE AND PAINT. COMBINATIONS OF DIVERSE MEDIA PRESENT PROBLEMS OF CLEANING, AND THEREFORE REQUIRE SPECIALIZED ATTENTION.

Stone and Marble Outdoors

For most people, marble and stone are equated with permanence and durability. Many of the oldest works of art in the world are carved in some form of natural rock, so it is difficult to understand that a stone sculpture requires the same amount of care as a painting, textile, or work on paper. The artistic value of any stone or marble sculpture depends on the quality of its surface finish. If that surface is removed by weathering or injudicious cleaning, the sculpture is irreparably damaged. A bruise or scratch on a marble statue presents as serious a loss as on a painting; but whereas a painting's losses can be "touched in," those on a marble sculpture are far less easy to disguise.

STONE DECAY

During the last three decades conservators and scientists have undertaken extensive studies into the nature of stone decay and its causes. Pollutant gases in the atmosphere, derived from the burning of fossil fuels for power generation or from vehicular exhaust, are seen as the prime reasons for stone decay. The popular term "acid rain" describes the chief agency of decay, a combination of gases mixed with airborne moisture to form weak acidic solutions that slowly dissolve the carbonaceous or siliceous base of which most marbles and stones are composed.

The other main agencies of decay in external stone are frost, ground salts, contact with corroding metals, structural movement, and organic growths such as lichens, mosses and ivies. The common factor in all these mechanisms of decay is water. Moisture, whether rain, rising damp or simply the humidity in a conservatory, will act as a catalyst for pollution, salts, biodeterioration, plant growths and metal corrosion. By keeping sculpture as dry as possible the rate of its decay can therefore be reduced.

COVERING SCULPTURE

Covering garden sculpture in winter has long been regarded as beneficial because it protects marble and stone against the mechanical stress associated with the freezing and thawing cycles of frost and snow. Unfortunately, some methods used to protect sculpture are often crude and can sometimes result in unnecessary damage, such as covering a sculpture with straw and then tying a tarpaulin around it. It is difficult to be certain that any stone sculpture or urn is completely dry when it is covered. Surrounding it with straw and tarpaulin merely ensures that it will remain wet throughout the winter, and salts and biological growth will continue their expansion and metal cramps and fixings will corrode.

The best form of covering for a sculpture allows the free passage of air around it, thus helping it to dry out during the winter. A form of sentry box with a pitched roof made of marine plywood (appropriately sealed or varnished), with air vents at the top and bottom and a secure method for fixing it to the ground so that it will not blow over in the wind, has proved the best method for this task. Neither the sculpture nor its pedestal should come into contact with the box, nor should they be used as securing points for the construction of the box.

External statuary is often used for architectural decoration, and in classical and Gothic schemes was usually protected from the effects of water by hood moldings or niches. However, in many old buildings these architectural moldings have been allowed to decay. The rainwater that would have been directed away from the building by the moldings, falls instead on the sculpture. It is therefore important to ensure that all moldings are kept in good order and perform their functions properly.

REBUILDING SUPPORTS

Rising damp, a very common cause of decay in sculpture, cannot be alleviated without rebuilding the support or pedestal beneath the object. As most sculptures and urns are attached to stone-clad pedestals with a brick core, they are in direct contact with the earth and will readily absorb ground moisture and salts. The continuous migration of salts through stone and their gradual efflorescence and expansion beneath the dry outer surface of the stone cause harmful flaking, which in extreme cases can lead to a complete loss of surface detail.

To cut off the source of damp, the sculpture and its pedestal should be dismantled and rebuilt. To ensure that the whole structure is based on a strong foundation, a concrete raft should be laid, which is greater in width than the sculpture to give stability and avoid subsidence. A lead, damp-proof membrane should be placed on top of the raft to stop the absorption of salts and moisture. Over the membrane a new core of brick or stone can be

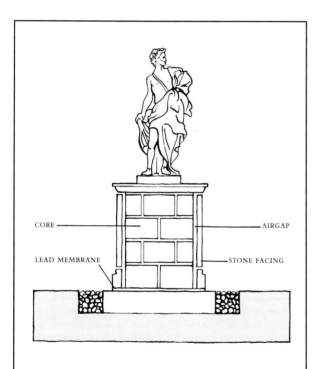

CORE — AIRGAP

LEAD MEMBRANE — STONE FACING

Displaying and mounting garden sculpture
Garden sculpture should be mounted on a plinth of traditional materials over an impermeable membrane. The pedestal should be set in firm concrete foundations in a trench filled with gravel for drainage, again protected by a damp-proof membrane.

17th-century marble bust, attributed to Jan Pieter van Baurscheit
THE ELABORATELY CARVED SURFACES OF SUCH PIECES ARE OFTEN BLURRED BY APPLICATIONS OF WAX AND CONSTANT BUFFING.

Marble bust of Alexander Pope, Roubiliac, 1741
THIS IS AN UNUSUALLY WELL-PRESERVED VERSION OF THIS
PORTRAIT. OTHER EXAMPLES HAVE LOST THEIR DELICATE SURFACE
TEXTURE DUE TO REPEATED CLEANING WITH ABRASIVES OR
STRONG ACIDIC OR ALKALINE CLEANERS.

constructed and, finally, the stone cladding of the pedestal can be reconstructed around it. Avoid using portland cement in reconstruction, as this can damage old stone. If new cramps and dowels are used to secure stone or marble, they should be of the best-quality stainless steel. Copper and bronze are not suitable as they can cause copper staining and are not as strong as stainless steel.

PLANT GROWTH

One of the most disfiguring features commonly encountered on garden sculpture is plant growth. Many people may find the appearance of a sculpture half-buried in lichens or mosses somewhat romantic, but plants do cause considerable damage to stone. Not only do they stain the surface of sculpture, but they often secrete weak acids that damage the structure of marble. In seeking moisture in the stone, ivies often dig into the surface with their tendrils, creating numerous pits and boreholes. The removal of such growths is a skillful operation and should not be attempted by the amateur. Attempting the removal of

algae and lichens with commercial biocides can, in fact, do more harm than good, for many of these preparations deposit chemicals in the stone that may stain it or – worse – cause it to break down.

Often vegetal growth can be discouraged by siting sculpture in an appropriate setting. For instance, if a sculpture is placed under a tree not only will rainwater drip onto it, but it will remain wetter and damper than one sited in an open, airy surrounding and so encourage plants to establish themselves. Shrubs that are allowed to grow up around a sculpture will not only keep it damp, but the branches will scratch the surface.

Stone and Marble Indoors

External sculpture is not the only type of statuary affected by atmospheric pollution, as anyone living in an urban environment or near a busy road will have found out when their marble sculpture has yellowed from the build-up of pollutant gases. Indeed, marbles kept near doors or windows often become noticeably yellow within a year. Although such discoloration will not cause surface loss, it can be unappealing and does provoke some people to clean sculpture more often than is necessary.

CLEANING

A marble sculpture should only be cleaned thoroughly once every thirty or forty years. Constant cleaning damages the surface polish and blurs the details. Much of the sculpture kept in historic houses, museums and churches has been routinely cleaned in the past with strong acids, alkalis and even abrasives. To treat a fine marble carving in this way is akin to scrubbing the surface of a fine painting, and does irreparable harm.

All marble and stone sculpture should be cleaned by a professional conservator. The only treatment advisable by the untrained person is dusting the surface with a fine white-haired bristle brush to remove surface dust. The metal ferrules of the brush should be bound with masking tape so that they do not scratch the marble. Feather dusters and polishing cloths should not be used to remove dust from sculptures, as these will often redeposit the dirt that has previously accumulated.

Should marble sculptures, fireplaces or tabletops be stained by wine, grease or paint, no attempt should be made to remove the mark with a damp cloth or detergent. The stain should be left to dry and the services of a professional conservator sought to draw it out. Vigorous rubbing with a cloth while the stain is damp will only serve to drive it in further and make it permanent.

DISPLAY AND PROTECTION

One of the fundamental misconceptions that people have about marble and stone is that because they are heavy, they are necessarily strong. This is not the case. A marble bust mounted on a marble, wooden or scagliola (imitation marble) column is essentially a vulnerable object, top-heavy and unstable, and an inadvertent push could shatter it into many pieces. Whenever heavy sculpture is being displayed, always consider the substratum on which it is to stand. To place a bust and supporting pedestal on top of a carpet is unsafe because the carpet is flexible. A sprung wooden floor will also cause similar problems. Wherever possible heavy sculpture should be sited on a solid masonry, brick or concrete floor; if this is not possible, it may be necessary to place metal plates under the pedestal to provide a stable foundation.

Damage to sculpture commonly results from a lack of care during house refurbishment or decoration. Simply covering a bust or figure with a dustsheet will afford little protection against scaffolding, ladders and wooden planks. Sculpture should be protected during decoration with boxes made of heavy-duty plywood and battening.

STAINING

Both marble and stone surfaces can often be disfigured by unsightly stains. In Carrara marble this can result from a number of causes, such as repeated washing, which will turn marble brown or orange because the natural iron in the marble (iron pyrites) has corroded when saturated with moisture. A brown or yellow stain can result from the use of strong acid or alkali solutions. Metal cramps or dowels used for securing a bust to its socle will also create strong local staining. The use of fats, soaps and oils to clean, protect or seal a marble during molding (casting) can also produce similar stains. The staining of some Classical and Renaissance sculptures may result from the residues of paint media from surfaces that were once brightly colored or gilded. Some stains may also result from bacterial activity. Whatever their origin, stains should never be tampered with by the amateur as they will invariably become worse.

SITING SCULPTURE

The siting of sculpture in a domestic environment is of considerable importance. Sculpture often forms a signifi-cant feature in both marble and stone fireplaces. If the fireplaces are in use, the stone will necessarily suffer some discoloration from the resultant currents of fumes, smoke and warm air. With wood fires some degree of blackening in both stone and marble is to be expected, but this can be

Sculptures from Petworth House, England
MARBLE AND STONE BUSTS ARE BOTH HEAVY AND FRAGILE. THE SLENDER BASES ON WHICH THEY ARE FREQUENTLY MOUNTED MUST THEREFORE BE SECURELY ANCHORED TO THE FLOOR OR WALL.

prevented from occurring in an undamaged fireplace by seeking professional advice to find a suitable sealant. However, where the soot and smoke are deeply ingrained, one can only hope for limited success.

Placing reliefs or other sculpture above radiators or heating vents is to be discouraged. Convected warm air passing over marble and stone will not only carry dust and dirt with it, but the warmth will dry out any wooden frames supporting the sculpture, creating the threat of warping and permanent damage.

PACKING AND MOVING

The packing and transportation of marble and stone sculptures, which are both brittle and porous, often result in losses and disfigurements. If a marble figure is inadequately or incorrectly supported during lifting or moving, it will often crack in one of the more vulnerable parts, such as the ankles, neck, arms or fingers.

Wooden cases are flexible by nature, so every attempt should be made to reinforce them with battens or metal

plates. Cases should always be screwed together, never nailed. The use of nail and hammer can create immense stresses on the brittle sculpture inside the case.

Because stone and marble are porous, the packing materials used for wrapping should not contain any dyes. Colored felt, wadding or straw should be avoided at all cost. Where possible only acid-free tissue, inert foam, bubble wrap or polystyrene pellets should be allowed to come into contact with the surface of the sculpture. If marble or stone has a weathered or deteriorating surface, a conservator should be called in to carry out some consolidation or other appropriate protective treatment before the object is packed and moved.

Slate and Other Impermeable Stones

Monumental and decorative carvings made of slate, Istrian stone, Purbeck marble, Verona marble and other impermeable stones do not readily absorb moisture. Their maintenance therefore requires a quite different approach from that needed for porous stones.

SURFACE COATINGS

It is very dangerous to put surface coatings on porous rocks such as Carrara marble or Portland stone, since the moisture absorbed under an impervious coating will cause exfoliation and spalling (splintering) as it migrates towards the surface, but dense materials such as slate and Istrian stone do not suffer from this problem. They can be treated by a conservator with a surface coating such as microcrystalline wax and acrylic resins. These should be applied on a cyclical basis of five to ten years.

CONDENSATION DAMAGE

Purbeck marble, which is truly a limestone, has commonly been used for monuments in English churches since the early Medieval period. The main agency of decay would appear to be condensation. Whereas hard stones such as slate and Purbeck marble often weather well outside, they can deteriorate badly indoors when subjected to prolonged exposure to high humidity. Slate (and some marble) memorials are often disfigured by condensation streaks. Because the stones are very cold and have highly polished surfaces, condensation forms on the surface when heating is turned on in buildings. Over a period of years – sometimes several hundred – the rivulets of water will etch into the stone, removing the polish and disfiguring the surface. The only treatment in this case is to try to balance the humidity and temperature, and to treat the stone with a moisture-proof coating.

Coade Stone and Terracotta

Although the product manufactured by the Coade factory in Lambeth, south London, in the eighteenth and early nineteenth centuries was described as an artificial stone, it is in fact a ceramic and shows many of the characteristics of terracotta, a hard, unglazed, brownish earthenware. Coade stone (and many of its later nineteenth-century imitations) is commonly found in garden statuary, or as decoration on building façades. Its durability is well attested by the large numbers of sculptures and architectural decorations that have survived to this day. The success of the material apparently lies in both the blending of clays and other minerals and their prolonged firing (up to four days) to a temperature of between 2012°F and 2102°F, which produces a highly vitrified material.

COADE STONE DETERIORATION

Due to its manufacturing process, Coade stone occasionally deteriorates. It was produced by casting the ceramic body into plaster piece-molds, a technique resulting in a very dense skin on the surface (which is increased by firing), and a much coarser and more porous body beneath it. When subjected to the movement of capillary moisture or salts, the thin hard skin often spalls from the surface, leaving the more porous body beneath as vulnerable to weathering and pollution as is limestone.

TERRACOTTA DISPLAY

Within conservatories terracotta suffers the usual problems caused by high humidity and light levels – disfigurement by algae and other organic growths. Within a domestic environment the two most serious causes of damage are mechanical damage and the absorption of dirt and grease into the surface. Terracotta is extremely brittle and, if knocked over or exposed to structural stress during transportation, will easily break or shatter. If an accident occurs, great care should be taken to make sure that every fragment is carefully picked up and placed in labeled boxes so that the conservator can readily identify fragments for the work of reconstruction.

Unlike glazed ceramics (such as those produced by the della Robbia family in Florence), terracotta sculpture does not have a hard coating to stop the absorption of grease and dirt. In common with Parian ware, it has a highly absorbent surface. Just as early collectors of Parian protected their sculptures by keeping them under glass domes, so terracotta sculpture is best kept in glass showcases. Without this protection such pieces will invariably become marred by patches of ingrained dirt.

Although terracotta sculpture is usually thought of in its natural color, it has been a common tradition in both Europe and Asia to paint terracotta. Today it is rare to see full naturalistic polychromy on a sculpture (much of it having been removed by nineteenth- and twentieth-century aesthetes and restorers who objected to the vulgarity of the painting), but monochromatic schemes can sometimes be found intact. The terracotta sculptures of eighteenth-century artists such as Clodion, Roubiliac and Rysbrack were often painted with thin washes of terracotta-colored paint to disguise any damage that may have occurred during firing. Such treatments are original and they should not be removed.

Lead figure of a shepherd boy, 1710
WHILE LEAD SCULPTURE MAY NOT DISPLAY OUTWARD SIGNS OF CORROSION, CRACKING AND SPLITTING ARE COMMON PROBLEMS. (RIGHT)

Bronze and Lead

Metal sculpture is often considered "durable," and is commonly encountered in the form of garden sculpture or fountain ornament. It is, however, highly susceptible to attack from moisture, salts and many forms of moisture-aggravated corrosion. The public's image of external bronze statuary is most frequently of objects that have developed a pronounced patina. The chemical changes that can take place on the surface of a bronze during years of exposure are sometimes the result of natural ageing or in other cases the signs of rapid disintegration. To attempt to arrest these changes by applying impervious coatings may well trap corrosion and accelerate the decay.

CORROSION OF SUPPORTS

One of the most common causes of decay in bronze sculpture is the corrosion of the iron support, or armature, inside. Bronze and lead sculptures are composed of thin shells of cast metal, which are relatively weak and easily bent or cracked by lateral movement. To give structural strength and coherence to the metal, a supporting frame of ferrous metal is put inside to make the sculpture more rigid and to provide sound anchorage to the supporting pedestal, which is usually of stone or marble. Ferrous metals are usually much more susceptible to corrosion from moisture and salts, and the resulting expansion and distortion of the iron often cause cracks and failure in the bronze or lead sculpture. Sadly, in the past, attempts were made to reinforce failing leads and bronzes by pouring cement inside them. Such action only creates more complex chemical reactions within the sculpture and generally increases the rate of decay of all metals that come into contact with the strongly alkaline cement.

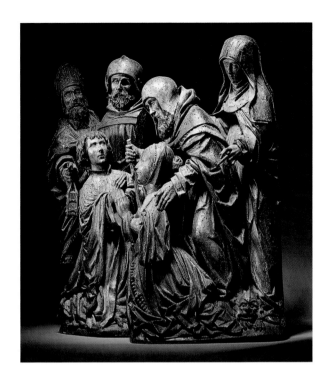

English 15th-century alabaster of the Entombment
THIS NOTTINGHAM ALABASTER RETAINS TRACES OF ORIGINAL
POLYCHROMY, WHICH IS SUSCEPTIBLE TO DAMAGE. (ABOVE)

Two German painted limewood sculptures
of Groups of Donors, c.1510–20
MOBILE WOOD WITH BRITTLE PAINT AND GESSO IS VULNERABLE
TO CHANGES IN HUMIDITY AND TEMPERATURE. (ABOVE RIGHT)

HANDLING AND CARE

Both bronze and lead can be easily scratched or scarred by
other metal objects. Gardening tools used carelessly or left
leaning against statuary will often result in deep scarring
(particularly in lead), which is often difficult to remove
without damaging the patination of the surface.

All types of metal sculpture can be covered during
winter, but great care must be taken to ensure that
moisture is not trapped within the protective covering as
this will aggravate metal corrosion.

Small bronzes present one of the most difficult areas of
conservation. Although they are usually not exposed to
weathering and are kept in the domestic environment,
they are easily damaged by abrasion, injudicious washing,
and over-zealous polishing. Very few bronzes retain the
patinations that were originally intended for them; most
result from later ages. The wisest approach is to accept the

appearance of the sculpture and simply dust it once or
twice a year with a soft hogshair brush. Carefully dislodge
more stubborn dirt with a wooden cuticle stick with
cotton wool wrapped around its tip.

Alabaster

Alabaster, a type of gypsum, is readily dissolved in water
and cannot withstand prolonged weathering, so such
sculpture is usually found indoors. Although external
examples of alabaster sculpture exist in Spain, the material
is usually treated as a more delicate form of marble, since it
is extremely brittle and easily bruised. In England alabaster
is commonly found in churches in the form of large
monuments dating from the thirteenth to the twentieth
century. The finest creamy-white alabaster of the Medieval period was highly prized because its smooth surface
provided a perfect ground for painting.

Alabaster sculpture and monuments were usually
painted, but now many have been divested of their paint
by over-enthusiastic washing and scrubbing. For those
responsible for the care of such a monument in a church
the main threat of damage comes from condensation,
rising damp and the migration of soluble salts. Prolonged
exposure to attack results in spalling and powdering of the
surface, with a resulting loss of pigment and carved detail.
The corrosion of iron cramps will lead to structural

disruption in the monument. The professional approach to treating a monument in this state is to dismantle it completely, consolidate and strengthen it, and then rebuild it against a damp-proof membrane to insulate it as far as possible from further attack from moisture and salts.

In a normal domestic situation alabaster should be very stable. The main cause of damage is scratching or bruising. Once damaged in this way it is almost impossible to disguise the blemish. Since it is also extremely brittle and the sheets of alabaster used for relief carving are often very thin, any wooden frame in which a panel is contained should be protected from distortion which may result from changes in temperature and humidity.

Plaster

Much of the plaster sculpture seen today dates from the eighteenth and nineteenth centuries. In many cases the pieces are casts – often from classical antiquities – that were either brought from Italy or manufactured by companies that specialized in reproductions. It was also common in the nineteenth century for artists to make models of sculptures in plaster for exhibition to a client or for a competition rather than presenting the original object.

Whereas stucco is made from calcium carbonate (or lime) and has some durability outdoors, plaster – which is derived from alabaster – does not. It is easily damaged by contact with moisture, and will readily grow mold if stored in damp conditions. As it is a very brittle material and cannot support much weight, plaster sculpture is often reinforced with metal armatures. These frequently corrode badly, and will cause severe orange and brown staining and cracking when affected by moisture.

To protect the absorbent surface of plaster against dust and damp, many sculptors treated the surfaces with shellac, paint and even gilding. The cleaning of such surfaces is an extremely delicate matter, and the private collector should never do anything beyond gentle dusting with a soft white hogshair brush.

Painted and Lacquered Wood

Sculpture carved in wood is sometimes unpainted, but it is more often painted or lacquered. Usually sculptors preferred fine-grained woods that carved easily, were not brittle, and would not split readily. In Europe the common carving woods were lime, boxwood, pine, oak, walnut and a number of fruitwoods. Although pine was a common carving wood in China and Japan, more exotic species such as magnolia and foxglove were also used.

WESTERN AND EASTERN METHODS

There was a marked difference of approach to the technique of making wooden sculpture in Europe from that used in the Far East. In Europe much Medieval and later sculpture is either carved from sawn planks of wood (for relief work) or from a solid tree trunk that has had the heartwood removed (so that the sculpture dries more evenly and does not split apart too readily).

The system of construction used in the Far East is very different and consists of "building up" a figure out of a number of small blocks of wood, and then joining them together with wooden dowels and animal glue. Often these blocks are individually hollowed so that the sculpture itself is composed of a wooden shell that is little more than $\frac{1}{2}$–$1\frac{1}{2}$in thick. By thinning the wood in this way, oriental sculptors were often able to avoid the damage that befalls much European sculpture, which is frequently marked by cracks and splits.

MOBILE AND BRITTLE SURFACES

Painted or lacquered wood presents a continual maintenance problem for the sculpture conservator. Wood is constantly mobile and extremely sensitive to changes in moisture and humidity – a range of 63–68°F temperature and 50–60% humidity is preferable (see page 181). Gesso, paint and lacquer are less flexible than wood and therefore react less rapidly than the wooden substrate in changing conditions, with the result that paint and gesso become detached from the mobile surface beneath.

Lacquer, which was originally applied in conditions of high humidity, is also an extremely brittle material. The large number of applications needed to form the finished surface results in a very thick, very heavy layer that will readily detach itself from the sculpture if the wood then either swells or contracts.

Beyond controlling environmental conditions there is little anyone can do to improve the state of a decaying sculpture of this type without seeking professional advice from a sculpture conservator. Displaying it in a well-constructed, airtight case will help to reduce dramatic changes to the sculpture caused by fluctuations in humidity and temperature. It will also prevent dust from gathering on the surface, and is thus to be encouraged since even the gentlest regular dusting will cause damage to a flaking polychrome or lacquered surface.

Light levels should be carefully controlled, as painted surfaces on sculpture (and pigment in lacquer) are just as vulnerable as oil paintings. They should be kept under similar light levels and, where necessary, adjustable blinds should be fitted to windows.

Head of Guan Di showing results of cleaning tests
COMBINATIONS OF DIFFERENT MATERIALS WITH WIDELY DIVERGENT CHARACTERISTICS, SUCH AS WOOD AND LACQUER, POSE PARTICULAR PROBLEMS FOR THE CONSERVATOR. WOOD IS HIGHLY MOBILE, AND LACQUER EASILY BECOMES DETACHED FROM IT.

Chinese lacquered and gilt-wood sculpture representing the god Guan Di, Ming-Qing Dynasty, 1640–1700
FAR EASTERN TECHNIQUES OF SCULPTING IN WOOD WERE VERY DIFFERENT FROM EUROPEAN PRACTISES. FIGURES SUCH AS THIS WOULD BE BUILT UP FROM SMALL BLOCKS OF WOOD JOINED TOGETHER WITH WOODEN DOWELS AND ANIMAL GLUE.

FAILING JOINTS AND PEST DAMAGE

Most sculptures have some joints or restorations, which will disintegrate. Failing glue joints and warped or cracked wood will slowly damage the sculpture. Do not glue back detached bits, as great care must be taken to choose the correct strength of glue.

The second major cause of deterioration is insect damage. Surprisingly, Chinese and Japanese sculpture does not seem to suffer as much as European sculpture. The holes made by worms or beetles are readily identified, and the appearance of a fine powdering of wood denotes that activity is still in progress and urgent treatment is necessary. The infestation should be treated by a professional, as an amateur's application of solvent-borne insecticides can permanently stain gesso and paint, as well as disrupt repairs and weaken adhesives.

Ivory and Bone

Ivory can originate from a very wide range of animal and vegetable sources. These include elephant (both African and Indian), walrus, hippopotamus, narwhal and sperm whale (all now subject to an international ban), and vegetable ivory derived from the nut of a tropical palm.

Bone is often confused with ivory (and has many similarities in its decay characteristics), but is readily distinguished by an expert, being generally lighter in weight, thinner, and more brittle. Careful inspection also shows small black dots or holes not found in ivory.

One of the most commonly collected forms of ivory carving is the tiny Japanese netsuke. Many of these carvings were originally pigmented, and where they are in very good condition much of this pigment still survives. They should be handled with great care and should never be rubbed or carried in a pocket.

Mounting netsuke can often be a problem because they are usually carved completely in the round, often making it difficult to find a suitable point of attachment for a base or shelf. However, since they are often pierced to accommodate the cords by which they were traditionally suspended, it is sometimes possible to insert a small Plexiglas peg into these holes, which also fits into a hole in the base, and thus achieve reasonable security.

CARING

Ivory can be very sensitive to moisture and humidity changes and, because of their small scale, ivory carvings can be seriously disfigured by cracks and splits. Ivory tends to grow in annual rings and therefore cracks and splits often develop in a circular pattern around the growth rings, as well as longitudinally. Because carvers often needed to use the whole thickness of the tusk, they could not hollow the tusk as readily as they could a tree trunk. This means that the tensions between the inner growth rings and the outer rings can be considerable, eventually leading to flaking and splitting.

Although ivory is best kept in an airtight case, measures can be taken to prevent its "drying out." Like human skin, ivory tends to flake when it is no longer fed by natural oils. Careful treatment of a sculpture with almond oil on an annual basis can restore some of the elasticity to a dry bone or ivory piece. Of course, nothing should be applied to the surface of ivory that is painted or gilded without first seeking expert advice. The almond oil can be painted on with a fine sable brush until the whole surface of the ivory has an oily appearance. After leaving the sculpture overnight in a cool, dry place, any surplus oil can be gently removed with cotton-tipped swabs.

DISPLAY

Ivory sculpture often changes color quite dramatically over a period of time. It is common to find that the front of a sculpture is a bright white while the back is a dark yellow or brown. This disturbing variation of color is caused by the action of light: strong daylight will bleach ivory, constant darkness will cause it to darken. When displaying ivory sculpture, put it in a filtered light and, if at all possible, move it around annually so that the source of the light is not constant, but variable.

When mounting ivory or bone sculpture, be careful not to place it on a mount covered with dyed fabrics. Many modern adhesives give off fumes that react with dyestuffs in the fabric. The resulting vapor may be acidic and cause a reaction with the ivory that results in staining. If enclosed in a case, the fumes will build up over a period of time and can sufficiently disturb the coloring agent in, for instance, a red velvet, which will transfer to the ivory and turn it pink. Many types of wood are also acidic, so if ivory is to be displayed in a wooden cabinet or on a wooden mount seek expert advice to make sure that the chosen wood will not cause instability.

Jade and Hard-Stone Sculpture

Jade is one of the hardest carving stones and, like ivory, tends to be used for small-scale sculpture. It is also extremely brittle and will shatter if dropped. The two most common types of stone used for carving are jadeite

Danish 17th-century ivory relief of Cephalus and Procris, Joachim Henne
IVORY CAN CRACK VERY EASILY IF THERE ARE CHANGES IN HUMIDITY AND TEMPERATURE. SUCH CRACKS BECOME DARK AND UNSIGHTLY, ARE EXTREMELY DIFFICULT TO CLEAN, AND ARE PARTICULARLY NOTICEABLE ON SMALL OBJECTS.

and nephrite, and these can range in color from a milky white to dark green or brown.

Jade does not suffer from the changes of temperature normally encountered in domestic situations and therefore can be readily left on open display. Its surface is also very dense and does not easily absorb dirt or even grease. Dusting with a soft white hogshair brush is all that is required to remove superficial dust.

As jade is brittle but can also be carved intricately, the most common form of damage is breakage. The repair of thin pieces of jade sculpture, such as the legs of a horse, can be extremely difficult for the conservator. The translucency of the material means that glass or other translucent dowels have to be used for pinning, and drilling into the hard jade can be very hazardous. In some cases it may be impossible to disguise damage satisfactorily, so it is important that the greatest care be taken when handling jade in order to avoid breakage.

Other common materials for hard-stone carving are rock crystal, rose quartz, agate and onyx. These stones share much the same characteristics as jade and can be maintained in the same manner. They also suffer from brittleness and should be handled with extreme care.

GENERAL CARE

This concluding chapter takes an overview of the general considerations that should be accorded works of art in the home environment. As the foregoing chapters have shown, excesses of light and heat, fluctuations in humidity, and the presence of pollution in the atmosphere each cause damage to works of art in varying degrees. Ideal conditions have been recommended for many, very different materials. Methods of measuring and monitoring light, heat and humidity, and of adjusting them in the domestic environment to reduce their damaging effects, are described below.

The following advice does not suggest that attempts should be made to replicate the special conditions and microclimates created for specific objects in museums, but describes simply how it is possible, within the realms of reason, to create an environment which is safer for most works of art but still congenial to individuals who must conduct their daily lives around them.

Pest control, general guidelines for avoiding accidents while pieces are *in situ* and during transportation, and simple security measures are also outlined, and the necessity of documenting a collection is explained.

Light

Light has a detrimental effect on many materials, particularly organic materials such as wood, paper and textiles which contain cellulose and protein. It is the ultraviolet (UV) radiation in the light spectrum that is the most harmful to objects, causing paper to become brittle and discolored, textiles to perish, and pigments to fade.

Although all light, provided it is strong enough, causes damage, sunlight and bright daylight are the most harmful since they contain the highest levels of ultraviolet radiation. Fluorescent tubes also emit ultraviolet rays. Incandescent light, from tungsten bulbs and from fires and candles, contains the smallest amount of UV rays. Nevertheless, the effects of light are cumulative; an equal amount of damage is caused by exposing an object to strong light for a short period as is done by exposing it to weak light for a long period.

The amount of visible radiation and of ultraviolet radiation (which is not visible) are measured by two different instruments. The intensity of light is measured in units of lux, registered by a light meter such as that used by photographers. The measurement made is known as the illuminance. A maximum of 50 lux (a measure of illuminance) is recommended for the most light-sensitive works of art; these include watercolors, prints, miniatures, manuscripts, textiles, paintings in distemper, and objects containing natural dyes. A maximum illuminance of 150 lux is safe for less light-sensitive objects, such as furniture, paintings in oil and tempera, undyed leather, Oriental lacquer, bone, and ivory.

Never underestimate the levels of illuminance in the everyday living and working environment, nor the ease with which the human eye adjusts to compensate for widely different levels of illuminance. Fluorescent tubes in the average well-lit office, for example, produce an illuminance of 500–700 lux, many times above that recommended for the least light-sensitive works of art. The average domestic living room on a relatively bright afternoon would produce an illuminance of 250–300 lux, provided it is out of direct sunlight.

Ultraviolet radiation is measured with a UV monitor. Although this is not a difficult instrument for the layperson to use, it is a relatively expensive piece of equipment which individual collectors are unlikely to want to acquire. Those with particularly sensitive objects to protect will find it easier to ask a conservator to take a reading with a UV monitor in various parts of the house on an average summer's day. If necessary, the conservator will suggest how UV radiation can be reduced. Either light blinds or curtains can be fitted to windows, or the window panes can be coated with UV-absorbent filters (thin transparent films of plastic applied directly onto the glass). Filters may also be applied to fluorescent tubes and other sources of strong UV radiation.

If these measures cannot be taken, or if recommended levels of illuminance cannot be constantly maintained, then simple, common-sense measures such as drawing blinds, covering objects up, or putting them away in drawers or cupboards to reduce their exposure to light will make a positive difference to their preservation.

When considering lighting delicate works of art for display, it is worthwhile consulting an expert who specializes in museum lighting. To avoid heat build-up in an enclosed space, it may be possible to install fiber-optic lighting in a display cabinet. Also, cool-beam lamps with a controllable output of both quantity and quality of light and heat can be custom-made for the safe illumination of pictures and textiles.

Humidity and Temperature

All organic materials, and some inorganic ones, contain moisture, and need to be kept in conditions at which their proper moisture levels can be maintained. To some degree, all organic materials are hygroscopic; that is, they absorb moisture as the atmosphere becomes more humid, and exude it as the atmosphere becomes drier. An over-dry atmosphere causes hygroscopic materials to shrink, crack or become distorted, and an over-humid atmosphere causes them to expand and can also cause distortion. Damage is exacerbated when humidity levels fluctuate, causing hygroscopic materials to expand and contract repeatedly. Over-humid conditions also encourage some materials to absorb surface dust and dirt, which then becomes permanently embedded.

The materials that are most sensitive to incorrect or fluctuating levels of humidity include wood, textiles, leather, parchment, works of art on paper, bone, and ivory. Each, according to their chemical composition, contains different proportions of moisture, so that, ideally, each should be kept in an atmosphere adjusted to their individual requirements. In practice, because a mixture of objects – furniture, watercolors, oil paintings, tapestries and ivories, for example – are normally displayed in a single room in a domestic environment, this is impossible and a compromise must be reached.

Temperature, the effects of which are closely allied to those of humidity, must also be controlled. Unsuitably high temperatures combined with arid conditions damage organic materials by causing the breakdown of the cellulose or protein which they contain. Heat and moisture combined cause mold spores to germinate and become active, feeding on the cellulose and starch in wood, paper, parchment, fabrics and other organic materials. Heat also accelerates corrosion in metals and the chemical reactions caused by acids in the atmosphere.

TAKING MEASUREMENTS
Moisture in the atmosphere is measured in terms of relative humidity (RH). This is the amount of water in a given quantity of air measured as a percentage of the maximum amount of water that air can hold at a given temperature. Relative humidity is measured with a hygrometer, several types of which are available.

In a whirling hygrometer, the moisture-sensitive mechanism is manually rotated in the air at speed, and a reading taken on a calibrated scale. In a psychrometer, which works on a similar principle, a fan draws air into the instrument, which measures its relative humidity. Chem-ically treated paper is another, though less accurate, method of measuring relative humidity. A thermohygrometer measures relative humidity and temperature simultaneously. A thermohygrograph records temperature and humidity on a moving chart over a period of time, allowing fluctuations to be monitored. Each of these instruments is relatively straightforward to use.

DESIRABLE CONDITIONS
A constant relative humidity of 55% (±3%) and a temperature of 64°F are generally regarded as safe for most objects. It is worth bearing in mind that a hall, for instance, may be cooler or more humid than a living room, where for human comfort a drier atmosphere and a temperature of 70°F need to be maintained. To an extent, it is therefore a case of displaying the object according to the atmospheric conditions of the room.

The special requirements of certain objects, such as photographs and vellum manuscripts, which need either more or less humidity or lower temperatures than the norm, are indicated in the preceding chapters. In exceptional circumstances, or if an object is important enough, one may consider adapting a room for the object.

The hygroscopic nature of organic materials may sometimes thwart good intentions. Objects that have been kept in constantly dry or humid conditions tend to adjust to those conditions and reach an equilibrium. A piece of furniture kept for years in a damp farmhouse or a collection of ivories displayed in an arid town house, both ostensibly unfavorable conditions, may have adjusted and achieved stability. Well-intentioned actions to move them or create a "correct" atmosphere for them may actually cause rather than prevent damage. If an object must be moved, it should be allowed to acclimatize to new conditions gradually for the period of time recommended for the particular object.

ADJUSTING HUMIDITY
Central heating, which can create arid, desert-like conditions, is a frequent cause of damage to objects made of organic materials. Humidifiers, which replace moisture and maintain a constant level of relative humidity, are the best means of compensating for the effects of central heating. Various models exist to suit different-sized rooms. Those fitted with a built-in hygrostat, allowing the machine to switch itself on or off according to a pre-set level of humidity, maintain the most constant conditions. Humidifiers designed to be used over radiators are the least effective, frequently drying out and offering little control of humidity levels.

Dehumidifiers may also be installed to combat excessive humidity. When using either of these devices, it is wise to check relative humidity with a hygrometer. Temperature can, of course, be monitored with a thermometer.

Pollution and the Atmosphere

Although oxygen in the atmosphere cannot be regarded as a pollutant, it is a component of many chemical reactions. The embrittlement of oil paints and varnish, the rusting of ferrous metals, and the breakdown of certain plastics are all processes of oxidation.

Air pollution, a man-made phenomenon, takes various forms. Unnaturally high levels of carbon dioxide accelerate corrosion in ferrous metals; sulfur dioxide, produced in certain industrial processes, oxidizes in the atmosphere to form sulfur trioxide, which combines with moisture to form sulfuric acid and falls as acid rain, which attacks stone and metals; unnaturally high levels of ozone, produced by photocopying machines and electronic equipment, break down plastics and cause oxidation in many materials. The presence of particulate dirt in the atmosphere, most of it greasy grime, is caused almost entirely by the burning of fossil fuels.

Pollution in general is at its worst in industrial or urban areas. Although the ambient atmosphere can be controlled by air-conditioning and filtering, these measures are very costly. Designed primarily for museums and art galleries with extremely delicate items to protect, they are not usually suitable for private houses.

Certain steps can nevertheless be taken to minimize the effects of air pollution. Vulnerable objects in the home should not be placed near windows, where pollution is usually highest. Small, delicate objects can be kept in glass or Plexiglas cases, and garden statuary that is evidently suffering can be brought indoors. The possibility that pollution can be produced in the home should not be overlooked: candles and coal- and wood-burning fires emit soot, and heavy smoking of pipes and cigarettes coats surfaces in sticky tar.

Insect, Vermin and Mold Damage

Cellulose, protein and starch in organic materials are the chosen food of a variety of insects. In northern Europe, North America and other temperate climates, the most common are the larvae of woodworm and other beetles; the larvae of clothes moths; silverfish; and tiny mites known as thrips or thunder flies. Tropical climates encourage a multitude of other insect pests of this type.

In all cases it is important to isolate infested pieces and, where possible, to wrap them in plastic sheeting to avoid scattering any eggs, larvae or adult insects and thereby helping to spread the infestation. Although various insecticides and repellents are available, few are suitable for works of art as the chemicals they contain may damage the material from which the objects are made; it is best to seek the advice of a conservator in this regard.

In temperate climates, insect infestations do not usually get out of control quickly or cause extensive damage – as long as vigilance is exercised and action to treat the object is taken fairly quickly. Regular inspections – twice a year for furniture and every two months for books and textiles – should be enough to forestall most damage.

In contrast to insects and mold, mice, rats and gray squirrels can cause serious damage in a very short time. Books, pictures, frames, photographs, textiles and small wooden objects which have unwisely been put away in an attic or cellar (without due care to their storage), particularly in houses in rural areas, are at risk from the attentions of rodents, which may gnaw on them or shred them to make nests. For this reason, quite apart from the fact that humidity levels are unlikely to be congenial, works of art should never be stored in those parts of the house unless measures have deliberately been taken to provide an adequate environment for them there.

FUMIGATION

Fumigating antiques and works of art as a method of killing insects and mold spores is only worth pursuing if the piece is going back into an insect- and mold-free environment as fumigation does not protect against future attack, but simply kills what is presently in or on the object. To prevent mold growth in the future the object should be housed in an environment dry enough not to allow mold spores to germinate, at 55% relative humidity ($\pm 3\%$). The only way to prevent reinfestation is to establish a sealed and air-conditioned environment.

Fumigation may be recommended for insect-infested upholstered furniture. In such cases, insects will have invaded either the wood frame or upholstery which is original to the piece and cannot be removed. However, it should be noted that some modern fumigation substances can be harmful to some materials in an object as well as to the person doing the fumigating. For this reason, the use of freezing and of gamma-radiation are currently under trial to take the place of chemical fumigation in killing mold spores and insects. These methods are being investigated to discover whether they will cause damage to the structure of the various materials.

Avoiding Accidents

Careless handling and the inadequate packing of objects for transportation account for a large proportion of avoidable damage, both to large pieces like furniture and statuary and to smaller ones like ceramics and glass. Accidents can also happen when rediscovering collections of small pieces that may have been put away in less-than-ideal conditions.

Lift boxes gently, as the bottom may have disintegrated, and unwrap pieces carefully on a padded surface, as small ones easily fall out and shatter or dent. Never lift objects by any weak, protruding part. Carry fragile objects about the house on a trolley or in well-padded trays. Before displaying fragile objects on flat, open surfaces, bear in mind that vibration from traffic or movement from loose floorboards can cause them to "walk" and fall to the floor.

Correct packing for transportation is of paramount importance, both for the physical preservation of the object and for its security (see below). Small objects should not be crammed into boxes without proper protection from knocks and vibration. Large ones should be well padded and wrapped, and placed in a crate if necessary. If the crate is to be exposed to the elements, it must be made waterproof. If a very valuable or delicate work of art is to be transported, it is wise to employ a firm that specializes in fine-art transport.

Security

The decision to fortify doors, install window bars, and fit electronic security devices depends as much on the nature of a collection and where it is housed as on the inclinations of the owner. A basic rule is to make a photographic and written record of every item in a collection. Another is not to invite trouble by displaying valuable or eye-catching objects in a window under the gaze of passers-by. Also remember that· objects outdoors – garden statuary in particular – are at risk from theft.

Marking an inconspicuous area of objects with inks that become visible only under ultraviolet light can also be useful in verifying ownership in case of theft. However, the long-term effects of such inks on the surface of an object are as yet unknown.

When transporting works of art, observing the recommendations for wrapping them well (as given above) also conceals their nature. If you have to leave a piece of furniture or other large object in the back of a car, do not leave it exposed to view; cover it with a rug or blanket.

Photography and Documentation

Documenting objects in almost any collection is of the utmost importance, firstly for security reasons and secondly to monitor their condition accurately and record any conservation, restoration or other treatment those objects may have undergone in the past.

Every piece in a personal collection should be photographed, preferably in color, with additional shots taken of the back, sides and underside of pieces, where appropriate. An inventory should then be made, describing each piece in detail, including its shape, color and dimensions, patterns and inscriptions, and any fractures, cracks or dents. Where possible, a note or drawing of factory marks (on ceramics) and hallmarks (on silver and some other metals) should also be made.

Owners of particularly valuable collections should consider lodging a copy of their photographic record and inventory with a bank. Should a burglary occur, this documentation both allows the owner to assess the extent of the theft, and increases the likelihood of stolen objects being identified and returned.

The inventory should also record the condition of each piece, particularly in cases where the condition is unstable or deterioration suspected. Regular checks to monitor condition should then be made and any developments carefully noted. Checking items in storage is especially important since, out of sight and all too easily forgotten, they can suffer unseen from the onset of deterioration.

Photographing watercolors, paintings, carpets and tapestries to monitor possible fading of their pigments is unfortunately of no great value unless carried out with highly sophisticated equipment and under controlled lighting conditions. As colour photographs often fade or change color, it is museum practice also to photograph all items in a collection in black and white. Such prints alter less and certain changes in condition are more detectable on a black and white photograph.

Where appropriate, a note of any cleaning or other treatment carried out at home, as well as any conservation or restoration the object has undergone, should also be made. A full and detailed record of the nature and extent of conservation or restoration should always be provided by the professional who carried out the work, and carefully kept as part of that object's documentation. The record will consist of a full description of the original condition of the object, the date of examination, the treatment given and the types of material used, all of which are absolutely essential should that object need professional attention in the future.

SELECT BIBLIOGRAPHY

Anderson, B.W.: *Gem Testing*, London, 1990

Baillie, G.H.: *Watch and Clockmakers of the World*,
vol. 1, London, 1966 (see Loomes)
Bailly, Christian: *Automata, The Golden Age*, London, 1987
Baynes-Cope, A.D.: *The Study and Conservation of Globes*, Vienna,
1985
Bennett, Ian: *Rugs and Carpets of the World*, London, 1977
Blackmore, Howard: *Guns and Rifles of the World*, London, 1962
Blair, Claude: *Pistols of the World*, London, 1965
Blair, Claude: *European Armour 1066–c.1700*, London, 1972
Britten, F.J.: *Old Clocks and Watches and their Makers*, London, 1973
Brommelle, N.S. and Smith, P.: *Conservation and Restoration of
Pictorial Art*, London and Boston, 1976, pp.129–33
Brown, Yu-Ying: *Japanese Book Illustration*, London, 1988

Cameron, Elisabeth: *Encyclopedia of Pottery and Porcelain*, London,
1986
Carter, John: *ABC for Book Collectors*, London, 1980
Casey, P.J. and Cronyn, J.M. (eds.): *Numismatics and Conservation*,
Department of Archaeology Occasional Paper No.1, Durham,
1978
Clapp, Anne F.: *Curatorial Care of Works of Art on Paper*, Ohio, 1978
Coe, Brian and Haworth-Booth, Mark: *A Guide to Early Photographic
Processes*, London, 1983
Cohn, M.B.: *Wash and Gouache*, Boston, 1977
Conservation Standards for Works of Art in Transit and on Exhibition,
UNESCO, Switzerland, 1979

Dossie, R.: *Handmaid to the Arts*, London, 1764

Fletcher, E.: *Bottle Collecting*, London, 1972
Frank, S.: *Glass and Archaeology*, London, 1982

Geijer, A.: *A History of Textile Art*, London, 1979
Gernsheim, Helmut and Alison: *The History of Photography*, New
York, 1969

Hamilton, J.: *An Introduction to Wallpaper*, London, 1983
Harley, R.D.: *Artists' Pigments, c.1600–1835*, London, 1982
Holben Ellis, M.: *The Care of Prints and Drawings*, Nashville, 1987
Horton, Carolyn: *Cleaning and Preserving Bindings and Related
Materials*, Chicago, 1969
Hubel, Reinhard G.: *The Book of Carpets*, New York, 1970

Kahlert, H., Mühe, R. and Brunner, G.L.: *Wristwatches*, West
Chester, Pennsylvania, 1986
Kite, M.: 'The Conservation of the Jesse Cope', *Textile History, 20(2)*,
London, 1989, pp.235–43

Lambert, Susan; *Drawings, Technique and Purpose*, London, 1984
Landes, D.S.: *Revolution in Time*, Cambridge, MA, 1983
Landi, S.: *The Textile Conservators Manual*, London, 1985
Liddicoat Jr., Richard T., *The Jewelers' Manual*, Santa Monica, 1974
Loomes, B.: *Watch and Clockmakers of the World*, vol. 2, London, 1976
(see Baillie)

MacDowall, D.W.: *Coin Collections, their Preservation, Classification
and Presentation*, UNESCO, France, 1978
Martin, E.: *Collecting & Preserving Old Photographs*, London, 1988
Mayer, Ralph: *A Dictionary of Art Terms and Techniques*, New York,
1969
Mayer, Ralph: *The Artists' Handbook*, New York, 1970
Medley, Margaret: *The Chinese Potter*, Oxford, 1976
Mehlman, F.: *Phaidon Guide to Glass*, Oxford, 1982
Miner, D.: *The History of Bookbinding 525–1950 AD*, Baltimore,
1957
Morley-Fletcher, Hugo (ed.): *Techniques of the World's Great Masters
of Pottery and Ceramics*, London, 1984

Newton, R. and Davison, S.: *Conservation of Glass*, London, 1989

Petsopolous, Yanni: *Kilims*, London, 1979
Plenderleith, H.J. and Werner, A.E.A.: *The Conservation of Antiquities
and Works of Art*, Oxford, 1971
Plowden, A. and Halahan, F.: *Looking after Antiques*, London,
1987
Preserving our Printed Heritage, Trinity College Dublin, 1968

Reilly, James M.: *Care and Identification of Nineteenth-Century
Photographic Prints*, New York, 1986

Sandon, John: *English Porcelain of the 18th and 19th Centuries*, London,
1989
Sandwith, H. and Stainton, S.: *The National Trust Manual of
Housekeeping*, London, 1991
Staff, Donald and Sacilotto, Deli: *Printmaking, History and Process*,
New York, 1978
Stewart, Basil: *A Guide to Japanese Prints and their Subject Matter*, New
York, 1979

Tarrasuk, Leonid and Blair, Claude: *The Complete Encyclopedia of
Arms and Weapons*, London, 1979
Thomson, G.: *The Museum Environment*, London, 1978
Thompson, John M.A. (ed.): *Manual of Curatorship, A Guide to
Museum Practice*, London, 1984
de Tolnay, Charles: *History and Techniques of Old Master Drawings*,
New York, 1983
le Turner, Gerard: *Antique Scientific Instruments*, Poole, 1980

Vainker, S.J.: *Chinese Pottery and Porcelain*, London, 1991

Ward, Philip: *The Nature of Conservation, A Race against Time*,
California, 1986
Watrous, James: *The Craft of Old Master Drawings*, Wisconsin,
1957
Webster, Robert: *Gemmologists' Compendium*, London, 1975
Webster, Robert: *Gems*, London, 1983
Weinstein, R.A. and Booth, L.: *Use and Care of Historical Photographs*,
Nashville, 1977
Wilkinson, Frederick: *Collecting Military Antiques*, London, 1976
Wilkinson, Frederick: *The World's Great Guns*, London, 1987
Wingfield-Digby, G.: *Elizabethan Embroidery*, London, 1963

GLOSSARY

acid-free A term used to describe paper and board having an all-rag fiber content, or chemically purified wood fibers, manufactured to produce a neutral or slightly alkaline pH condition. These materials normally incorporate a neutral sizing agent such as calcium carbonate. Some **acid-free** materials may not include an alkaline buffer (e.g. those used to house photographic materials).

acid rain A term used to refer to rain water that has absorbed the pollutant gas sulfur dioxide, leading to the formation of sulfuric acid. Acid rain will attack limestone and marble leading to severe erosion. Sulfur dioxide will also attack paper, leather and metals.

acrylic resin Clear, colorless synthetic resin used as an adhesive, a filler for glass and ceramics, or for strengthening bronze or stone statuary.

alkali The name given to substances that give alkaline solutions in water (those that have a pH value of more than 7). Alkalies, such as lime and caustic soda, have the ability to neutralize acids.

alloy A mixture of two or more metals, such as copper and zinc (brass) or copper and tin (bronze).

alum-tawed A mineral tannage with aluminum salts.

ambient conditions See **environment**.

archival quality Also called **museum quality**. Refers to board or paper that conforms to museum standards for long-term storage or display of objects. See **acid-free**.

armature Internal, skeletal metal support used to strengthen statuary or ceramic figures.

atmospheric conditions Levels of heat, humidity and purity of air that affect objects. See **environment**.

base metals Those that are corruptible, or prone to **tarnish** or **corrosion**, such as copper, brass and iron. The baser the metal the more **unstable** it is.

biocide A substance or liquid capable of killing plants and other life forms.

biodegradable Refers to material that is capable of being decomposed biologically, usually by the action of damp or mold.

bleed To seep out and stain, e.g. as dyes do from textiles and inks from paper. See **migration**.

bloom Cloudy effect that appears on glass, caused by chemical imbalance in the glass; or on the varnish of paintings or polish on furniture. Caused by moisture or a defect in the varnish.

bluing Process by which steel is heated to give it a rich blue reflective surface. Used for the hands of clocks and watches; it protects metal against **corrosion**.

bronze disease Refers to bright green powdery spots, or a **corrosion product**, which forms on surface of ancient bronze. It is caused by damp conditions.

cellulose Fundamental material of plant cells and thus the main constituent of paper, card, cotton, linen, canvas and other textiles made from vegetable fibers.

cellulosics Textiles made from vegetable fibers. See **cellulose**.

chemical patination See **patina**.

chemical stripping Removal of surface of metals by action of acids to remove stains, heavy

tarnish or corrosion. Gives a pristine appearance and is not suitable for antique metalware.

cleavage 1. Accidental splitting of stones used in jewelry. 2. Lifting of paint from the surface of a canvas or other support.

cold pigments Paints used to decorate ceramics, which are not subjected to **firing** in the kiln.

composite An object consisting of a combination of materials, e.g. wood inlaid with brass, or metal set with gems.

composition A mixture of ground chalk, resin and **size**, commonly used to make molded and gilt ornamentation for furniture and picture frames.

compound A substance consisting of two or more chemically united elements. Most metal polishes work by forming a compound with, and removing, the surface layer of metals.

conservation Primarily the process by which damage and decay in objects are arrested, preventative treatment given and the deteriorating condition made **stable**.

conservation framing and mounting The conservation of works of art on paper onto **acid-free** card, using chemically **inert** fixing agents and glazing with built-in **UV protection**.

cool-beam lamp A spotlight fitted with a reflector that directs **visible light** forwards, and deflects **infrared** radiation and the heat that it generates through the back of the lamp.

corrosion Chemical deterioration of metals in reaction to their **environment**. **Corrosion products** can be **stable** (e.g. **verdigris** on copper) or **unstable** (e.g. rust on iron).

corrosion product Substance that forms on metals as the result of **corrosion**, e.g. rust on iron.

couched repairs **Conservation** to embroidered textiles in which the threads are attached to a secondary **support** by stitching.

craquelure Network of fine cracks on surface of oil paintings. Caused by drying of paint and varnish, and expansion and contraction of the **support**.

crizzling or **glass disease** Network of fine cracks in glass, sometimes accompanied by weeping (drops of moisture forming on the surface). Caused by chemical imbalance in the glass.

cuprous chloride or **copper chloride** A **corrosion product** that forms on copper and its **alloys** as the result of burial in salty soil. May lead to **bronze disease**.

degradation Deterioration of materials, particularly in situations involving chemical or biological decay.

delamination The gradual separation of any layers of material, such as wallpaper, through wear, natural detioration, or the breakdown of adhesives.

diffused light Light that emanates or is reflected from many sources, e.g. natural or artificial light reflected off the walls of a room.

direct heat Heat emitted from a specific source at close range, e.g. from a radiator, electric fire or light bulb.

direct light Light emanating from a specific source at close range, e.g. from a light bulb or bright sunlight.

efflorescence Deposit of salt crystals, e.g. on the surface of porous stone or terracotta, caused by the absorption of soluble ground salts and their **migration** to the surface of the stone.

electrical bonding, or **electrolytic exchange** Process by which gold or silver is plated onto a **base metal**. An electrical current in a salt solution dissolves the gold or silver and deposits it on the base metal, to which it is electro-chemically fused.

electrolytic exchange See **electrical bonding**.

environment, or **ambient conditions** The surroundings, i.e. temperature, humidity, light and purity of air, in which objects are stored or displayed.

epoxy resin Synthetic adhesive consisting of resin and a hardening agent which, when mixed together, harden and become insoluble.

esparto Rush-like grass used in paper-making.

exfoliation Term for the condition of surface flaking, especially of porous stone, that is caused by absorption of moisture.

ferrous metals Those made with iron, e.g. cast iron.

fiber-optic lighting Artificial light transmitted by thin fibers of glass or plastic rather than by an **incandescent** filament, and therefore producing very little heat.

firing The process by which a clay body is exposed to specific temperatures in a kiln to harden it, turning it into pottery or porcelain, and fusing the glaze to the body, or fixing enamels to the glaze. Porcelain and some pigments on pottery are high-fired (at 2012°F); enamel decoration is low-fired (at 1292°–1652°F).

fixative or **fixing agent** Consolidating agent sprayed onto pastel, chalk, charcoal or pencil drawings to secure the pigments to the **support** and protect them against rubbing. If at all possible, such applications should be avoided.

foxing Reddish-brown spots that develop on prints, drawings and old paper under damp or acidic conditions. Thought, but not proved to be a type of mold.

French-polishing Deep, lustrous finish applied to furniture by repeated application of dilute **shellac**.

glass disease See **crizzling**.

ground Substance with which a **support** (e.g. canvas) is covered to render it non-porous, thereby making it suitable for painting.

high-fired See **firing**.

hygroscopic Refers to a material that absorbs moisture as the atmosphere becomes more humid and exudes it as the atmosphere becomes drier.

hygrometer General term for any instrument used to measure **relative humidity** in the atmosphere. See also **psychrometer**, **thermohygrograph** and **thermohygrometer**.

illuminance Measurement of **visible light** level expressed in units of **lux**.

impasto Style of oil painting in which the paint is laid on thickly and is highly textured.

incandescent light Produced by a filament that is made to glow white-hot by the passage of electricity through it, as in a tungsten light-bulb.

inert Refers to a substance that contains no active chemicals and is thus unable to **tarnish**, corrode, stain or cause chemical deterioration in other materials.

infrared light Radiation with a wavelength beyond the red end of the visible spectrum and which is therefore invisible. Also known as **radiant heat**.

inorganic material Substance of mineral origin, as distinct from animal or vegetable origin, e.g. metals, glass, ceramics or stone.

inpainting Technique of

coloring the damaged area of a painting to blend with the surrounding color, without covering any original paint.

integrity State of completeness of an object, composed from the originality of its appearance, parts and structure.

lake color Pigment produced by chemical combination of a dye and an insoluble base. For example, Madder Lake.

lead carbonate Whitish **corrosion product** forming on lead as a result of exposure to **organic acid** vapor.

lead formate Whitish **corrosion product** forming on lead or zinc as a result of exposure to atmospheric **pollution**.

lead glass Made from flint, potash and lead. Clearer, heavier and more brilliant than **soda glass**.

light-sensitive Refers to materials that tend to fade, rot or discolor when exposed to **ultraviolet** and/or **visible light**.

lining 1. Fabric, usually new canvas, backing the damaged or fragile canvas of a painting to strengthen it. 2. Fabric backing a carpet or textile used in preparation for hanging or as a support.

low-fired See **firing**.

lux Unit by which the level of **visible light** incident on a surface, or the degree of **illuminance**, is measured.

mercury gilding A process by which a mixture of gold and mercury is applied to metals or ceramics, and then fired (see **firing**). The mercury is dispersed by heat, leaving a film of gold on object.

microclimate Artificially created **environment** in which heat, light and humidity are adjusted, and air is sometimes filtered, for the preservation or safe display of objects.

microcrystalline wax Solid, partly synthetic wax with very

small crystals that removes surface dirt, produces a sheen and protects a surface against moisture.

migration The movement of soluble salts through porous stone, or the seepage of dyes from one fabric to another, caused by the absorption of moisture.

mold bloom Fungal spores of various colors that develop on most surfaces under humid conditions.

museum-quality See **archival quality**.

nitrocellulose or **cellulose nitrate** Principal ingredient of the synthetic lacquer, which is made from **cellulose** and nitric acid.

non-ionic detergent Does not produce ions (electrically charged atoms) when mixed with water.

organic acid Emitted by an **organic material**, e.g. vinegar or fresh wood. Corrodes some metals such as lead.

organic compound Substance formed from carbon and other elements.

organic material Animal or vegetable substance, as distinct from minerals, e.g. wood, paper, ivory, leather or **parchment**.

organic solvent Made from an **organic** substance, such as oil, mineral spirits or acetone. Dissolves **organic compounds**.

oxidation Process in which oxygen reacts with materials to alter their chemical composition, e.g. causing iron to rust, oil paint or varnish to become brittle, or paper to yellow.

overpainting or **overspraying** Related techniques by which cracks or breaks in ceramics, or damage to the surface of oil paintings, are covered by painting or spraying the original surface.

parchment See **vellum**.

particulate dirt Particles of solid dirt suspended in the atmosphere and forming part of air pollution.

patina The surface sheen formed, particularly on wood, metal and stone, as a result of handling, polishing, burial, weathering, **oxidation** or discoloring. Usually occurs naturally over time but can also be chemically or artificially applied to some metals.

pH factor Measure of acidity or alkalinity.

plastics See **polymer**.

plumbago Graphite, or a drawing made with this material.

polymer A natural or synthetic substance made up of identical, linked molecules forming long chains. The basic material of plastics and **acrylic resins**.

precious metals or **noble metals** Those that are incorruptible, or not vulnerable to **tarnish** or **corrosion**, such as gold, pure silver and platinum.

pollutant Harmful gas, e.g. sulfur dioxide or hydrogen sulfide, or **particulate dirt**, released into the atmosphere generally by industrial processes or car exhausts. See also **acid rain**.

psychrometer Instrument used to measure **relative humidity**. Air is drawn into the instrument by a fan, its humidity measured and a reading given on a scale. A type of **hygrometer**.

radiant heat Heat that is transmitted by radiation, e.g. from the sun, a glowing electrical heater or a flame, as distinct from convected heat. See **infrared light**.

raking light Light that is beamed at an angle so as to reveal surface imperfections on paintings and other objects.

reagent Refers to a substance used to produce a chemical reaction, e.g. in order to clean metals or to dissolve varnish or greasy deposits.

relative humidity (RH) The amount of water in a given quantity of air, measured as a percentage of the maximum amount of water that air can hold at a given temperature.

restoration The process by which an object is, as far as possible, returned to its original condition and appearance.

reversible Refers to treatment given and materials used that can easily be reversed or removed at a later date without harming the object or leaving any trace.

RH See **relative humidity**.

shellac A natural varnish made from the resin secreted by a species of South-east Asian tree insect. Used as a protective coating on furniture. See also **French-polishing**.

siliceous stone A type of stone containing silica, e.g. sandstone and quartz.

silicone An **organic compound** resistant to water and used in some commercial furniture polishes, but not generally recommended for antique objects.

silver chloride A **corrosion product** that forms on silver as the result of exposure to salt in the earth or atmosphere.

size or **sizing** Gelatinous solution used for sizing paper to render it less absorbent (and thus suitable for printing with inks) and to protect it from scratches and abrasion. Also used for stiffening textiles.

soda glass Glass that is made of silica, soda and lime. It often has a smoky tinge and is lighter than **lead glass.**

Solander box Box with a side flap and hinged or removable lid, for storing unmounted or unframed prints and drawings. Made from **acid-free** cardboard.

solvent A substance that dissolves another.

spalling Splintering, as on the surface of porous stone; a condition caused by the absorption of moisture and **migration** of soluble salts.

stable Refers to a condition that will not continue to deteriorate. Stable **corrosion** does not develop further. A stable material is unlikely to react chemically to its **environment**.

stressed metal Metal that is tensioned, e.g. brass used for tubing in scientific instruments.

stretcher 1. Wooden frame on which canvas is mounted to keep it taut for painting. 2. The strut of wood between the legs of a piece of furniture.

sulfide Compounds of other elements with sulfur. Sulfides can decompose to produce hydrogen sulfide, a gas which will cause **tarnish** on silver, copper, brass and bronze. Sources of hydrogen sulfide gas include decaying vegetable matter, wool, felts, rubber based adhesives and velvet.

support Canvas, panel, paper, metal, ivory, fabric or any other material on which a painting, drawing, watercolor, textile or other work of art is executed.

tarnish A deposit which forms on the surface of metals such as silver, copper and brass as they react with **sulfides**. It is usually **stable** and harmless to metal.

thermal shock The adverse reaction of a material subjected to an abrupt temperature change.

thermohygrograph Instrument for measuring and recording temperature and **relative humidity** over a period of time on a graph. A variety of **hygrometer**.

thermohygrometer Instrument for measuring temperature and **relative humidity**. A variety of **hygrometer**.

thermoplastic adhesive Adhesive that softens and becomes malleable as it is heated, and hardens as it is cooled.

ultraviolet light (UV) Radiation having a wavelength beyond the blue (violet) end of the visible spectrum and which is therefore invisible. Causes fading and discoloration in paper, watercolors, dyes, some inks, and wood, and disintegration in textiles.

unfired pigment Paint used to decorate ceramics or glass, which is not subjected to **firing** in the kiln.

unstable Refers to a condition that will continue to deteriorate. Unstable **corrosion** will continue to develop. Unstable material is likely to react chemically or physically to its **environment**.

UV See **ultraviolet light**.

UV filter, barrier or **protection** Transparent film of plastic which, placed on window panes, over fluorescent tubes or other sources of light, filters out **ultraviolet light**.

UV monitor Instrument for measuring the amount of **ultraviolet light**.

vellum or **parchment** Animal skin used for writing or painting, prepared by drying under tension.

veneer Thin sheet of wood, usually chosen for its attractive color or grain, applied to wood as a decorative surface.

verdigris Bright green waxy **corrosion product** that forms on copper, brass and bronze, usually caused by humid conditions; generally **stable**.

visible light Ordinary daylight or artificial light, i.e. radiation having a wavelength between red and blue (violet) ends of the visible spectrum. See **infrared** and **ultraviolet light**.

weeping glass See **crizzling**.

whirling hygrometer Instrument used for measuring **relative humidity**.

DIRECTORY OF CONSERVATION ORGANIZATIONS

Sotheby's Restoration Company

Sotheby's Restoration Company offers professional advice on the conservation and restoration of works of art and fine furniture. It provides a high-quality service for items ranging from furniture to paintings, watercolors, prints, drawings, books, ceramics, and textiles. It also specializes in cabinet-making, polishing, lacquering and gilding. Since its foundation in 1980, the Company has grown into an international group of artists and artisans whose craftsmanship, combined with specialized knowledge of the latest scientific advances on conservation, ensures that works of art are given the best possible treatment.

Clients may make an appointment to bring damaged works of art for consultation. Alternatively, visits can be arranged throughout North America to examine items that are either too numerous or heavy to be moved easily.

Sotheby's Restoration accomplishes all forms of fine art restoration in two locations:

Sotheby's Restoration
1425 YORK AVENUE
NEW YORK, NY 10021
Tel: (212) 860-5446
Fax: (212) 876-1064

Sotheby's Restoration North
PO BOX 213
CLAVERACK, NY 12513
Tel: (518) 851-2544
Fax: (518) 851-2558

American Institute for Conservation of Historic and Artistic Works

AIC is the national organization of conservation professionals which sponsors conferences and publishes and sells a variety of conservation-related periodicals. Its nonprofit foundation, the Foundation of the American Institute for Conservation of Historic and Artistic Works (FAIC), offers educational programs, grants to conservators, and a referral system. A general bibliography on conservation is available on request.

AIC
1400 16TH STREET, NW
SUITE 340
WASHINGTON, DC 20036
Tel: (202) 232-6636
Fax: (202) 232-6630

CONSERVATION BODIES

Sotheby's and the publishers cannot accept responsibility for the advice given or actions taken by any of the bodies listed below.

Advisory Council on Historic Preservation
1100 PENNSYLVANIA AVENUE, NW
ROOM 809
WASHINGTON, DC 20004
Tel: (202) 786-0503

American Association of Museums (AAM)
1225 EYE STREET, NW
SUITE 200
WASHINGTON, DC 20005
Tel: (202) 289-1818

American Chemical Society (ACS)
1155 16TH STREET, NW
WASHINGTON, DC 20036
Tel: (202) 872-4600

American Society of Appraisers
PO BOX 17265
WASHINGTON, DC 20041
Tel: (800) ASA-VALU

Appraisers Association of America, Inc.
60 EAST 42ND STREET
NEW YORK, NY 10165
Tel: (212) 867-9775

Association for Preservation Technology International (APT)
PO BOX 8178
FREDERICKSBURG
VA 22404
Tel: (703) 373-1621

Center for Safety in the Arts (CSA)
5 BEEKMAN STREET
NEW YORK, NY 10038
Tel: (212) 227-6220

Commission on Preservation and Access
1785 MASSACHUSETTS AVENUE, NW
ROOM 313
WASHINGTON, DC 20036
Tel: (202) 483-7474

Getty Conservation Institute
4503 GLENCOE AVENUE
MARINA DEL REY
CA 90292
Tel: (213) 822-2299

Institute of Metal Repair
1558 S. REDWOOD
ESCONDIDO, CA 92025
Tel: (619) 747-5978

Mellon Institute
4400 FIFTH AVENUE
PITTSBURGH
PA 15213
Tel: (412) 268-6854

National Antique & Art Dealers Association of America, Inc.
15 EAST 57TH STREET
NEW YORK, NY 10022
Tel: (212) 826-9707

National Institute for the Conservation of Cultural Property (NIC)
THE PAPERMILL
SUITE 403
3299 K STREET, NW
WASHINGTON, DC 20007
Tel: (202) 625-1495

National Park Service Division of Conservation
HARPERS FERRY CENTER
HARPERS FERRY
WV 25425
Tel: (304) 535-6854

National Trust for Historic Preservation
1785 MASSACHUSETTS AVENUE, NW
WASHINGTON, DC 20036
Tel: (202) 673-4000

Professional Picture Framers Association
4305 SARELLEN ROAD
RICHMOND, VA 23231
Tel: (804) 226-0430

Society of Gilders
PO BOX 50179
WASHINGTON, DC 20091

INDEX

ACKNOWLEDGMENTS

The publisher thanks the following organizations and photographers for their kind permission to reproduce the photographs in this book:

10 Photography: Bill Batten; Styled: Claire Lloyd; **16** Angelo Hornak (Courtesy of Birmingham Museums & Art Gallery); **20** National Trust Photographic Library; **21** Graham Challifour/ National Trust Photographic Library; **22** Rob Matheson/ National Trust Photographic Library; **28** below Rob Matheson/ National Trust Photographic Library; **32** James Mortimer/ World of Interiors; **37** Private Collection; **44** Connaissance des Arts/R Guillmot/Edimedia; **51** Sandra Davison, The Conservation Studio, Thame; **54** Reproduced by courtesy of the Trustees of the British Museum; **62** above Reproduced by courtesy of the Trustees of the British Museum; **73** left The National Galleries of Scotland; **89** Patek Philippe, Geneva; **96–7** National Maritime Museum, Greenwich; **98** above Derby Museum & Art Gallery; **98** below National Maritime Museum, Greenwich; **101** left Richard Bryant/Arcaid; **111** By permission of the Statens Museum for Kunst, Copenhagen; **112** Jim Murrell (By permission of the Sir David Ogilvy Trust); **114** Agnews, London; **117** Jane McAusland; **119** The Tate Gallery, London; **123** Photography: Paul Hirst at AI McDermott Restoration; **124** Agnews, London; **131** The National Gallery, London; **134** Courtesy of the Board of Trustees of the Victoria & Albert Museum; **137** Photography: Paul Hirst at AI McDermott Restoration (Courtesy of The Fletcher Moss Museum, Manchester); **138** Photography: Paul Hirst at AI McDermott Restoration; **139** National Trust Photographic Library; **142** Cathedral of St Bavo, Ghent/Giraudon/Bridgeman Art Library; **152** Before and after restoration by Richard Lannowe Hall; **153** English Heritage Photo Library; **154** Angelo Hornak; **157** Marion Kite; **160** ET Archive (Courtesy of the Board of Trustees of the Victoria & Albert Museum); **161–2** The Antique Textile Company; **163** above Courtesy of the Board of Trustees of the Victoria & Albert Museum; **163** below The Fan Museum (Collection of Hélène Alexander); **165** The Antique Textile Company; **168** Neil Campbell-Sharp/National Trust Photographic Library; **173** J Pipkin/National Trust Photographic Library; **175** D'Agar & Gifford Antiques; **178** Courtesy of the Board of Trustees of the Victoria & Albert Museum.

The following photographs were specially taken for Conran Octopus by Lucy Mason:

1 (Courtesy of the Edward James Foundation); **3**; **13** (Courtesy of the Ashmolean Museum, Oxford); **15** (Courtesy of the Edward James Foundation); **38** (Courtesy of the Ashmolean Museum, Oxford); **41** (Courtesy of the Ashmolean Museum, Oxford); **43** (Courtesy of the Ashmolean Museum, Oxford); **47–9**; **55** (Mrs R Hughes); **57** (Sotheby's, London); **69–71** (Private Collection), **73** right (Sotheby's, London), **76–8** (Sotheby's, London), **80, 84–5, 87, 90–2, 93** left, **93** right (Menno Heoncamp), **102, 105–9, 132–3** (Elizabeth Martin), **140** (Courtesy of the Edward James Foundation); **143–7** (Courtesy of the Edward James Foundation).

The following photographs were provided by Sotheby's:

Sotheby's, London/photographer Ken Adlard: **2, 34, 52, 59, 94**.

Sotheby's, London: **8, 12, 14, 19, 23, 26–7, 28** above (Clifford Tracey), **29, 30** left, **30** right (James Lindsay of Wm. Galbraith, London), **31, 40, 42, 56, 60–1, 64–7, 74–5, 79, 88, 101** right, **121–2, 125–9, 130** left (© Roy Lichtenstein), **130** right, **148, 158, 166, 167** (Courtesy of the Textile Conservation Centre, Hampton Court), **170–2, 176, 179**.

Sotheby's, New York: **25, 62** below.